ON
THE ROAD
TO
COMMUNISM

On
THE ROAD
TO
COMMUNISM

ESSAYS ON
SOVIET DOMESTIC AND FOREIGN POLITICS

Edited by
Roger E. Kanet and Ivan Volgyes

THE UNIVERSITY PRESS OF KANSAS/LAWRENCE/MANHATTAN/WICHITA

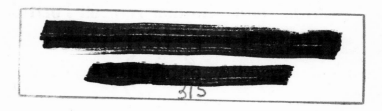

PREFACE

Since the successful seizure of power by the Bolsheviks in 1917, the leadership of the Communist party of the Soviet Union has been faced with the problem of creating the foundations for Communist society. According to the 1961 Party Program, the USSR has already completed the tasks of creating a socialist society and is now in the process of completing the construction of the basis for the full development of this Communist society. The articles that compose this volume deal with a number of the problems that have been handled by the Soviet leadership during the past five and a half decades, both in the area of domestic politics and in foreign policy. All but the articles by Kanet and Lee were originally delivered as papers at the Sixth Annual Bi-State Slavic Conference (Kansas-Missouri), held at the University of Kansas, Lawrence, Kansas, November 17–18, 1967, and have since been revised.

The editors wish to express their appreciation to those who have made the publication of this volume possible. The authors to the articles complied promptly and willingly with the requirements of updating and necessary editorial changes. The University of Kansas provided the financial support for the original conference, for typing, and for editorial assistance. Thanks are also due to Dr. John Alexander and Mr. Karl Kappelman of the University of Kansas for their assistance in organizing the conference at which most of the papers were first delivered. In addition, the editors wish to express their appreciation to the University Press of Kansas for encouragement and assistance.

Finally, the editors wish to acknowledge their indebtedness to two stimulating scholars, Dr. Samuel L. Sharp and Dr. Harold H. Sprout, under whose tutelage they were introduced to the complexities of the political process and to whom this volume is gratefully dedicated.

Roger E. Kanet
Ivan Volgyes

CONTENTS

PREFACE v

PART I
Essays on Soviet Domestic Politics 3

1
PAUL ROLEY
Flexibility and Dogmatism: The Ambiguous
Legacy of Leninism 6

2
ERIK P. HOFFMANN
Ideological Administration under Khrushchev:
A Study of Intraparty Communication 15

3
ROBERT SHARLET
A Conceptual Framework for Mass Political Socialization
in Soviet Political Development 47

4
NICHOLAS DeWITT
The October Revolution and Soviet Education 60

5
WILL ADAMS
Capital Punishment in Soviet Criminal Legislation,
1922–1965: A Code Content Analysis and
Graphic Representation 78

6

GEORGE M. ENTEEN
Soviet Historians Review Their Own Past: The
Rehabilitation of M. N. Pokrovskii   122

PART II
Essays on Soviet Foreign Policy   139

7

ROGER E. KANET
Changing Soviet Attitudes toward the
Developing Countries   142

8

JAAN PENNAR
The Arabs, Marxism and Moscow: A
Historical Survey   158

9

ARTHUR JAN KLINGHOFFER
The Soviet View of African Socialism   176

10

CHAE-JIN-LEE
Strategic Aspects of the Sino-Soviet Dispute: A Study
of Recent Chinese Arguments and Positions   190

Notes on Contributors   211

On
THE ROAD
TO
COMMUNISM

PART I

ESSAYS ON
SOVIET DOMESTIC POLITICS

PART I: ESSAYS ON SOVIET DOMESTIC POLITICS

During the past fifty years the Soviet Union has evolved from an underdeveloped country to one characterized by a relatively high level of economic and political development. Economically and militarily it is the world's second most important power. In addition, Soviet society is relatively stable and its members are generally content with much of the progress that the Soviet state has made. Politically the power of the Communist party of the Soviet Union is unchallenged by the existence of another political party or of any organized groups.

While the development of the Soviet Union solved many of the problems that faced tsarist Russia at the end of World War I, it also created new ones that were not envisioned by the makers of the Revolution of 1917. A number of these problems are dealt with in the first part of this book.

Paul Roley discusses two trends in Leninist ideology—dogmatism and flexibility. Roley argues that the organization principle is not the central element in Leninism but, rather, that the major characteristic of Lenin was "a willingness to compromise with reality on the tactical level." Lenin's desire for a disciplined party organization was primarily the outgrowth of his political realism. However, although Lenin was flexible in the selection of tactics, he was among the most dogmatic of ideologues on basic philosophic questions, Roley maintains.

In the second essay, Erik Hoffmann analyzes some of the problems of communication within the Agitation-Propaganda section of the Communist party of the Soviet Union. Treating Agitprop as an administrative unit and applying concepts of communication theory, he concludes that "there are definite limits to Agitprop's power of command" and that "the key to efficient ideological administration lies in the ability of Agitprop to persuade provincial officials that what it wants of them is also in their own best interests." By pointing out the inefficiency of intraparty communication, both vertically and horizontally, Professor Hoffmann shows that Soviet bureaucracies face problems similar to those which exist in the bureaucracies of other industrialized countries.

Robert Sharlet focuses on the question of the transmission of values from one generation of Soviet citizens to the next in his article on political socialization in the Soviet Union. He examines the various instruments employed by the Soviet government in its attempt to bring about significant changes in the political attitudes and values of the Soviet population. Although he does not arrive at definite conclusions concerning contemporary political socialization processes, he points to the importance of Soviet desires to create the new Soviet man and the attempts that have been made to accomplish this goal.

Nicholas DeWitt surveys the aims and tasks of Soviet education. Professor DeWitt argues that Soviet education, like many of its Western counterparts, is unable to respond adequately to the needs of both the state and the individual. The state expects to train useful producers in the sectors it considers the most important, while the individual expects to be educated so that he may participate in the type of economic activity where his personal rewards can be maximized.

Will Adams, in his study of capital punishment in the Soviet Union, points to an increasing regularization of Soviet criminal legislation. Although he observes that the death penalty has been readmitted for certain crimes against the state, he concludes that these crimes are much more clearly delineated than they were in the past. Professor Adams has employed content analysis in a thorough study of Soviet criminal codes in order to document changing attitudes in the Soviet Union toward the death penalty.

In the concluding essay in Part I, George Enteen examines the Soviet reevaluation of the historical importance of M. N. Pokrovskii, one of the greatest historians of the Soviet Union, whose writings were banned and name and reputation as an historian were maligned during the Stalin era. Professor Enteen argues that the rehabilitation of Pokrovskii was closely tied to the process of de-Stalinization. He concludes that, although Soviet historiography is no longer called upon to indulge in the same type of falsification that existed during the thirties and forties, it will continue to remain mostly nonobjective, as long as it is subordinated to the task of propagating a particular world view.

1

PAUL ROLEY
Western Washington
State College

FLEXIBILITY AND DOGMATISM:
THE AMBIGUOUS LEGACY OF LENINISM

The eminent American historian of the French Revolution, R. R. Palmer, claims that Maximilien Robespierre is "one of the most argued about and least understood men of modern times."[1] However accurate Palmer's assessment, it strikes one that this description might also be applied to V. I. Lenin, whose character and doctrines have proved to be so elusive as to baffle even his closest colleagues.

It is indicative of the complexity of the man that in the great party debates of the mid-1920s both the right- and left-wing Bolsheviks, who were espousing essentially opposed policies, could with complete sincerity appeal to the example of the departed leader. Thus one of Trotsky's closest supporters, G. L. Piatakov, is reported as arguing in a private conversation in 1928 that

> the essential Lenin . . . was not to be found in the creator of NEP and in the leader's last articles, which were . . . the product of weariness and sickness. The real Lenin was the man who had had the courage to make a proletarian revolution first, and then to set about creating the objective conditions theoretically necessary as a preliminary to such a revolution.[2]

Just a year later, however, N. I. Bukharin, the foremost right-wing theoretician, addressing a memorial meeting on the fifth anniversary of Lenin's death, called the last five articles from the hand of the great leader "Lenin's Political Testament" and described them as his "wisest words" and "final instructions."[3]

Bukharin was probably correct in his claim that the course charted by Lenin in 1921 and after was the policy line he had intended to pursue over an indefinite period of time.[4] More to the point, however, is that these contradictory assessments of "the essential Lenin" by leading party figures, both of whom claimed to be true disciples of the master, are indicative of the difficulty of distilling the "essence" of Leninism, of distinguishing the fundamental characteristic or characteristics composing that complex and elusive creed.

The error one hazards in attempting to discover the "essence of Leninism" is that committed by the three blind men in the fable who undertook an examination of the elephant. It will be recalled that each isolated a particular feature of that curious beast and thereupon proceeded to identify the whole with the part he had happened to encounter, thus arriving at diametrically opposed conclusions concerning its physical nature. In the opinion of this author this is precisely the error that most Western students of the subject have been guilty of when they identify the Leninist organizational principle as the central element of Leninism.[5]

It is true, of course, that from at least 1902 Lenin was a vigorous exponent of a highly centralized, tightly disciplined party organization. Yet for approximately the first eighteen years of their existence the Bolsheviks were an unruly, contentious group whose congresses and central committee plenums were often the scenes of vociferous disagreement and impassioned debates.[6] Indeed, such a basically hostile observer as Leonard Schapiro admits that "it was not . . . until 1921 . . . that it [Lenin's doctrine on party organization] began to be put into practice."[7] The fact is that, except in those instances where issues he considered fundamental were involved, Lenin was not intolerant of dissent. As early as 1909, for instance, he stated that "a party may include a whole gamut of opinions, the extremes of which may even sharply contradict one another";[8] and toward the end of his life he wrote Bukharin: "If you are going to throw out all the not-always-obedient but clever people and keep only the obedient fools, you will *definitely* ruin the party."[9]

One should not carry this argument too far, however: Lenin was a firm believer in the *principle* of party discipline and, on occasion, strictly insisted upon it. Nevertheless, the organizational principle was not the essential characteristic of Leninism, but rather was a consequence of an outlook that was fundamental to his whole approach to politics (though always within the framework of an ideologically tight Marxist program), that which Louis Fischer calls "Lenin's practicality, which swept away considerations of theory, principle, precedent, and previous policy."[10]

This trait has been variously labeled as "pragmatism," "realism," "flexibility," and even "opportunism," or, according to this author's view, as a willingness to compromise with reality on the tactical level. This latter formulation admits both the possibility of changes in tactics as conditions warrant and the permissibility of compromise and retreat when necessary. Lenin was an advocate and practitioner of both types of maneuvers. Thus we find him on one occasion stressing the virtue of flexibility, which he described as ". . . the ability to effect swift and sudden changes of tactics if changes in objective conditions demand them, and to choose another path to our goal if the former path seems inexpedient or impossible at the given time."[11] Such flexibility might also on occasion require that distasteful compromises be undertaken, but "to reject compromises 'on principle,' to reject any possibility of compromises in general, no matter what kind, is childishness, which is difficult even to consider seriously."[12] These two tactics are but opposite sides of the same coin, however, and must be viewed as arising out of the same pragmatic or practical outlook.

Whatever term is used to describe this trait, none can doubt that it was one of Lenin's most distinctive characteristics. The most commonly cited examples of this are the reversal of the decision to boycott the Duma in 1906, the submission to the onerous German terms dictated at Brest-Litovsk in 1918, and the abrupt about-face executed in March 1921, when the New Economic Policy was adopted. Yet it may be argued that this tactical flexibility, this willingness to compromise with reality, was one of the basic principles guiding Lenin's approach to politics and thus exerted a strong influence on the shaping of his entire program. If this be the case, his article "Left-Wing Communism, An Infantile Disease," in which he most clearly enunciated his tactics of flexibility and compromise, is an even more fundamental statement of the Leninist creed than is the oft-cited "What Is To Be Done."

The latter, of course, contains the classic exposition of the organizational principle. Since the question of the significance of this to the whole creed of Leninism is central to our discussion here, it should be closely examined. A reading of Lenin's text reveals that the need for a tightly organized, highly disciplined party was justified on the basis of three premises.

In the first place, it was argued that the Russian proletariat, while capable of revolutionary spontaneity—i.e., of on occasion rising up in revolt against its oppressors—was not possessed of revolutionary consciousness. It did not understand the basic dynamics of its own situation and therefore was not aware of its own long-range interests. It was for this reason that the proletariat was susceptible to the seductions of trade unionism, which would possibly gain it economic advantages but which could not free it from its bondage. According to Lenin, "The history of all countries shows that the working class, exclusively by its own effort, is in a position to work out only a trade-union consciousness."[13] Thus to have the ranks filled with large numbers of politically untutored workers who could, in a democratic framework, swing the balance of power within the party would be to expose it to the risk of swerving from its revolutionary mission and taking the road to revisionism.

Secondly, the party should therefore be made up of a small vanguard of politically conscious revolutionaries who would preserve its doctrinal purity and could serve as political tutors to the proletariat. "No revolutionary movement can endure without a stable organization of leaders maintaining continuity," Lenin opined. Furthermore, "The more widely the masses spontaneously drawn into the struggle form the basis of the movement and participate in it, the greater is the necessity for such an organization and the more stable this organization must be."[14]

Finally, strict organizational discipline was necessary to combat the tendency toward argumentativeness, indecisiveness, and excessive willfulness on the part of the intellectuals, who composed the bulk of the party membership.

Who can doubt the essential accuracy of these three premises? Had not the examples of the German Social Democrats and the Russian Economists clearly indicated the dangers of revisionism, of a dilution of the revolutionary thrust of Marxism? Indeed, has not the history of Western Marxism since the 1900s revealed the likelihood of such distortions of the movement? Did not the experience of the Mensheviks and other non-Bolshevik Marxist factions indicate that the revolutionary intelligentsia, if not properly harnessed, could reduce a political party to impotence? As for the central issue concerning the political sophistication of the workers: Were they or were they not innately imbued with revolutionary consciousness as Marx had claimed and most Social Democrats believed? The fact is that both Marx and Engels had themselves developed doubts concerning this topic after 1848.[15] Furthermore, Richard Pipes has shown that neither Lenin nor his Marxist comrades in St. Petersburg had enjoyed much success in the political agitation among the proletariat in the mid-1890s, that, indeed, they had to involve themselves in the workers' economic struggle and eschew political agitation, and that this experience had given impetus to the development of Economism. Professor Pipes further suggested that this experience had led Lenin to the realization that, left to their own devices, the workers were capable of developing only a trade union outlook.[16] Lenin was right in this respect, just as he was right in his other two premises. These considerations were firmly grounded in the realities of the situation. According to Robert Daniels:

> Lenin's organizational ideas were not ill adapted to Russian conditions and the Russian temperament. It was precisely the evils which Lenin warned against—inadequate discipline, overconcern with theory at the expense of practical work, the excessive individualism of the intellectuals, failure to adjust tactics to changes in the political situation—that proved the undoing of [Bogdanov's group.][17]

Thus Lenin's demand for a centralized, disciplined party organization was based on very practical considerations. The organizational principle may be seen, then, as a direct outgrowth of his political realism, and the latter in turn reveals itself as a basic element of Leninism.

It would be mistaken to claim that pragmatism was the very essence of the Leninist creed. Though it is, in the author's opinion, the *main* characteristic, part of the complexity of Leninism arises from the fact that it is composed of seemingly contradictory elements. Thus, in addition to a large dose of tactical flexibility, one may also discover an only slightly smaller measure of doctrinal rigidity, which could be identified as the second most important element in the composition of Leninism.

There are those who would question Lenin's Marxist orthodoxy,[18] who, indeed, would go so far as to label Lenin as more revisionist than those whom he so often denounced for that sin. This seems to obfuscate our understanding of Lenin and his work. The misconception arises from that very flexibility that has been discussed above. The fact is that in fundamentals, in matters involving basic doctrine or tending to dull the revolutionary thrust of Marxism, he was rigidly doctrinaire. According to one of his earliest associates, Lenin ". . . could permit himself the luxury . . . of being opportunistic in matters of the method of the struggle, for he always knew how far one could go in such cases and at what moment questions of tactic began to affect purely programmatic issues, which demand complete obstinacy."[19] Thus at the tactical level, Lenin was a loose interpreter of Marxism, while on basic philosophic questions he was the most dogmatic of ideologues. He took the position that tactical flexibility, engaged in for the advancement of the cause, not only did no violence to the letter of Marxism but was squarely within the spirit of the creed. "Our theory is not a dogma, but a *guide to action*," he declared, quoting Engels.[20] But to tamper with the philosophic foundations of Marxism, to weaken its revolutionary impact was not permissible. "Any belittling of socialist ideology, *any departure* from it, means the same as strengthening bourgeois ideology," Lenin wrote in 1902.[21]

There can be no doubt, in fact, that Lenin was a committed Marxist, unreservedly accepting the world view the system outlined and the socialist vision it foresaw. "For [both] Marx and Lenin," wrote Alfred Meyer, ". . . the goal is . . . freedom from the forces of nature and society, freedom for the unhampered development of all potentialities inherent in man as an individual and as a species, most specifically, freedom of man from exploitation."[22] With this commitment, then, the overriding consideration was the attainment of the ideal, which was the absolute good for which everything else could be sacrificed. The same party comrade quoted above considered that for Lenin "every means of struggle . . . is good or bad depending on whether, in the given circumstances, it conduces to the attainment of those ends or, on the contrary diverts from them."[23] This was not merely the old rationale that the end justifies the means; it was also a commitment to tactical flexibility. Leninism admitted of only one other principle: an unswerving adherence to the philosophic system that foresaw and guaranteed the realization of the socialist goal.

Before the complexities of Leninism become coherent, these two principles must be viewed within the context of a singular element of Lenin's character: his absolute faith in his own judgment. It has often been argued that Lenin manifested a compulsive drive to dominate or destroy. There is probably more than a grain of truth in this assertion, but to attribute this drive to an inherently authoritarian nature is to disregard considerable evidence that in many ways Lenin was essentially a humane individual and was utterly immune to the corruptions of power. A more consistent and, perhaps, truer picture may be obtained if we accept the fact of his basic decency, add in the traits already discussed—a pragmatic outlook coupled with a total commitment to the Marxist *Weltanschauung* and to the socialist ideal—and postulate a third ingredient: an unswerving conviction of his own rectitude. What emerges, then, is an honest fanatic who was so absolutely convinced that his course was the correct one for the achievement of the great ideal that he was ultimately capable of almost any expedient. Such a man could be the kindest of comrades but the most inexorable of enemies, as he was in his continuing fight against ideological revisionism and tactical error. "Against any attempt to abuse Marxism or confuse the policy of the workers' party we will fight without sparing life," Lenin once wrote Gorkii,[24] thus clearly enunciating the two principles of his political creed.

Leninism, then, is compounded of equal parts of a total commitment to revolutionary Marxism and a healthy pragmatism on the tactical level. But was it possible to maintain that delicate balance over a long period of time? Starkov may have seen Lenin as knowing just how far he could compromise with reality without impinging on purely programmatic issues, but there remains the question of how long even an astute mind like Lenin's could differentiate between the two, particularly under the very real pressures of exercising state power and attempting to make a government and a society function in conditions Marx never foresaw. When does compromise cease to become a tactic and become a habit? Is not the first compromise something like the loss of virginity in that afterwards each succeeding temptation becomes more difficult to resist? Indeed, one could argue, as Piatakov did in essence, that during the last years of his life Lenin capitulated to reality, setting aside the claims of revolutionary Marxism and concentrating on the practical problem of making the system that existed work. And if Lenin were susceptible to seduction, how much more so were his successors? While the answer to this question lies in the eye of the beholder, it is perhaps the central problem in interpreting the Soviet experience.

For his heirs the legacy of Lenin was an ambiguous one. Bukharin, speaking for the right wing, identified the essence of Leninism as tactical compromise while Piatakov, representing the leftists, saw it as revolutionary purism.

What is undoubted is the enormous moral authority Lenin exercised even from the grave; the only problem was to identify the moral. Under the circumstances, then, the mantle was inevitably to descend upon the one who could most adroitly manipulate the Leninist scriptures to buttress his case and whose policies and programs were most in tune with the mood of the party and of the country in the transition period.

As it turned out, pragmatism triumphed over the revolutionary ethic, and it is probably fortunate for both Russia and the world that it did. Both would have been better off, however, if that pragmatism had been more principled.

But that, too, is part of the Leninist legacy, for just as tactical flexibility is always subject to being interpreted as unprincipled opportunism, so can unscrupulous men claim the sanction of precedent set by more decent predecessors. Thus was Stalin usually able to invoke the example of the master in defense of his most heavy-handed policies. For instance, those who opposed forced collectivization, he said in 1928, "are not Marxists or Leninists, but peasant philosophers. . . ."[25]

Lenin's main legacy, then, was a pragmatic flexibility that his successor prostituted into the most blatant and unprincipled opportunism, sacrificing ideological commitment to minute consideration of policy, prestige, and power, yes, and even to whim. Isaac Deutscher claims that in the days of the First Five-Year Plan "highly placed Bolsheviks" were saying that "one Soviet tractor is worth more than ten good foreign Communists."[26] Is this simply good sense or is it a negation of the purposes for which the Bolshevik revolution was made? One suspects that Lenin, while recognizing both the practical and ideological utility of tractors, would have denounced the terms in which the choice was made as utterly alien to the spirit of Marxism. But who is to say? The answer is the party leadership, which means in practice that Leninism may be invoked to sanction whatever the ruling group decides is needed and right—or merely expedient. While men may legitimately disagree on the extent to which Lenin is a flawed hero, few can doubt that much that was done by his successor under the imprimatur of Leninism was a perversion of what he stood for.

NOTES

1. R. R. Palmer and Joel Cotton, *A History of the Modern World*, 3rd ed., New York: Knopf, 1965, p. 359.
2. N. Valentinov (N. V. Vol'skii), "Sut' bol'shevizma v izobrazhenii Iu. Piatakova," *Novyi zhurnal* (New York), no. 52 (1958), pp. 140–61. Quoted in Leonard Schapiro, *The Communist Party of the Soviet Union*, New York: Random House, 1959, pp. 380–81.
3. *Pravda*, Jan. 24, 1929.

4. Although scholars have long inclined toward this view, taking Lenin's last works as an outline of his plans for the future, there is now even more substantial evidence indicating that this was the case. It was revealed by the late Boris Nicolaevsky that Bukharin told him in 1936 of a conversation with Lenin that occurred in the fall of 1922 in which the latter revealed his ideas concerning future policy. According to Bukharin, they were

partly set forth in Lenin's last articles, although his death cut short the full exposition of them. See Boris Nicolaevsky, *Power and the Soviet Elite: "The Letter of an Old Bolshevik" and Other Essays*, ed. Janet Zagoria, New York: Praeger, 1965, pp. 11–13.

I am indebted to Professor Sidney Heitman of Colorado State University for pointing out that passage in Nicolaevsky to me. Professor Heitman discusses the matter at some length in the introduction to his collection of Bukharin's writing, *Put' k sotsializmu v. Rossii: Izbrannye proizvedeniia N. I. Bukharina*, New York: Omicron, 1967, pp. 50–52.

5. See, for instance, Alfred G. Meyer, *Leninism*, New York: Praeger, 1962, p. 15.

6. See Robert V. Daniels, *The Conscience of the Revolution: Communist Opposition in Soviet Russia*, Cambridge, Mass.: Harvard, 1960, p. 3.

7. Leonard Schapiro, *The Origin of the Communist Autocracy: Political Opposition in the Soviet State—First Phase, 1917–1922*, New York: Praeger, 1965, pp. 343–44.

8. V. I. Lenin, *Polnoe Sobranie Sochinenii*, 5th ed., 55 vols., Moscow, 1958–65, XIX, 6. (Hereafter cited as *Soch*. This new, more complete, and magnificently edited edition,

which contains many significant new materials not previously in print, is, in my estimation, preferable to the standard second or third editions.)

9. *Pravda*, Sept. 12, 1928.

10. Louis Fischer, *The Life of Lenin*, New York: Harper & Row, 1964, p. 667.

11. *Soch.*, XLIV, 151.

12. *Ibid.*, XLI, 20.

13. *Ibid.*, VI, 30.

14. *Ibid.*, p. 124.

15. See Meyer, *op. cit.*, p. 12.

16. Richard Pipes, *Social Democracy and the St. Petersburg Labor Movement, 1885–1897*, Cambridge, Mass.: Harvard, 1963.

17. Daniels, *op. cit.*, pp. 25–26.

18. See, for instance, Meyer, *op. cit.*, p. 12.

19. V. Starkov, *Krasnaya nov'*, November 1925. Quoted in Fischer, *op. cit.*, p. 21.

20. *Soch.*, XLI, 55. Lenin had, in fact, misquoted Engels, but the spirit of the quotation was not distorted.

21. *Ibid.*, VI, 40.

22. Meyer, *op. cit.*, p. 11.

23. Starkov, *op. cit.* Quoted in Fischer, *op. cit.*, p. 21.

24. *Soch.*, LXVIII, 141.

25. *Pravda*, July 15, 1928.

26. Isaac Deutscher, *Stalin: A Political Biography*, 2nd ed., New York: Oxford, 1967, p. 405.

2

ERIK P. HOFFMANN
State University of
New York at Albany

IDEOLOGICAL ADMINISTRATION UNDER KHRUSHCHEV: A STUDY OF INTRAPARTY COMMUNICATION

A major concern of this study is the relationship between organizational communication and administrative efficiency. In an effort to bring Soviet data to bear on this question, empirical evidence has been gathered to identify communication patterns within the Communist party of the Soviet Union (CPSU) and to study intraparty communication on "ideological work" during the Khrushchev era. Particular attention will be paid to the Soviet leaders' perennial contention that "shortcomings" in domestic political education *result* from inefficient "leadership" or "guidance" (*rukovodstvo*) by regional party organizations.

The central hypothesis to be examined is taken from the general literature on administrative behavior. Confirmed in various contexts, the proposition is: "Organizations which have a high degree of vertical and horizontal communication are more likely to have a high degree of effectiveness than organizations which have a low degree of vertical and horizontal communication."[1] Data to test this hypothesis could be

This article is reprinted with permission from *Canadian Slavic Studies* IV (1970), 736–766.

drawn from organizations in any Communist or non-Communist nation. The present study focuses on Soviet experience from 1956 to 1964, a period during which intraparty communication on ideological work greatly increased. Some party leaders seem to have assumed that improved intraorganizational communication was the essential component, if not the equivalent, of *rukovodstvo*. Also, many officials apparently hoped that better communication between the central and regional party apparatuses, and among cadres of provincial CPSU organizations, would help propagandists have a greater impact on the thinking and behavior of Soviet citizens and on the growth of the economy.

Did increased intraparty communication have the effects intended and desired by Soviet leaders? Before hazarding answers to this question, it is first necessary to describe in some detail the prevalence and distribution of various kinds of communication within the CPSU, and to identify important communication channels, formal and informal, through which leadership was exerted.

Let us begin by defining some of the concepts used in this study. "Technical communication" refers to "messages" relevant to the performance of specific tasks—for example, the oral and written directives that inform a propagandist of his daily assignments or provide him with practical assistance in performing his official duties. Information of this kind might include anything from commonsense advice on the use of visual aids to empirical sociological data on the impact of different types of propaganda on various strata of the population. Technical communication facilitates the fulfillment of tasks already defined. It provides an employee with material, physical, and technological assistance in carrying out responsibilities he clearly understands and accepts as "legitimate."

"Normative communication," on the other hand, refers to messages that help to delineate tasks, rules, and responsibilities—for example, the expectations of higher-ranking officials that help to define or clarify the role of the provincial ideological secretary and to prescribe proper behavior in situations when he is forced to choose among seemingly conflicting professional, social, and personal responsibilities. Normative communication within an organization consists of the expectations of one's superiors, peers, and subordinates about one's behavior on the job. This kind of communication may also be intended to provide or in fact provide the psychological support or "satisfactions" needed to fulfill these expectations. Technical communication, in contrast, provides the tangible material assistance and instructions needed to carry out such expectations.[2]

A sharp distinction between "communication" and "interaction" will not be drawn. As Blau and Scott have succinctly observed, these concepts

> refer to the same processes but different aspects of them. The concept of social interaction focuses principally upon the formal characteristics of social relations: such terms as frequency, initiative, superordination, and reciprocity indicate its dimensions. The concept of communication, on the other hand, directs attention to the meaningful content conveyed in the encounter, and its characteristics are described by such terms as the flow of messages, obstacles, positive and negative reactions, and exchanges.[3]

The phrase "meaningful content" blurs an important distinction, however. For the *intent, substance,* and *effects* of communication differ profoundly. Although the researcher may be able to assess the purposes, content, and consequences of different communications, he must very carefully distinguish among his concepts in order to keep them logically and empirically discrete. In this study, "communication" refers exclusively to the substance or content of the written and oral messages transmitted.

A sharp distinction between "vertical" and "horizontal" communication must be drawn. Vertical communication refers to communication among party committees at different levels of the CPSU. For example, central party organs frequently communicate with republic and provincial CPSU committees, and provincial committees (*obkomy* and *kraikomy*) with city (*gorkomy*) and district party committees (*raikomy*). Horizontal communication, on the other hand, refers to communication among party organizations at the same level of the CPSU, and among different departments of the same party committee.

Specific kinds of communication do not necessarily flow through discrete channels, formal and informal. In other words, various kinds of technical and normative communication may be transmitted through the same channel. Moreover, the same message may be intended to serve very different purposes, and it may indeed have very different effects on various audiences within the CPSU and other Soviet organizations. With little interview data and direct observation, it is quite difficult to study the nature and impact of inter- and intraorganizational communication within the USSR. Thus, in an exploratory study such as this, it is probably best to limit the conceptualization and measurement of communication to the two general types described above.

The concept of "administrative efficiency," also broadly defined, relies heavily on Chester Barnard's classic analysis of organizational "effectiveness" and "efficiency." Effectiveness is a measure of material productiveness or, more generally, of the degree to which the central goal or purpose of the organization is being achieved. Efficiency refers to the willingness and capacity of the members of an organization to contribute their energies and talents toward attaining the primary goals of the organization as the leaders of the organization define those goals. It is virtually impossible to create an organization whose actions are in fact or are perceived as being equally beneficial to its various subgroups and to the organization as a whole. But an organization may be considered "efficient" to the extent that its employees believe that the stated purposes of the organization can and should be implemented, and that its executives generate for their subordinates and for themselves continuing material and nonmaterial satisfactions to sustain that belief. Barnard writes: "Efficiency of effort in the fundamental sense with which we are here concerned is efficiency relative to the securing of necessary personal contributions to the cooperative system."[4] For Barnard, the "effectiveness" of an organization concerns the relevance of its purposes to the environment in which it operates (goal attainment or maximization); the "efficiency" of an organization refers to the extent of coordinated effort and cooperative relationships among the members of the organization. With emphasis on the latter, *both* of these phenomena will be subsumed under the term "administrative efficiency" in this study.

It will now be argued that the available data substantially confirm each of the following descriptive generalizations and assertions:

1. Until 1959 there was surprisingly little technical and normative communication among departments of propaganda and agitation at the same and different levels of the CPSU. Also, there seems to have been relatively little interaction among leading cadres in different propaganda and agitation departments. Between 1956 and 1959 there was slightly more communication than before. This was brought about largely through the work of newly formed "propaganda groups" dispatched by *obkom* and *gorkom* bureaus to assist lower-level party committees with their ideological work.

2. Between 1959 and 1964 interaction among propaganda cadres and vertical intraparty communication of both types increased significantly. Important new channels of communication were created

between the upper and middle levels of the CPSU. New lines of communication were also opened up between provincial and lower-level party and government organs. The available evidence indicates that the increased flow of information about ideological work was transmitted mainly through four kinds of channels, the first three of which were created between mid-1958 and 1961: (a) investigatory and advisory activities of small itinerant teams of Agitprop officials; (b) numerous conferences on ideological work at all levels of the party; (c) "instructional groups" created primarily to improve communication between *raion* and primary party organizations; and (d) existing communication channels such as party journals, established lecture groups, and formal reports.

PROBLEMS OF INTRAPARTY COMMUNICATION, 1953–1959

In his classic study of public opinion in the USSR, published in 1950, Alex Inkeles asserts:

> the absolute control of all matters affecting public opinion
> is concentrated and centralized in the hands of the Depart-
> ment of Propaganda and Agitation, whose lines of authority
> reach out to include the lowliest secretary for propaganda
> and agitation in the smallest executive committee of some
> remote primary party organization in factory or village.[5]

In Soviet theory, of course, this is true. Decisions of higher party bodies are absolutely binding on lower bodies.[6] Nevertheless, many propaganda and agitation departments do not seem to have been closely supervised by their respective party bureaus or by the agitprop departments immediately above them in the party hierarchy. Inkeles's statement may more accurately describe desired conditions than actual ones—perhaps to an increasing degree after Andrei Zhdanov's death in 1948 and during the early 1950s.

It is possible of course that freer criticism of certain conditions merely reflects political leaders' renewed interest in changing those conditions, rather than the sudden emergence of new problems or the worsening of old ones. In September 1955, however, a *Kommunist* editorial bluntly asserted that "many Party committees still guide ideological work in an unsatisfactory manner. Delegates at Party conferences justly criticize the *raikomy*, *gorkomy,* and *obkomy* for paying insufficient attention to propaganda and agitation, bordering on non-chalance and indifference."[7]

These criticisms were elaborated upon in a *Kommunist* editorial of 1956. Allegedly the political education of party cadres was being conducted "almost exclusively" by propaganda and agitation department personnel.[8] Also, it was charged that workers in other departments—including CPSU secretaries—rarely participated in any kind of ideological work. When "the powerful weapon" of propaganda was placed "exclusively" *(bezrazdel'no)* in the hands of one department, an *obkom* could not efficiently direct the work of lower-level committees. Moreover, the editorial warned that party guidance of ideological work must not be allowed to sink to the level where *obkom* bureaus merely discuss *raikom* reports from time to time, and *raikomy* occasionally discuss reports from primary party organizations. CPSU secretaries were sternly reminded of their responsibility to organize ideological activities carefully and to participate personally in mass-political work. Furthermore, *kraikom* and *obkom* bureaus were urged to obtain accurate and up-to-date information about the administration of ideological work in their respective bailiwicks—especially information about the political training of Communists at the *raion* level. "Effective leadership" must be based on "careful study" and "first-hand knowledge," it was pointedly observed.[9]

In 1960 Leonid Ilichev summed up his views on the shortcomings of Soviet ideological administration. "In essence, the entire problem right now lies in organizational work."[10] But where was the necessary leadership to come from? Which party organs should bear the responsibility for planning, supervising, and carrying out ideological activities? During the 1950s CPSU leaders seem to have assumed that middle-level party committees could do the job largely by themselves —that is, conduct their own political education programs with minimal assistance and prodding from Agitprop. Numerous directives, instructions, and responses may have been communicated through private channels. But fragmentary evidence suggests that there was surprisingly little private communication and interaction among indoctrination specialists of the central and regional party apparatuses. Furthermore, public communication about ideological work was less frequent and less frank than in the 1960s. Problems of communication and coordination between national and provincial party organs were simply not acknowledged, for example.

One finds clear references, however, to the lack of vertical communication and interaction among officials within the same provincial party organization and to their allegedly insufficient leadership of ideological work. In 1956, for example, Ekaterina Furtseva delivered a blistering attack on the Moscow Party organization.

> It is very obvious that improvements in ideological work are inconceivable without a reorganization *(perestroi-ka)* and radical improvement of its guidance by party organizations—the *raikomy* and *gorkomy* of the CPSU. It will be necessary to reorganize the departments of propaganda and agitation ahead of all the others.[11]

Furtseva went on to express her opinions on the most important current problems of ideological administration. "The main shortcoming of propaganda and agitation departments is that they are still poorly acquainted with life"—that is, they are "linked" with only "a narrow circle of the *aktiv*," their workers "rarely associate with propagandists and agitators, do a poor job of studying the organization of party-political work in the localities, and weakly disseminate the experience of leading propagandists, agitators, and lecturers."[12]

Furtseva went on to describe a model *raion,* where conferences were regularly held for secretaries of primary party organizations. Important *raion* officials, including the first secretary, freely discussed questions of ideological administration with other cadres. *Obkom* officials also participated from time to time. But Furtseva concluded: "Unfortunately, examples such as this are few."[13]

By 1959 a more sensitive topic was openly discussed—the previous lack of communication and cooperation among republic and lower-level party organizations. A *Kommunist* editorial declared:

> It would be incorrect to assume that in the future local cadres should do all the work in explaining the materials of a party congress. It is necessary that groups from the *aktivy* of republic and oblast centers be sent regularly, systematically, into enterprises and *kolkhozy,* city and *raion* centers, to help local party committees organize mass-political work and to participate directly in explaining the materials of the Twenty-first Party Congress.[14]

The phrases "in the future," "all the work," "regularly," and "systematically" suggest that interlevel cooperation of this kind had not been common in the past.

A sweeping indictment of republic and provincial party organizations appeared in the important Central Committee decree of January

9, 1960. Implicitly, certain CPSU committees were charged with negligence in the field of ideological administration.

> The Party Central Committee considers that the main reason for the shortcomings in party propaganda is that some Central Committees of Union Republic Communist parties, *krai* and oblast party committees, and agencies and institutions engaged in questions of ideological work are doing a poor job of guiding this most important sector of party work.[15]

Communication aspects of this problem were illuminated by an anonymous writer in June 1961:

> The Central Committee of the CPSU notes the absence of a well-thought-out system *(otsutstvie produmannoi sistemy)* of work with full-time propaganda cadres of the party apparatus. . . . It is unfortunate that we rarely if ever organize oblast, *krai,* and republic seminars for the leaders of the permanently operating propagandists' seminars that are attached to the *raikomy* and *gorkomy* of the party and to the larger primary party organizations. Not less than twice a year the leaders of propagandists' seminars and the leaders of lecture groups should participate in seminars at the oblast, *krai,* and republic levels. The work of these seminars should be founded on creative discussion of Marxist-Leninist theory and the politics of the party, the most important economic-political tasks facing an oblast, *krai,* or republic, and also on the exchange of views concerning the practice and methods of propaganda work.[16]

By 1961 a still more delicate subject was publicly discussed: the previous lack of contact between central and republic officials. Addressing the All-Union Ideological Conference in December 1961, A. K. Kazakbaev, a secretary in the Central Committee of the Kirgiz Republic, requested that Agitprop officials visit his republic more often, preferably several times a year and on a regularly scheduled basis.[17] Kazakbaev explained his views in two revealing passages:

> Regular visits by teams of Agitprop officials would not only help the propaganda profession and enrich the content of local propaganda work, but they would also promote business-like collaboration and help to develop personal contacts between the Republic's ideological workers and

central ideological institutions, leading scholars, and out-standing figures in science, culture, and art. . . .

At the same time, it would be desirable to extend the network of permanently operating courses and seminars of the CPSU Central Committee, in order to give the ideo-logical workers of different republics a greater opportunity to exchange experiences, especially the workers of the re-public and central newspapers, journals, radio, and tele-vision.

It is also necessary to strengthen the ties *(sviazi)* be-tween central creative institutions and departments and republic institutions. The absence or weakness of these ties results in unfortunate blunders *(privodit k dosadnym pro-makham)* and undesirable misunderstandings.[18]

Evidence of this kind suggests that "the absolute control of all matters affecting public opinion" was not in fact "concentrated and centralized" in the hands of Agitprop. But one surely cannot conclude that all departments of propaganda and agitation were autonomous organs during the 1950s. When a party official cites specific examples of interlevel cooperation, there is little reason to doubt his word. I. Spiridonov, for example, described a fruitful series of seminars that were held in 1958 for the editorial staffs of *raion* newspapers and all heads of *raikom* propaganda and agitation sections of the Leningrad Oblast.[19] Regardless of the subjects discussed, these meetings almost certainly increased technical and normative communication and served their intended purpose—namely, to help disseminate accurate informa-tion about "the leading experience of agitational-propaganda work."[20]

An important attempt to increase communication among indoctri-nation specialists was the creation of "propaganda groups." After the Twentieth Party Congress, Soviet leaders stepped up their efforts to improve technical communication between middle- and lower-level party committees. *Kraikom* and *obkom* bureaus were strongly urged to gather accurate information about the state of ideological work in their respective provinces and to disseminate useful information about polit-ical education. To do so, party organizations were ordered to form small itinerant teams of propagandists. A directive to this effect is not contained in any published decree of the Central Committee, but later accounts suggest that the first of these "propaganda groups" were created in 1956.[21] By 1958 all *kraikom* and *obkom* organizations in the RSFSR had dispatched propaganda groups to their *raiony*.[22] During

1958, for example, teams of indoctrination specialists visited every district in the Moscow and Leningrad oblasty at least three or four times.[23] In turn, *gorkomy* and *raikomy* also began to send propagandists directly into factories, collective farms, and brigades.

Ideally, an *obkom* propaganda group consisted of four or five leading party, soviet, and trade union officials. In a major source of information on the subject, the professions of individual cadres are carefully noted.[24] They include instructors in departments of propaganda and agitation, members of the editorial board of a local newspaper, the head of an oblast Society for the Dissemination of Political and Scientific Knowledge, and lecturers from the same institution. Members of propaganda groups were to be "experienced organizers of mass-political work," as well as competent lecturers.[25] Furthermore, cadres were to receive detailed instructions from various *obkom* secretaries, and could also expect careful briefings on local conditions from other important party, soviet, and *sovnarkhoz* officials.[26] In theory, at least, propaganda groups were well prepared to render "valuable assistance" to lower-level party organizations.

In fact, the quality of the personnel selected for propaganda groups seems to have fallen far short of the high standards described above. The usefulness of their work also left much to be desired in some, perhaps many, provinces. Although propaganda groups were rarely criticized in the press, at least three serious "shortcomings" have been acknowledged, each of which clearly impeded upward and downward vertical communication within the party.[27]

First, cadres assigned to this job were often inexperienced in administrative work and did not receive adequate assistance or instructions from leading regional officials. Second, many teams merely delivered speeches to informal gatherings of citizens and did not meet with important *raion* officials. Third, leaders of propaganda groups were sometimes not even asked to submit reports on the work they had performed, "so that their activities [could] be discussed in the *obkomy* and *kraikomy* of the party."[28]

For example, a certain provincial committee had "frequently" received "signals" about the neglect of ideological work in one of its *raiony,* and the *obkom* bureau eventually sent a propaganda group to investigate and correct the situation.[29] But members of this team merely delivered a few critical speeches and then departed. Reportedly they did not render any assistance to the *raion* party committee and were not at all interested in investigating the current state of mass-political work. The *obkom* continued to receive "signals" after the return of the propaganda group and was soon forced to send another team of cadres back into the same district.

What was the nature of these "signals"? Were they sent through channels within the party apparatus or party Control Committee? Were they received directly from private citizens or perhaps forwarded by the oblast press? In this particular case we simply do not know. But in a rare reference to the subject, a Voronezh *obkom* secretary noted that fifty propaganda groups had been dispatched to the *raiony* in 1959 and had visited over seven thousand schools, seminars, and study circles.[30] He then added: "As a means of checking up on them (*v poriadke kontrolia*), about 300 experienced lecturers listened to their performance and evaluated their work."[31] It is not stated that these "lecturers" actually transmitted critical reports or "signals" to the *obkom* bureau. But these cadres did perform "checking" (*kontrol'*) functions clearly designed to open up new channels of communication to the party bureau and presumably to encourage the flow of accurate information from propaganda groups to permanent party organs.

Lack of data makes it difficult to evaluate the achievements of propaganda groups. Some provided their party bureaus with valuable information; others did not. Some party bureaus utilized accurate information; others ignored it. Surely propaganda groups opened up important new communication channels in certain provinces. But, more important, this did not necessarily improve the quality of ideological administration or "administrative efficiency." For propaganda groups reported directly to their respective *obkom* and *kraikom* bureaus, not to Agitprop. And the available evidence suggests that provincial party bureaus were often quite reluctant to pass on unfavorable information to central party organs.[32]

In 1956 leading CPSU officials had reassessed the state of ideological administration and apparently concluded that provincial party committees must continue to perform much of the "organizational work" needed to eliminate current problems. But, despite the proliferation of propaganda groups, little progress seems to have been made in the years immediately thereafter. The major Central Committee decree of January 9, 1960, not only specifies measures to improve ideological work, but is itself a tacit acknowledgment that past programs had not been very efficient or effective ("efficient" in the sense of administrative efficiency; "effective" in the sense of influencing significantly the attitudes, beliefs, and behavior of Soviet citizens). A need was registered between 1956 and 1959, but problems were not resolved. What seems to have happened is that the Central Committee said to the regional party organizations, "Do this! Do that!" And nothing happened.[33]

IMPROVEMENTS IN VERTICAL COMMUNICATION, 1959–1964

The foregoing discussion suggests that prior to 1960, when and if "operational measures" were taken to improve the quality of political education work, the success of these measures depended to a very great extent on the initiative and administrative skills of officials in middle-level party bureaus and propaganda and agitation departments. If *obkom* cadres lacked these qualities, lower-level committees were left to shift for themselves. Despite careful top-level planning by Agitprop, the dedicated efforts of individual propagandists, and the increased vertical communication that may have been achieved by the newly created propaganda groups, the overall efficiency of the CPSU's ideological activities could not be significantly improved without competent management at the provincial level.

Did most *krai* and oblast party committees have the trained personnel needed to implement the new policies formulated in 1956 (e.g., the deliberate proliferation of seminars and study circles, increased economic studies for propagandists, recruitment of technical specialists into propaganda work)?[34] It seems not. Even if they had wanted to, *krai* and oblast organizations could not have created out of thin air a sizable group of cadres skilled in organizing ideological activities and able to direct the work of other propagandists—that is, "management executives" capable of formulating political education programs, training personnel at different levels of the regional apparatus, and deploying cadres with greater efficiency.

Ilichev discussed this problem publicly in December 1960. His remarks were summarized in an account of a party ideological conference:

> As a result of the lack of coordination and unified planning of lecture propaganda, it frequently happens that a very large number of lectures are given in some organizations, and very few in others; and in some areas, despite the comparatively broad scope of lecture propaganda, significant segments of the population remain outside the sphere of its influence. . . . "The need has arisen," said Ilichev, "to turn the attention of the party committee's lecture groups in the

direction of organizational work. The lecture groups must concentrate a significant part of their efforts on questions of organizing lecture propaganda: working out the themes of lectures, planning lecture propaganda, controlling the quality of the contents of the lectures, helping lecturers, conducting seminars, etc."[35]

Ilichev noted that "until a few years ago" most lectures were delivered by staff and volunteer workers of the party committees, but that currently the overwhelming majority of lectures were delivered by members of the All-Union Society for the Dissemination of Political and Scientific Knowledge. The message seems clear: lecturers must now assist ideological officials with important administrative tasks such as organizing entire political education programs and supervising other full- and part-time propagandists. It is noteworthy that these are very different kinds of jobs, each demanding skills that are not automatically or easily transferable to the other. Good lecturers are not necessarily good administrators, and vice versa.

A Western scholar has observed that "the department of propaganda and agitation under the Central Committee of the party is much more an operative agency in itself than are most of the other departments which are concerned to supervise the work of the ministries in the state structure."[36] However, Agitprop officials could not personally retrain large numbers of propaganda cadres with any less difficulty than could the bureau of a republic party committee or of an *obkom*. The limited staff of Agitprop also could not direct the day-to-day administration of the policies set forth in 1956 and reaffirmed in 1960. But the Central Committee *could* exert considerably greater pressure on an *obkom* to improve the quality of its ideological work and to fulfill directives previously ignored, circumvented, or only partially implemented. Moreover, Agitprop *could* render greater technical assistance to lower-level departments of propaganda and agitation. In essence, this seems to be precisely what happened in the years from mid-1958 to 1964.

Investigatory and Advisory Activities of Agitprop

The first part of this two-pronged program relied heavily on the investigatory work of small teams of Agitprop officials. One of the earliest references to the activities of these groups was made by Furtseva at the Twenty-first Party Congress.[37] The work of Agitprop cadres was also referred to indirectly in the Central Committee decree of January 9, 1960. It was noted that "a study of the state of ideological work" had been recently conducted "in Moscow and Leningrad, in the Ukrainian, Belorussian, Kazakh, Georgian, and Uzbek Republics, and in Sverdlovsk, Saratov, Ulianovsk and certain other provinces of the Russian Republic."[38] This evidence suggests, and of course is intended to suggest, that the recent investigations by Agitprop were being carried out on a large scale.

Agitprop officials did intensively examine the work of some provincial party organizations, as was clearly revealed in a series of detailed Central Committee decrees. These resolutions reflect meticulous on-the-spot investigation and careful analysis of information gathered. Both the investigations themselves and the highly authoritative way in which they were publicized opened important new channels of communication between the upper and middle levels of the party. Not since the immediate post-World War II period had the Central Committee launched a sustained public campaign to improve the quality of ideological work and so forcefully demanded that all indoctrination specialists contribute their time and skills to this effort.[39]

A similar method of prodding middle-level party committees was introduced in 1960. Reporting in *Partiinaia zhizn'* or *Politicheskoe samoobrazovanie,* high-ranking indoctrination specialists discussed the malfunctioning of party organizations they had recently visited. In December 1960, for example, A. P. Kosul'nikov, then deputy head of the Central Committee's Department of Propaganda and Agitation for the RSFSR, wrote a very critical article about the Karelian *obkom.* Kosul'nikov states that he found "a lack of sharp and concrete criticism and self-criticism about shortcomings in the field of propaganda."[40] He supports this familiar allegation by describing in detail a meeting he or some of his aides had attended personally—a meeting of the Karelian Party *aktiv* that was called to discuss the January 9, 1960, decree and to evaluate the extent to which the oblast was fulfilling the directives contained therein. Kosul'nikov commented:

> In the speech by the *obkom* secretary, Comrade Smirnov, and likewise in the discussion session, not one of the leading party or soviet workers, not one secretary, not one head of a *raikom* department of propaganda and agitation, subjected to criticism the existing shortcomings in ideological work. And the Petrozavodsk *gorkom* secretary, Comrade Martynov, addressing the *aktiv,* did not even in general terms refer to shortcomings, to unresolved problems

in the field of ideological work, having given no evidence to justify this complacency.[41]

Another article of this kind was written by V. Fedinin, possibly an instructor in the Central Committee's Department of Propaganda and Agitation for the RSFSR.[42] Fedinin tells of attending a lecture that had been well publicized in the Vologda Oblast newspaper and held in an *obkom* and *gorkom* Political Education Center. The lecture was so poor that members of the audience openly criticized the speaker at the end of his presentation. Fedinin talked to the man afterward and learned that he was not, in fact, familiar with the subject matter and had merely been "helping out." This was by no means an isolated event, asserted Fedinin, citing other inferior political lectures he had recently attended or learned about.[43]

What caused problems of this kind and other deficiencies in the ideological work of the oblast? Fedinin's answer is extremely interesting. He argues that the basic cause is poor communication between the *obkom, gorkom,* and *raikom* party committees:

> In our view [the problems of ideological administration] can be largely explained by the fact that the CPSU *obkom* is not sufficiently demanding of local party organizations in matters concerning the content and quality of ideological work. Questions of agitational-propaganda work are often discussed in the *obkom* bureau, but decisions are poorly implemented.[44]

To support these general assertions, Fedinin presents detailed and revealing illustrations such as this:

> More than half a year ago, the bureau of the party *obkom* discovered serious shortcomings in the propaganda work of the Babaevo *raion* and demanded that the *raikom* of the CPSU pay greater attention to questions of political work among the masses. However, half a year later, when some interest was shown in the state of affairs there, it turned out that there was just as much blundering and negligence as before.
>
> All of this can be explained by the fact that workers in some party committees quickly forget about decisions that have been made and do not carry out the necessary organizational work to implement them. *During the last six months, not one worker in the propaganda and agitation*

department of the CPSU obkom traveled to the raion and
took an interest in these matters, and not once did they in-
quire—even by telephone—to find out what was being done
to implement the decision of the CPSU obkom. The party
raikom *also forgot about it.*[45]

The effect of Fedinin's criticisms on the subsequent behavior of party officials in the Vologda Oblast and elsewhere is difficult, if not impossible, to measure. The same is true for the statements of Kosul'nikov. But articles of this kind (by observers from Agitprop at public lectures, study circles, *aktiv* and bureau meetings) are unmistakable attempts to transmit messages with normative content to cadres in the regional party apparatus. Reports such as these are not only excellent sources of information about interlevel communication within the CPSU, but are themselves a significant new channel of normative, and to a lesser extent, technical communication.

In the years 1959 to 1964 Agitprop officials also rendered increased technical assistance to indoctrination specialists at middle and lower levels of the party. Although information on this subject is surprisingly difficult to obtain, several republic and provincial officials acknowledged the assistance they had received in speeches at a party conference in December 1961.

The head of the Department of Propaganda and Agitation of the Azerbaijan Republic noted that "propaganda groups of the CPSU Central Committee" had been of "great assistance" to the republic Central Committee in recently organizing a large-scale program of ideological activities. Three-day seminars were conducted for lower-level propaganda cadres in four major cities, and teams of indoctrination officials had been dispatched to all rural *raiony*.[46] A secretary of the Georgian Central Committee also noted that "a propaganda group from the Central Committee of the CPSU" had recently visited his republic. The group consisted of "workers" from the Academy of Social Sciences, the Higher Party Schools, and "other scientific institutions of Moscow."[47] The team reportedly conducted two-day seminars in five different cities and also delivered lectures on the significance of the Twenty-second Party Congress. The Georgian official concluded: "Hopefully, teams of this kind will be sent to the Union Republics on a systematic basis and will take an active part in the scientific and theoretical conferences we hold."[48] Similar sentiments were expressed by other officials.

Evidence of this kind clearly implies that visits by officials of the central party apparatus had not been made frequently in the past, and possibly not at all, except to help disseminate information about a party congress or Central Committee plenum. After the Twenty-second Party Congress, however, Agitprop officials continued to render greater assistance to lower-level CPSU organizations. In September 1962, for example, the editors of *Partiinaia zhizn'* clearly indicated that the scope of these activities was rapidly expanding. Many *obkomy, kraikomy,* and central committees of Union Republics had conducted seminars for ideological workers and leaders of *raion* propaganda groups during the past year. "Propaganda groups of the CPSU Central Committee took an active part in the work of these seminars," and "were also sent to *obkomy, kraikomy,* and Central Committees of Union Republic Communist Parties."[49] In short, Agitprop officials seem to have significantly increased personal contacts with provincial party committees in the early 1960s.

Party Conferences for Indoctrination Specialists

During the 1960s the number of *obkom* and *gorkom* conferences on ideological work proliferated rapidly, greatly increasing the opportunities for interaction among propaganda cadres. In 1959 many party plenums and *aktiv* meetings were convened to discuss the first of the important Central Committee decrees, which criticized in detail the ideological work of the Stalino Oblast party organization. However, the activities of these republic, province, city, and district conferences were not well publicized. One of the rare references to such meetings concluded with the limp observation that "party organizations and committees can now engage in political work among all sectors of the population more concretely and operationally than a year ago."[50]

In July 1960 *Politicheskoe samoobrazovanie* began to publicize the activities of the many ideological conferences now being held. One writer meticulously describes a three-day "methodological conference" in the Chkalov (Orenburg) Oblast from its planning stages to concluding speeches and informal seminar reports.[51]

"Representatives from a number of central ideological institutions" were present at the conference.[52] Yet all arrangements seem to have been made and carried out by oblast officials. According to the report, the meeting was organized primarily by two groups—the Orenburg *obkom* and *gorkom* Political Education Center and the *obkom* department of propaganda and agitation. The Political Education Center made a concerted effort to include many propagandists, lecturers, and agitators in both the planning and proceedings of the conference.[53] To prevent "only a narrow circle of propagandists" from doing all the work, "consultants" from the center traveled to many cities and *raiony* to explain the aims of the conference to rank-and-file cadres and to edit speeches that were being prepared for presentation.[54]

Interaction among propagandists was strongly encouraged during the preparation of the conference and at the meeting itself. The writer notes that "in the course of preparing for the conference much was done to promote genuinely fruitful conversations about the propaganda profession."[55] He asserts that some formal talks are necessary at gatherings of this kind. But he quickly adds that "methodological conferences should focus their attention on questions of Marxist-Leninist theory, methods, detailed analysis of lessons, and *concrete discussions* among leaders of circles and seminars."[56] In hopes of achieving these ends, the agitprop department of the Orenburg *obkom* distributed a specially prepared pamphlet to all participants at the conference. This pamphlet analyzed the shortcomings of a previous conference and suggested numerous subjects for informal discussion.[57]

Evidence of this kind indicates that interaction among indoctrination specialists was deliberately encouraged to increase and did in fact increase technical communication and administrative efficiency within the party. Middle-level ideological conferences were not convened primarily to exchange views on the content of Marxist-Leninist theory or current Soviet policy; they were convened to discuss methods of disseminating this information and thereby presumably to influence the behavior of citizens in different age, occupation, and ethnic groups. In brief, these conferences were intended to stimulate new ideas on various forms and methods of political socialization, and to enable propagandists to exchange views on the comparative utility of techniques already in use.

Republic and oblast conferences also helped to increase normative communication among indoctrination specialists and were almost certainly intended to do so. Although it is impossible to document the nature and extent of this communication, it is known that participants engaged in countless informal discussions. Seminars at the Orenburg conference, for instance, produced many lively exchanges of opinion.[58] Serious disagreements on methods and techniques of political education were not uncommon. Describing in detail the conflicting recommendations and rejoinders of two propagandists, the writer observes that "the discussion was very active, one might almost say stormy."[59]

It is not possible to ascertain the ways in which face-to-face contact influenced the role expectations of individual propagandists.[60] It is also impossible to determine how their views on the status of their profession were affected. At provincial conferences some cadres may have made new friends and acquaintances, accumulated useful ideas to improve their work, and acquired a greater sense of group identification and professional pride. Others may have been appalled at the low intellectual level and apparent incompetence of their senior ideological officials and colleagues. In any case, local indoctrination specialists were provided with new opportunities to exchange technical information, which in turn very probably increased normative communication of various kinds—especially among regional party *apparatchiki* of the same status and from the same oblast party organization.

All-Union conferences on ideological work also were convened with much greater frequency during the early 1960s. In December 1961, for example, thirteen hundred local party officials and fourteen hundred representatives of national institutions attended the All-Union Conference on Questions of Ideological Work in Moscow. The following types of cadres were present: ideological secretaries of republic, *krai,* and oblast party committees; heads of agitprop departments at all levels of the CPSU; leaders of study circles and lecture groups; editors of national and provincial newspapers, journals, and publishing houses; representatives of the radio and television industries; instructors in the party school system; and a handful of rank-and-file propagandists and agitators.[61].

At the Moscow conference much time was spent listening to brief formal speeches, and apparently no discussion groups or seminars were held.[62] However, there was probably a considerable amount of interaction among leading central and regional indoctrination specialists. An even larger number of informal contacts might have developed had there been fewer speeches and small loosely structured discussion groups. Once again, important opportunities were created for normative and, to a lesser extent, technical communication. It is not unreasonable to assume, though it cannot be proven, that considerable interaction and significant (i.e., influential) communication did take place.

In short, the many national and regional conferences of this kind almost surely increased intraorganizational communication through both vertical and horizontal party channels. Most important, the evidence above suggests that greater technical and normative communication—especially at the oblast conferences—helped to coordinate provincial ideological activities, clarify the goals and priorities of key national and regional leaders, disseminate successful techniques of persuasion, and secure greater psychological support from local indoctrination specialists—all important elements of administrative efficiency.

Instructional Groups

Party conferences were the most important but not the only means of increasing communication between middle- and lower-level indoctrination specialists. In addition to the existing "propaganda groups," a variety of new "instructional groups" were formed in the early 1960s. Although these new organs were rarely referred to in the party press, a book on ideological work in Moscow provides interesting information on their structure, composition, and operations.[63]

V. Anikin, a Moscow *raikom* secretary, noted that eight instructional groups were created by his party committee shortly after the Twenty-second Congress.[64] Each group included three leading *apparatchiki,* one each from the Department of Propaganda and Agitation, the Department of Organizational Work, and the Department of Industry and Transport. Most teams were rounded out by eight or ten volunteers from the nonstaff *aktiv.* Although some instructional groups included only one or two full-time party cadres, Anikin emphasizes that the groups composed of staff members from three different departments were particularly effective; allegedly they provided an excellent means of improving both horizontal *and* vertical communication.[65] Anikin bases this conclusion on the experience of his own *raikom,* which organized several instructional groups on an experimental basis before the Twenty-second Party Congress:

> Having generalized carefully the work of our best instructors, we came to the conclusion that *the influence of the party* raikom *on the activities of the primary party organizations is significantly greater where all three* raikom *department instructors work hand in hand* (vzaimosviazanno), *in close contact with one another.* The formation of instructional groups was based on this conclusion.[66]

These assertions are significant. They suggest that greater interdepartmental communication within a *raikom* helped to produce more efficient ideological administration at the primary organization level. Anikin's findings indicate that local party secretaries may be more responsive to directives and suggestions backed by the authority of several *raikom* departments, not merely by the agitprop department.

Moreover, the technical content of the information transmitted was probably of higher quality than before, or at least *partkom* officials seem to have thought so.

Anikin also asserts that instructional groups had "a positive effect" on the selection and training of leading cadres in the primary party organizations.[67] CPSU secretaries and lesser officials were previously appointed on the basis of recommendations from the *raikom* Department of Organizational Work, and the opinions of instructors from other departments were not taken into consideration. Under the new system instructional groups assumed the responsibility of selecting cadres, thus making possible "a many-sided evaluation" of all candidates for a position.[68]

Anikin goes on to point out that improved interdepartmental communication within a *raion* committee reduces the quantity of vertical communication needed to guide primary party organizations. Before the formation of instructional groups a *partkom* secretary was obliged to report to three or more *raikom* departments; now the secretary reported only to the instructional group.[69] Moreover, the officials of this group provided a new and direct line of communication from primary party organizations to meetings of the bureau and *aktiv*. Anikin explicitly states that only department heads had delivered reports at previous party conferences and meetings.[70] Under the present system instructional groups were expected to present detailed accounts of their activities. These reports were prepared at monthly meetings that were frequently attended by *raikom* secretaries and department heads.[71]

It is puzzling that the activities of instructional groups did not receive more publicity in the party press. Perhaps these bodies were created in very limited numbers or only in urban *raiony*. It seems more likely, however, that most instructional groups were simply not as successful as those in Anikin's *raion*. Indifference to ideological work, preoccupation with economic responsibilities, and problems of interdepartmental communication are possible causes of failure. The head of the propaganda and agitation department of the Moscow *gorkom*, N. Ivan'kovich, alluded to these factors in 1962. Having praised the accomplishments of Anikin's *raikom*, Ivan'kovich added: "There is not and cannot be any kind of wall between the departments of a party committee; only their joint efforts can produce the best results. . . . Unfortunately, there are still instances where various leading workers do not engage in ideological work and do not even consider it necessary to do so."[72]

Ivan'kovich blurs the distinction between existing and desired conditions. "Walls" do exist between the departments of virtually all organizations. Moreover, there are numerous psychological and sociological barriers that impede effective communication and administrative efficiency within Communist party committees, especially between party bureaus and departments of propaganda and agitation. In short, many instructional groups may have become inactive, or actually disbanded, largely because of difficulties in maintaining a high level of interdepartmental communication.

Increased Use of Existing Communication Channels

Up to now our discussion has focused on newly created communication channels such as propaganda groups, Agitprop investigations, national and regional conferences for ideological workers, and instructional groups. However, existing channels were also increasingly used in the early 1960s. For example, the journals *Partiinaia zhizn'*, *Politicheskoe samoobrazovanie,* and *Kommunist* publicized all the activities discussed above, especially the work of Agitprop and regional party conferences. *Politicheskoe samoobrazovanie* presented many detailed reports on ideological conferences, sometimes even including the text of the major speech.[73] Although conferences of this kind were held in the 1950s, they were merely announced in the party press, not described, and thus meaningful communication was limited to conference participants and leading CPSU officials.

Existing channels within provincial party organizations were also used to transmit considerably more information about ideological work. The first secretary of the Kalinin *obkom* made some revealing statements on this subject in June 1962:

> *Two or three years ago* [raikom] *first secretaries would usually come to the* obkom *only to discuss economic problems.* Now a meeting of *raikom* first secretaries in the oblast center does not pass by without an examination of questions concerning political work among the masses, without a detailed discussion of measures to improve the effectiveness of party propaganda.[74]

Written communication also increased in new and interesting ways. In the Orenburg Oblast, for example, the *obkom* department of propaganda and agitation distributed questionnaires to all participants at the 1961 ideological conference. Here are excerpts from the published responses of three candid study circle leaders:

It is of utmost importance that methodological work with propagandists be conducted SYSTEMATICALLY (*planomerno*) and in accordance with a carefully worked out plan, not EPISODICALLY as it is now performed.[75]

It is always necessary to prepare our own visual aids, to hunt for appropriate passages from fictional writing. Much time is spent on this. Isn't it possible and expedient to have many visual aids manufactured CENTRALLY? . . . Fictional works on various subjects are usually enumerated at propaganda seminars. But why don't we receive more SPECIFIC instructions (*ukazaniia*)? Also, it would be very useful to have films on various study topics suitable for both film projectors and slide projectors.[76]

Why does the oblast publishing house produce so few books and pamphlets about the skills and achievements of individual propagandists? I think that the local press and radio also should play a larger and more productive role in this matter; certainly they could describe the work of the best lecturers, propagandists, and leaders of study circles.[77]

Questionnaire replies of this kind greatly increased the quantity and quality of information available to provincial party bureaus. The publication of constructive but frank criticism was almost surely intended to stimulate freer discussion of professional matters among indoctrination specialists at all levels of the party. One could come to other conclusions only if the comments selected for publication had merely repeated hackneyed formulas and evaded real issues. On the contrary, the editors of *Politicheskoe samoobrazovanie* chose to emphasize the central issues and deliberately capitalized words and phrases that directly refer to major problems.

Communication between middle- and lower-level party committees increased in still other ways in the early 1960s. Provincial indoctrination officials made increasingly frequent visits to the *raiony*.[78] Also, more and more outstanding industrial and agricultural workers, who had been drawn into the ideological activities of their factories and kolkhozy, were now assigned to various itinerant teams that included both technical specialists and professional propagandists. As part-time propagandists, production "innovators" were expected to disseminate technical information about their specialties, and above all to inspire others by their exemplary (i.e., "typical") behavior. No doubt some of these workers were less than enthusiastic about their time-consuming "second profession," and factory managers surely tried to keep their better workers on the job full time. But the participation of production specialists in lecture groups almost certainly helped to enhance the prestige of the propaganda profession and thereby greatly increased the flow of technical and normative communication among indoctrination specialists, other party workers, and the general public.

CONCLUSION

We are now in a position to reexamine our central hypothesis regarding the impact of increased intraparty communication on administrative efficiency. The former, of course, does not by definition or automatically produce the latter. Although greater technical and normative communication may be generated, senders and receivers may or may not be willing and able to act on it—that is, translate the information communicated into greater administrative efficiency. The foregoing evidence—pre- and post-1959—suggests a fairly strong relationship between these factors under certain circumstances, such as the provincial party conferences. But there is ample evidence to indicate that greater intraparty communication often did not have the effects intended by CPSU leaders. Conversely, infrequent communication between national and regional agitprop departments does not always seem to have impeded efficient ideological administration.

In June 1962, for example, the Central Committee charged that most competent ideological workers of the Minsk and Kuibyshev *obkomy* were spending much of their time in various conferences and meetings preparing countless reports and documents.[79] Although these activities certainly increased communication among some indoctrination officials, it seems that interaction was limited to a fairly small number of leading cadres. Also, much of the increased communication was apparently paper shuffling. And, in these particular cases, the flow of interlevel communication seems to have increased in only one direction: the *obkom* bureau transmitted occasional directives to the *raiony,* but chose to ignore the many reports and messages received from the *raiony* in return. Even more important, improved vertical communication within the *obkom* was apparently achieved at the expense of, and on some occasions in lieu of, daily administrative work. Evidence in support of these assertions is contained, for example, in the Central Committee decrees of June 6, 1962, and June 26, 1962.[80]

Further evidence regarding the relationship between intraorganizational communication and administrative efficiency is contained in a

Partiinaia zhizn' article entitled "The Ideological Department of a Party Committee."[81] In this rare and unsigned report, the reader is given a detailed view of the day-to-day operations of the propaganda and agitation department of the Krasnodar *kraikom*. The evidence indicates that in past years this department had little internal cohesion and considerable freedom from outside supervision and control. Until recently there had been few carefully planned activities, and staff propaganda cadres had apparently received few instructions from central organs or the *kraikom* party bureau. In short, a general state of aimlessness seems to have prevailed.[82]

Interestingly, the agitprop department of the Krasnodar *kraikom* still seemed to be very much on its own in December 1963. A formal work plan was now formulated four times a year. But there is no mention of general guidelines set down by Agitprop to help the *kraikom* organize its activities. Also, there is no reference to orders issued by indoctrination officials at the republic level, and no reference to specific "suggestions," "assistance," or "advice" from the *kraikom* bureau or first secretary. Apparently the propaganda and agitation department planned and organized all of its own work—and this is precisely what the anonymous writer affirms. "In brief, the department plans its own activities, in accordance with the vital daily needs of communist construction."[83]

If the experience of the Krasnodar *kraikom* is at all typical, the agitprop sections of provincial party committees had surprisingly little outside interference in conducting their ideological activities. Moreover, *raion* and primary party organizations probably tended to follow the example set by their respective oblast and *krai* committees. Some organized very creditable political education programs, while others ignored ideological work almost altogether. Some *raion* party committees had not even bothered to organize departments of propaganda and agitation, as Ilichev disclosed in December 1961.[84] He bemoaned the fact that this deficiency "clearly . . . harmed ideological work, especially in rural *raiony*."[85]

In short, increased communication between the central and regional party apparatuses, and within provincial party organizations, did not automatically increase the efficiency of Soviet ideological administration. It was probably a necessary but not a sufficient condition. National, republic, and provincial party committees issued many directives pertaining to political education, but these were not always followed up with careful or sustained administrative efforts. On the other hand, infrequent private communication between national and regional party organs did not make impossible efficient and effective ideological work at the provincial level. This was perhaps largely due to the considerable independence of oblast agitprop departments and to the existence of many important vertical communication channels—especially the central press and the other mass media.

The foregoing suggests some general conclusions about the relationship between Agitprop and middle- and lower-level party committees. Agitprop is an important operative agency, but not an overpowering one. Under Khrushchev it rendered increased technical assistance to many provincial CPSU organizations and made numerous spot checks of their work. But Agitprop does not select, train, and deploy vast numbers of professional propagandists; nor does it come close to having the necessary resources—money, personnel, and time—to direct and supervise the day-to-day administration of ideological work throughout the USSR.

To be sure, there is considerable uniformity in official policy toward propaganda and agitation work. Each year the party education system emphasizes a common theme that is studied throughout the Soviet Union.[86] From time to time the highest CPSU policy-making bodies encourage lower-level organs to create new institutions, organizational forms, and roles. And lower-level organs are usually quick to comply—formally, at least—with these recommendations.

But the uniformity of propaganda and agitation themes and the sudden proliferation of similar institutions do not undermine two main contentions of this paper—namely, that agitprop sections of regional party organizations enjoyed a surprising degree of autonomy in the 1950s, and that interlevel communication on ideological work increased significantly in the early 1960s. Although republic and provincial committees set in motion programs outlined by central organs, there was often little follow-through—that is, daily administrative work by *obkom* and *gorkom* bureaus and their departments of propaganda and agitation to implement these programs. Thus, while official policy may have been uniform, administrative practices varied considerably. Khrushchev's experience with "propaganda groups" and "ideological commissions" are good examples.[87]

In sum, there are definite limits to Agitprop's power of command. Its departments for the RSFSR and Union Republics possess an awesome array of formal powers. But the key to efficient ideological administration lies in the ability of Agitprop to persuade provincial officials that what it wants of them is in their own best interests—not in some future Communist society, but in the immediate here and now.

Given the overriding importance of purely economic "success indicators," the frequent transferring of provincial officials, and the disruptive bifurcation of the regional party apparatus in 1962, for example, this did not prove an easy task. Nevertheless, Khrushchev made a significant attempt to improve Soviet ideological work by increasing the flow of technical and normative communication among national and provincial party organs. By so doing, the central party apparatus assumed a much more active role in the "guidance" of domestic political education. This effort seems to have enjoyed modest success in improving administrative efficiency, but quite possibly had little effect on the beliefs and behavior of the Soviet citizenry.

This last assertion raises the important issue of the "effectiveness" *(effektivnost')* of ideological work—that is, the degree to which the values and beliefs party ideologists seek to inculcate do in fact promote officially sanctioned behavior among different groups in the population and among members of the Communist party themselves. To what extent were the political education efforts of the Khrushchev regime—particularly mass-political work and the activities of the party school system—"effective"? To what extent did greater intraparty communication increase the impact of party propaganda on the thinking and behavior of Soviet citizens? Such questions are virtually impossible to answer, and the data above permit only speculation as to the nature of the many complex relationships involved. But one might guess that domestic political education efforts under Khrushchev—despite greater intraorganizational communication and interaction among professional propaganda cadres—did not make a significant contribution toward creating "the new Soviet man" or toward accelerating the growth of the economy.

Consider the fragmentary evidence. First, recall that Khrushchev tended to evaluate the "effectiveness" of Party propaganda largely by one criterion—its contribution to Soviet economic progress. Especially after the bifurcation of the party apparatus in November 1962, the first secretary demanded that propaganda cadres master additional technical knowledge, administrative skills, and techniques of mass and small-group persuasion. Many were unable or unwilling to do so. Under Brezhnev and Kosygin, however, the impact of ideological work is assessed on numerous levels—intrapersonal, interpersonal, technological, organizational, and others. In contrast to Khrushchev, who seems to have soured on professional propagandists and concluded that they could not "directly" influence the economy, the present party leaders emphasize that ideological workers have *many* important responsibilities but can only influence the economy "indirectly."[88] Khrushchev's debunking of the propaganda profession and his heavy emphasis on production propaganda almost surely lowered the morale of many ideological cadres, confused them about the nature and value of their work, and reduced their prestige in the eyes of other party officials and the public. Each of these factors probably reduced the overall "effectiveness" and "efficiency" of party ideological work.[89]

Moreover, the current Soviet leaders seem very much aware of "the difference between sheer *comprehension* of a message and the receiver's *subsequent behavior* with respect to the originator's intentions."[90] Under V. I. Stepakov, until recently the head of Agitprop, significant steps were taken to make party propaganda "scientific"— that is, to collect empirical sociological data to determine which forms of propaganda have what kinds of effects on different strata of the population. To be sure, collection of such data was begun under Khrushchev. But concerted efforts to coordinate the activities of party organs and the social science research institutes, and to seek through empirical investigation new methods of shaping the values and behavior of Soviet citizens, are clearly a hallmark of the Brezhnev-Kosygin regime. Briefly stated, "conservatism in ideology should not be confused with a refusal to modernize methods."[91]

Under Khrushchev, Stalin, and Lenin the Communist party simply did not have a large amount of accurate feedback information about the impact of its domestic political education programs. Greater intraparty communication during the late 1940s and early 1960s (e.g., the oblast conference and Central Committee decrees) reflected renewed official awareness of this problem. But the lack of systematic Soviet research on political socialization—and the absence of such data in the formulation and implementation of policies—almost surely limited the capability of party leaders to shape the behavior of Soviet citizens by persuasive means.[92] This probably still held true after the major reorganization and centralization of party ideological work in 1938.[93] In any case, greater intraparty communication on political education, while probably a necessary condition, is surely not a sufficient condition of "effective" ideological work. Far more important than the quantity of information communicated is the nature of that communication, the characteristics of its receivers, and the prevailing system of sanctions. One's conclusions are crucially influenced, however, by one's fundamental assumptions about the basic *purposes* of Soviet ideological work. And the goals of Soviet leaders, as well as the social functions that ideology in fact performs, do not remain constant over time.[94]

NOTES

1. James Price, *Organizational Effectiveness: An Inventory of Propositions,* Homewood, Illinois: Richard Irwin, 1968, pp. 163, 167ff. For an extensive bibliography and survey of the literature on communication in organizations, see Lee Thayer, "Communication and Organization Theory," in Frank Dance, ed., *Human Communication Theory: Original Essays,* New York: Holt, Rinehart and Winston, 1967, pp. 70–115. See also the present author's "Communication Theory and the Study of Soviet Politics," *Canadian Slavic Studies,* II, (Winter 1968), 542–58.

2. Normative communication may be conceptually refined by distinguishing among the types of norms communicated—for example, "norms indicating general prescription of behavior, those indicating appropriate behavior for all members of a group, norms prescribing behavior for particular social roles and subgroups, those describing behavior in ambiguous situations, and norms outlining possible role choices." S. N. Eisenstadt, "Communication Systems and Social Structure: An Exploratory Comparative Study," *Public Opinion Quarterly,* no. 2 (Summer 1955), pp. 154ff.

3. Peter Blau and W. R. Scott, *Formal Organizations: A Comparative Approach,* San Francisco: Chandler, 1962, p. 116. See also Lee Thayer, *Communication and Communication Systems in Organization, Management, and Interpersonal Relations,* Homewood, Illinois: Richard Irwin, 1968; and the chapter "Communication and Interaction," in Barry Collins and Harold Guetzkow, *A Social Psychology of Group Processes for Decision-Making,* New York: Wiley, 1964, pp. 166–87.

4. Chester I. Barnard, *The Functions of the Executive,* Cambridge, Mass.: Harvard University Press,
1938, p. 92. See especially pp. 82–95. Cf. Herbert Simon, *Administrative Behavior,* New York: The Free Press, 1965; James March and Herbert Simon, *Organizations,* New York: Wiley, 1958; Blau and Scott, *op. cit.;* Daniel Katz and Robert Kahn, *The Social Psychology of Organizations,* New York: Wiley, 1966.

5. Alex Inkeles, *Public Opinion in Soviet Russia,* rev. ed., Cambridge, Mass.: Harvard University Press, 1958, p. 37. See also the discussions of party ideological work in John Armstrong, *The Soviet Bureaucratic Elite,* New York: Praeger, 1966, pp. 88–104; and Jerry Hough, *The Soviet Prefects: The Local Party Organs in Industrial Decision-Making,* Cambridge, Mass.: Harvard University Press, 1969, pp. 126–48.

6. On the principle of "democratic centralism," see Alfred G. Meyer, *The Soviet Political System,* New York: Random House, 1965; and Merle Fainsod, *How Russia Is Ruled,* Cambridge, Mass.: Harvard University Press, 1963.

7. "Tesno sviazyvat' ideologicheskuiu rabotu s khoziaistvennym stroitel'stvom," *Kommunist,* no. 18 (September 1955), pp. 9–10.

8. "Usilit' rukovodstvo partiinoi propagandoi," *Kommunist,* no. 14 (September 1956), p. 13.

9. *Loc. cit.*

10. Leonid Ilichev, "K novomu pod'emu ideologicheskoi raboty," *Kommunist,* no. 14 (September 1960), p. 38.

11. E. Furtseva, "Ukrepliat' sviazi ideologicheskoi raboty s zhizn'iu," *Kommunist,* no. 2 (February 1956), p. 87. See also, for example, B. Konoplev, "Voprosy vospitaniia kadrov i metody rukovodstva khoziaistvom," *Partiinaia zhizn',* no. 9 (May 1956), p. 26.

12. *Loc. cit.*

13. *Ibid.,* pp. 87–88. See also, for ex-

ample, "Protiv nedootsenki ideologicheskoi raboty (S partiinykh konferentsii i s'ezdov)," *Partiinaia zhizn'*, no. 3 (February 1958), p. 24.

14. "Massovo-politicheskuiu rabotu—na uroven' zadach semiletki," *Kommunist*, no. 4 (March 1959), pp. 8–9.

15. "On the Tasks of Party Propaganda in Present-Day Conditions," Central Committee decree of January 9, 1960, *Pravda*, January 10, 1960, pp. 1–2, in Leo Gruliow, ed., *Current Digest of the Soviet Press*, 12, no. 2 (1960), 18.

16. "Rabota s propagandistami—na uroven' sovremennykh zadach," *Politicheskoe samoobrazovanie*, no. 6 (June 1961), p. 80.

17. A. K. Kazakbaev, Speech to the All-Union Conference on Questions of Ideological Work, December 25–28, 1961, in *Dvadtsat' vtoroi s'ezd KPSS i voprosy ideologicheskoi raboty*, Moscow, 1962, pp. 335–37.

18. *Loc. cit.*

19. I. Spiridonov, "Leningradskaia organizatsiia v bor'be KPSS," in B. A. Pokrovskii, ed., *V tesnoi sviazi s zhizn'iu—iz opyta propagandistskoi i massovo-politicheskoi raboty partiinykh organizatsii Leningrada i Leningradskoi oblasti*, Moscow, 1958, p. 33.

20. *Loc. cit.* See also B. A. Pokrovskii, "Obobshchat' i rasprostraniat' opyt agitatsionno-propagandistskoi raboty," in B. A. Pokrovskii, ed., *op. cit.*, pp. 66–92.

21. See, for example, V. Ansimov, *Propagandistskie gruppy*, Moscow, 1959 (a 45-page pamphlet). Also "Propagandistskie gruppy," *Partiinaia zhizn'*, no. 1 (January 1959), pp. 16–18.

22. V. Ansimov, *op. cit.*, p. 7.

23. *Ibid.*, pp. 7–8.

24. *Ibid., passim.*

25. *Ibid.*, p. 8.

26. *Loc. cit.*

27. See Ansimov, *op. cit.*, pp. 40–41; and "Propagandistskie gruppy," *op. cit.*, pp. 17–18.

28. V. Ansimov, *op. cit.*, pp. 40–41.

29. "Propagandistskie gruppy," *op. cit.*, p. 17.

30. I. Smirnov, "Tesnaia sviaz' s zhizn'iu —vazhneishii printsip partiinoi propagandy," *Partiinaia zhizn'*, no. 18 (September 1959), p. 26.

31. *Loc. cit.*

32. See "Communication Theory and the Study of Soviet Politics," *op. cit.*, pp. 554–55.

33. The phrasing of this last sentence was suggested by an old anecdote from another context. See Richard Neustadt, *Presidential Power*, New York: Wiley, 1962, p. 9.

34. See "Ob itogakh uchebnogo goda v sisteme partiinogo prosveshcheniia i zadachakh partiinykh organizatsii v novom uchebnom godu," Central Committee decree of August 21, 1956, in *Spravochnik partiinogo rabotnika*, Vypusk 1, Moscow, 1957, especially pp. 350–53.

35. "Vsesoiuznoe soveshchanie po voprosam lektsionnoi propagandy," *Politicheskoe samoobrazovanie*, no. 2 (February 1961), p. 38. An official report of the speech delivered by Leonid Ilichev at the All-Union Conference on Questions of Lecture Propaganda, December 1960.

36. Derek Scott, *Russian Political Institutions*, New York: Praeger, 1966, p. 191.

37. E. Furtseva, Speech to the Twenty-first Party Congress of the CPSU, *Pravda*, January 30, 1959, pp. 5–6, in Lee Gruliow, ed., *Current Soviet Policies*, vol. 3, New York: Columbia University Press, 1960, p. 91.

38. Central Committee decree of January 9, 1960, *op. cit.*, p. 17.

39. See "Communication Theory and the Study of Soviet Politics," *op. cit.*, pp. 555–56.

40. A. P. Kosul'nikov, "O rukovodstve propagandoi v Karel'skoi partorganizatsii," *Partiinaia zhizn'* no. 20 (October 1960), p. 22.

41. *Ibid.*, pp. 22–23.

42. V. Fedinin, "Kogda net konkretnogo rukovodstva," *Politicheskoe samoobrazovanie*, no. 7 (July 1961), pp. 108–10.

43. *Ibid.*, p. 108.
44. *Ibid.*, p. 109.
45. *Loc. cit.* (italics mine).
46. A. A. Kaziev, in *Dvadtsat' vtoroi s'ezd KPSS i voprosy ideologicheskoi raboty*, p. 401.
47. D. G. Sturua, in *ibid.*, p. 182.
48. *Loc. cit.*
49. "Politicheskoe proveshchenie v novom uchebnom godu," *Partiinaia zhizn'*, no. 17 (September 1962), p. 7.
50. V. I. Snastin, "Za vysokuiu ideinost' i konkretnost' massovo-politicheskoi raboty," *Kommunist*, no. 18 (December 1959), p. 58.
51. G. Eligulashvili, "Propagandisty obmenivaiutsia metodicheskim opytom," *Politicheskoe samoobrazovanie*, no. 8 (August 1961), pp. 116–25.
52. *Ibid.*, p. 116.
53. *Ibid.*, p. 117.
54. *Loc. cit.*
55. *Loc. cit.*
56. *Loc. cit.* (italics mine).
57. *Loc. cit.*
58. *Op. cit.*, pp. 118–19.
59. *Ibid.*, p. 119.
60. See Erik P. Hoffmann, "Role Conflict and Ambiguity in the Communist Party of the Soviet Union," in Roger Kanet, ed., *The Behavioral Revolution and Communist Studies*, New York: The Free Press, 1971.
61. Nikita Khrushchev, in *Dvadtsat' vtoroi s'ezd KPSS i voprosy ideologicheskoi raboty*, pp. 5–6; and "Ideologicheskuiu rabotu na uroven' novykh zadach," *Politicheskoe samoobrazovanie*, no. 1 (January 1962), p. 9.
62. "Ideologicheskuiu rabotu na uroven' novykh zadach," *op. cit.*, pp. 9–22.
63. *O edinstve ideologicheskoi i organizatorskoi raboty*, Moscow, 1962. This book contains materials from a Moscow city ideological conference, May 12–13, 1962, conducted by the Moscow *gorkom*, The Academy of Social Sciences of the Central Committee, The Higher Party School of the Central Committee,

and the journals *Partiinaia zhizn'* and *Kommunist*.
64. V. Anikin, in *O edinstve ideologicheskoi i organizatorskoi raboty*, p. 34.
65. *Loc. cit.*
66. *Loc. cit.* (italics mine).
67. *Ibid.*, p. 35.
68. *Loc. cit.*
69. *Loc. cit.*
70. *Loc. cit.*
71. *Ibid.*, pp. 35–36.
72. N. Ivan'kovich, in *O edinstve ideologicheskoi i organizatorskoi raboty*, pp. 82, 87.
73. "Vsesoiuznoe soveshchanie po voprosam lektsionnoi propagandy," *Politicheskoe samoobrazovanie*, no. 1 (January 1961), pp. 121–22. "Vsesoiuznoe soveshchanie po voprosam lektsionnoi propagandy," *Politicheskoe samoobrazovanie*, no. 2 (February 1961), pp. 37–41. A. Filippov, "Ukrepliat' sviaz' s zhizn'iu, povyshat' ideinyi uroven' lektsionnoi propagandoi," *Politicheskoe samoobrazovanie*, no. 3 (March 1961), pp. 48–57.
74. N. Korytkov, "Partiinye komitety i rabota s propagandistami," *Politicheskoe samoobrazovanie*, no. 6 (June 1962), p. 86 (italics mine).
75. G. Eligulashvili, *op. cit.*, p. 125 (emphases in original).
76. *Loc. cit.* (emphases in original).
77. *Loc. cit.*
78. See, for example, "Ideologicheskii otdel partiinogo komiteta," *Partiinaia zhizn'*, no. 24 (December 1963), pp. 47–48.
79. "O rukovodstve Minskogo obkoma kommunisticheskoi partii Belorussii ideologicheskoi rabotoi," Central Committee decree of June 6, 1962, and "O rukovodstve Kuibyshevskogo obkoma partii ideologicheskoi rabotoi," Central Committee decree of June 26, 1962, *Spravochnik partiinogo rabotnika*, Vypusk 4, pp. 429–47.
80. *Ibid.*
81. "Ideologicheskii otdel partiinogo komiteta," *op. cit.*, pp. 43–53.
82. *Ibid.*, p. 45.

83. *Ibid.*, p. 47.

84. Leonid Ilichev, in *Dvadtsat' vtoroi s'ezd KPSS i voprosy ideologicheskoi raboty*, p. 84.

85. *Loc. cit.*

86. See Ellen Mickiewicz, *Soviet Political Schools: The Communist Party Adult Instruction System*, New Haven: Yale University Press, 1967.

87. See "Communication Theory and the Study of Soviet Politics," *op. cit.*, pp. 546–48.

88. On the activities of ideological officials in budgetary politics and the fields of "health, education, and welfare," see Jerry Hough, "Ideology and Ideological Secretaries as a Source of Change in the Soviet Union," unpublished paper presented at the Mid-West Association for the Advancement of Slavic Studies, April 11, 1969, Lincoln, Nebraska; and Jerry Hough, "The Party *Apparatchik*," in H. Gordon Skilling and Franklyn Griffiths, eds., *Interest Groups in Soviet Politics*, Princeton: Princeton University Press, 1971.

89. See "Role Conflict and Ambiguity in the Communist Party of the Soviet Union," *op. cit.*, and Thayer, *Communication and Communication Systems in Organization, Management and Interpersonal Relations, op. cit.*

90. Thayer, *ibid.*, p. 137. On different aspects of this subject, see Richard Dawson and Kenneth Prewitt, *Political Socialization*, Boston: Little, Brown, 1969; and Mark Hopkins, *Mass Media in the Soviet Union*, New York: Pegasus, 1970.

91. David W. Benn, "New Thinking in Soviet Propaganda," *Soviet Studies*, XX, no. 1 (July 1969), 54.

92. This is not to say that individual leaders have not demonstrated impressive persuasive skills, and that intuitive knowledge cannot produce effective systems of persuasion. See Inkeles, *op. cit.*, especially on oral agitation and "opinion leaders."

93. See especially the important document, "O postanovke partiinoi propagandy v sviazi s vypuskom Kratskogo Kursa Istorii VKP (b)," Central Committee decree of November 14, 1938, in *Resheniia partii o pechati*, Moscow, 1941, pp. 172–86.

94. See Alfred G. Meyer, "The Functions of Ideology in the Soviet Political System," *Soviet Studies*, XVII, no. 3 (January 1966), 273–85; and David Joravsky, "Soviet Ideology," *Soviet Studies*, XVII, no. 2 (October 1966), 2–19.

3

ROBERT SHARLET
Union College

A CONCEPTUAL FRAMEWORK FOR MASS POLITICAL SOCIALIZATION IN SOVIET POLITICAL DEVELOPMENT

A great deal of research has been done both in the United States and abroad on the various components and individual institutions by means of which the Communist political leadership of the USSR attempts to induct the broad population into the Soviet political culture. This is an interesting and significant socio-political process fundamentally interrelated with the past, present, and future development of the Soviet political system. Yet, there has been to date no systematic effort to integrate the available research towards the eventual discovery and verification of generalizations about how mass political socialization has contributed and does contribute to Soviet political development. By drawing on this body of scholarship, I have tried in this essay to map out a conceptual framework as the necessary first step towards the more ambitious task of rendering understandable in terms of discernible patterns the first fifty years of political development in the USSR.

PRINCIPAL TERMS OF REFERENCE

Mass political socialization: the process by which the individual is inducted into the prevailing pattern of attitudes, beliefs, and sentiments which shape and condition political behavior. This incessant

47

process of indoctrination is carried out by primary and secondary agents of socialization performing latent and manifest functions during the formative and mature years of the individual.[1]

Soviet political development: the process by which the ruling stratum of the Communist party, in its role as a modernizing elite, constructs, controls, and manipulates the systemic processes of political socialization, social regulation, political mobilization, and economic development in order to attain a hierarchical set of prescriptive ideological goals, culminating in the ultimate goal of revolutionizing human behavior through the creation of the "new Soviet man."[2]

COMPONENTS OF THE MASS POLITICAL SOCIALIZATION PROCESS

The following is an attempt to isolate and concisely characterize (in random order) the major components of the mass political socialization process of Soviet political development, 1917–1967.[3]

(1) The *family*, the primary agent of Soviet mass political socialization, carries out both its latent and manifest functions during the formative years of the individual. The family is the least manipulable and, consequently, the least predictable component of the mass political socialization process. The modernizing elite has tended to regard the Soviet family ambivalently as both the indispensable primary agent of political socialization and a dispensable counteragent.[4]

(2) The *educational system*, the major secondary agent, performs its manifest socialization function during the formative years of the individual and, for a part of the population, during the mature years as well. The educational system is centralized, standardized, and potentially able to reach a large part of the population from the preschooler in nursery school to the adult enrolled in high school or university evening or correspondence courses. Highly manipulable, this component can be altered through modification in teachers' training, curricular changes, textbook revisions, and other levers at the disposal of the modernizing elite.[5]

(3) *Peer groups* such as the individual's *kollektiv*, the comrades' court, and the peoples' volunteer patrol perform important latent and manifest functions of mass political socialization during the formative and mature years of the individual. Nearly everyone from the nursery schooler to the pensioner in an old age home is considered a member of at least one *kollektiv*. The average adult may belong to two, the *kollektiv* of his place of residence and that of his place of work. Al-

though a diffuse social institution, the *kollektiv* exercises considerable latent influence on the individual's political behavior. The comrades' court and the peoples' volunteer patrol are derivative peer groups and, in part, draw their legitimacy as agents of mass political socialization from the parent *kollektiv*. The comrades' court performs both manifest and latent functions, primarily during the individual's mature years; the person brought before the comrades' court is subject to manifest political socialization while the audience, which is urged to participate in the proceedings, is subject to latent political socializaton. The peoples' volunteer patrol, in addition to its primary quasi-police function, symbolizes model civic behavior and in this capacity serves as a latent political socializer of the general public among whom they patrol. The modernizing elite has consistently relied upon peer groups as secondary agents of mass political socialization, although these groups are not always subject to effective control, occasionally tend to exceed their mandate, and, consequently, are sometimes dysfunctional for the mass political socialization process.[6]

(4) *Occupational groups,* such as the production brigade in the factory or on a collective farm, also perform a latent political socialization function during the individual's mature years until the time of retirement. The modernizing elite has consistently extolled the virtues of work, especially factory work, but of all the agents of political socialization in the factory, the occupational group is probably the least manipulable compared with overlapping peer and intermediate groups.[7]

(5) The modernizing elite tends to place heavy reliance on a network of *intermediate groups* in the mass political socialization process. These groups, of which the trade union system, the Young Communist League, and the local soviets are the largest, encompass approximately half of the population. The trade union system, embracing the industrial, clerical, and professional labor force, reinforces the peer and occupational groups' latent political socialization functions, especially among the urban adult labor force. Added to this is the manifest impact of the trade union system through its communications system, which includes a publishing house, a daily newspaper, specialized newspapers and periodicals, as well as wall newspapers. The Young Communist League, frequently overlapping in membership among the younger trade unionists, includes a high percentage of the teenagers and young adults in the high schools, universities, factories, and offices, and to a lesser extent on the collective and state farms. The YCL, through its communications system and by means of its inter-

action with peer groups and occupational groups, is charged by the modernizing elite with the responsibility of manifest political socialization of the nation's youth. Finally, the periodic soviet elections perform a diffuse latent political socialization function for a majority of the adult population, while for a smaller group of citizens elected as deputies, the impact of the experience tends to be far more intense. How effectively the modernizing elite's huge, unwieldy, bureaucratic intermediate groups perform their mass political socialization functions in Soviet political development is still largely an uninvestigated empirical question.[8]

(6) The *Communist party* itself is directly involved in the mass political socialization process along with its manifold other functions. Through its political schools, its agitational-propaganda machinery, its extensive party communication system, and programmatic ideological statements, the party directly undertakes the systematic mass inculcation of the dominant political values and systemic goals of the modernizing elite.[9]

(7) Integrating the various group communications media (party, trade union, YCL), the national *communications system* serves as one of the major mass political socialization resources at the disposal of the modernizing elite. Through the press, radio, and television as latent political socializers, the modernizing elite manipulates media content to ensure consistency and maximize congruence between systemic goals and the content of the mass political socialization process. However, the modernizing elite must constantly attempt to reconcile the benefits of uniformity and intensity with the costs of overloading the political communications lines and creating mass apathy.[10]

(8) Closely related to the media in the mass political socialization process are the *arts*. Through the media of fiction, poetry, the canvas, and the film, the modernizing elite has managed to harness, or at least to identify, the arts with its longer-term systemic goals, but not without occasional difficulty. By imbedding standard political messages in heroic themes and positive heroes, the arts perform the latent function of mass political socialization. However, the indirect cost of cultural management for political purposes has frequently been less credible and hence less persuasive artistic work.[11]

(9) For the relatively small part of the population that comes into contact with it, the *judiciary* performs significant manifest and latent mass political socialization functions. The dual functions of the Soviet criminal judiciary expressed in Berman's "parental concept" of Soviet justice are punishment and education of the criminal. An incidental

by-product of the court's manifest political socialization of the criminal is the latent political socialization to which the witnesses and spectators are exposed in a trial. Throughout the Soviet political development process, the educational function of Soviet "parental" criminal justice has received varying degrees of emphasis. However, negative political socialization by comparing the antisocial behavior of the hapless miscreant to the image of the "new man" has definite limitations, as recidivism among so-called hardcore criminals indicates.[12]

(10) Finally, for most of the qualified young males of the population, the *military*, especially the threshold experience of basic training, plays a positive mass political socialization role. The military political indoctrination system includes special newspapers, magazines, periodical literature, monographs, documentaries, barrack displays, parade oratory, and, of course, the ubiquitous lectures delivered by political information officers. Although the military conscript is a captive audience, it would seem unlikely that the modernizing elite overestimates the value of military indoctrination of essentially civilian values and goals.[13]

This discussion has been an effort to define the parameters of the Soviet mass political socialization process without by any means exhausting the multiplicity of agents within the ten designated components. Various other mass political socialization agents, such as the Pioneers, sports societies, public lecture organizations, the atheist group, DOSAAF, and even the Constitution of the USSR can be classified within this framework.[14]

BUILDING THE SOVIET MASS POLITICAL SOCIALIZATION PROCESS

The mass political socialization process has been systematically constructed and reconstructed by the modernizing elite as one of the systemic variables of Soviet political development. This system-building task can be periodized according to the hierarchical goals of Soviet political development: (1) the preliminary goal of preparation for rapid industrialization; (2) the intermediate goal of rapid, heavy industrialization; and (3) the ultimate goal of creating the "new man."

MASS POLITICAL SOCIALIZATION AND THE PREPARATION FOR RAPID INDUSTRIALIZATION

The preliminary developmental goal of preparing the society for rapid industrialization was mainly achieved by the end of the New

Economic Policy. During this period, the modernizing elite began to construct a mass political socialization process to assist in facilitating the realization of the preliminary systemic goal. The result was a loosely integrated pattern of unevenly developed components. The *family*, generally weakened by Soviet divorce law in 1917, was regarded as a potential transmitter of prerevolutionary attitudes, sentiments, and beliefs. The *educational system*, gradually regaining its pre-World War I number of schools, was noncompulsory and reached relatively few children in the rural areas beyond the fourth grade. This was an experimental period in Soviet pedagogy that tended to destabilize the educational system and diminish its effectiveness. *Peer groups* such as the comrades' courts were first created in the Red Army and later in industrial enterprises in 1919. The number of comrades' courts gradually increased during the 1920s, but they were largely concentrated in state-owned industrial enterprises in urban areas.

Occupational groups, especially industrial or agricultural production brigades, included only a small percentage of the total labor force. The still overwhelmingly rural population included 75 percent who were classified as individual peasants and only 2.9 percent as collective farm peasants. Of the 6.6 percent (or 9.9 million people) of the population engaged in nonagricultural occupations in 1928, approximately one-third (or 3.9 million people) were industrial personnel.

Among the *intermediate groups*, the trade union system was the most developed, but its recruiting, organizing, and collective-bargaining functions in both the public and private sectors of the industrial economy consumed a large part of the leadership's energy. The intraparty struggle further diverted the attention of the trade union leadership during the middle and late 1920s. During this period, the Young Communist League was essentially an elitist organization and also became one of the arenas of the intraparty struggle. While interest in the local soviets was growing, only 29.9 percent of the women in the rural areas voted in the RSFSR elections of 1927.

Within the *Communist party*, the adult political education system was launched during the 1920s, ranging from basic schools for "political literacy" to Communist universities in several of the major cities. However, due to the underdeveloped condition of Soviet education at that time, party education had to undertake many of the responsibilities of a general educational system. *Agitprop* was created within the party secretariat in 1920, and agit-collectives were first established in 1923. The latter spread very slowly, while during the 1920s the secretariat was preoccupied to a large extent with organizational improvements and consolidation of control. The *communications media,* especially the press, developed rapidly during NEP, but the campaigns to wipe out illiteracy did not keep apace. Soviet radio, which began in 1920, developed much more slowly. By 1928, there were twenty radio broadcasting stations in the Soviet Union. The *arts* flourished during NEP, but spontaneously, pluralistically, and frequently with contradictory political orientations. Small independent publishing houses and emigré publications contributed to this aesthetic and political diversity.

Finally, the *judiciary* and the *military* were heavily staffed with former tsarist personnel due to the shortage of qualified Communists. Marxist jurists during the 1920s were primarily engaged in theoretical struggles with "bourgeois" legal philosophy and were too few in number to supervise the administration of justice as well. In the military, the party was mainly concerned with penetration of the officer corps, a slow process involving the training of Communist military cadres.

Consequently, it is only possible to identify in broad outline the major components of the developing mass political socialization process of the 1920s. A number of these components barely penetrated the rural areas, where 84 percent of the population lived as of 1928. Other components were not fully operative as agents of mass political socialization. A few were partially neutralized due to staffing problems, technical limitations, political conflict, or excessive diversity and diffusion of the political socialization function. However, it can be stated that during NEP the modernizing elite succeeded in supplanting the prerevolutionary agents of political socialization with the crude framework for a far more complex and sophisticated mass political socialization process. This accomplishment was a contribution to the goal of preparing the society for rapid industrialization.

MASS POLITICAL SOCIALIZATION AND RAPID INDUSTRIALIZATION

Beginning in 1928 with the First Five Year Plan, the systemic goal of Soviet political development became rapid, heavy industrialization, and the modernizing elite reconstructed the systemic processes, including mass political socialization, in order to facilitate and expedite realization of the new priority goal. As a result, a better integrated, and more effective mass political socialization process began to emerge from the flow of party resolutions and government laws. The individual components of the 1920s began to knit into a matrix of political instruments and social mechanisms subject to control and manipulation by the modernizing elite.

The structure of the *family* was gradually strengthened through legislation, culminating in the family law of 1936. Divorce was made more difficult and the family was restored as the primary agent of mass political socialization. The *educational* system was reconstructed beginning in 1930, bringing the experimental period to an end and introducing universal compulsory four-year education. From 1929–1931, comrades' courts as a *peer group* agent of mass political socialization spread throughout the industrial economy and were extended into the rural areas, where forty-five thousand functioned during the 1930s. During this period, millions of people moved from the rural areas to the urban-industrial centers mushrooming across the country, a labor migration institutionalized in the collective labor contract, which was introduced in 1931. As a result, millions of women and younger people, heretofore less exposed to the mass political socialization process in the countryside, were now encompassed by *occupational groups* such as the factory production brigades. By 1939, women composed a quarter or more of the labor force in the coal, iron, chemical, rubber, and machinery industries.

After 1928, *intermediate groups* became more conspicuous agents of mass political socialization. The rapid growth of the industrial labor force swelled the ranks of the trade unions, which were integrated into the state apparatus in 1933. The Young Communist League was gradually converted into a mass organization, a change institutionalized in the Program of the Young Communist League of 1936. The local soviets also began to assume a major role in mass political socialization. The number of people participating in the 1929 RSFSR elections was 25 percent greater than in 1927. This reflected, among other things, increased political participation by women, a large percentage of whom had been nonparticipants in the early 1920s, and a 14 percent total voting increase in the rural areas. In addition, more women (27 percent in the cities and 20 percent in the villages) were elected as deputies to the local soviets in the 1929 election. Mass political socialization through mass political participation continued to grow in the 1930s.

Within the secretariat of the *Communist party,* the mass political socialization machinery underwent reorganization in 1930, 1934, and 1939 in order to adapt it to the increased demands of the industrialization period. The party educational system, now able to concentrate primarily on political training, grew rapidly, increasing by 1933 to

210,000 party schools and study circles and 4.5 million students, an increase of 400 percent over 1930. Simultaneously, the national *communications* network began to expose a larger part of the population to political stimuli. After 1928, the circulation of the Soviet press grew considerably, increasing by 45 percent between 1934 and 1939. Concomitantly, the literacy rate rose to 90 percent by the early 1930s. Radio, a newer medium, grew more slowly but by the end of 1934 there were 64 broadcasting stations, 2.5 million receiving sets, and an estimated audience of 10–15 million listeners. The size of the audience was greatly augmented by "group listening" in clubs, reading rooms, and other public places where radios were installed.

Beginning in 1928–1929, the Soviet film industry was brought under more effective party control, and in 1932, the *arts* as a whole were integrated into the mass political socialization process by means of the policy of "socialist realism." Throughout the 1930s, the *judiciary* became a more effective component of this process as Soviet legal education was stabilized and began to produce more trained Marxist jurists for the bench. Finally, by 1931, over half of the Red Army officer corps were Communists, greatly improving the potential of the *military* as an agent of mass political socialization.

The reconstructed mass political socialization process was gradually perfected by the modernizing elite throughout the 1930s and after World War II, consistent with achieving the intermediate goal of rapid, heavy industrialization. Although the comrades' courts declined in the late 1930s, the family was further strengthened in 1944, total school enrollment climbed, the labor force grew enormously, trade union and YCL membership increased substantially, party propaganda-agitational work was improved, newspaper circulation and radio listening gained, the contribution of the arts became quantitatively more significant, professionalization of the judiciary advanced, and the armed forces became far more important as agents of mass political socialization. All of these components were manipulated by the modernizing elite as part of the integrated process of inducting the individual into the prevailing pattern of attitudes, beliefs, and sentiments which shape and condition his political behavior.

In the present phase of Soviet political development, the modernizing elite has reformulated the prescriptive ideological goals for the future. According to the 1961 Program of the CPSU, the Soviet Union has entered the stage of the transition to communism during which the intermediate goal of industrialization (the material-technical basis of communism) still has priority along with increased emphasis on the ultimate goal of creating the "new man." Consistent with the more sophisticated requirements of raising labor productivity and instilling greater civic consciousness, the modernizing elite has been modifying individual components of the mass political socialization process during the past decade. Family law has been reformed, curricular changes are underway, comrades' courts have been revived, peoples' volunteer patrols have been created, electoral reforms are being discussed, television has been introduced, the arts are being allowed more latitude within "socialist realism," and the administration of criminal justice has been reformed to give more emphasis to the court's educational function. Since many of the components are still undergoing modification, it would be premature at this time to attempt a fuller description of the changing mass political socialization process in the USSR today.

NOTES

1. This stipulated definition represents a selective synthesis of the definitions of political socialization of Hyman, Sigel, Greenstein and others, especially Gerald J. Bender, "Political Socialization and Political Change," *Western Political Quarterly*, XX, no. 2 (1967), 390–407; Gabriel A. Almond and James S. Coleman, eds., *The Politics of Developing Areas*, Princeton: Princeton University Press, 1960, pp. 26–31; Lewis A. Froman, Jr., *People and Politics*, Englewood Cliffs, N.J.: Prentice-Hall, 1962, pp. 18–28; and Robert K. Merton, *On Theoretical Sociology*, New York: Free Press, 1967, pp. 104–09. The term "function" is used to designate the consequences of a component of a system for the system as a whole. As such, this usage involves no commitment to a distinctive functional approach and is intended to be analytically distinct from Merton's concept of "function." See Ernest Nagel, *The Structure of Science*, New York: Harcourt, Brace, 1961, pp. 525–26, for this distinction between Merton's and the stipulated meaning of "function." The concept of "political behavior" which is used is Easton's conception of behavior that affects or is intended to affect the authoritative allocation of values. Finally, for the distinction between "mass" and "elite" political socialization in a Communist system, see John W. Lewis, "Party Cadres in Communist China," in James S. Coleman, ed., *Education and Political Development*, Princeton: Princeton University Press, 1965, pp. 408–36. For an analysis of the agents of "elite" political socialization in the Soviet system, see Milton Lodge, *Soviet Elite Attitudes in the Post-Stalin Period*, New York: Charles Merrill, 1969, ch. 4.

2. For an elaboration of this stipulative definition, see Robert Sharlet, *Soviet Modernization*, New York: Bobbs-Merrill, forthcoming. By the phrase "the ruling stratum of the Communist party in its role as a modernizing elite" is meant the membership of the Politburo/Presidium, the Central Committee, and the Party Congress. The concept

"social regulation" is meant as the process by which the norms of interpersonal behavior and the relations between the citizen and the state are defined, sanctioned, and regulated by the legal system, the administrative apparatus, and peer groups. The concept "political mobilization" is used as the process by which the individual is recruited and coopted for participation in the policy implementation process through an inclusive network of intermediate groups. And the concept "economic development" is defined as the process by which all necessary human and material resources are committed to the task of constructing, operating, maintaining, and administering the national economy by means of a number of social structures and manipulable technical devices.

3. For general discussions of political socialization in the Soviet Union, see Frederick C. Barghoorn, *Politics in the USSR*, Boston: Little, Brown, 1966, chs. III and IV; Alfred G. Meyer, *The Soviet Political System*, New York: Random House, 1965, ch. XIV; and Zbigniew Brzezinski and Samuel P. Huntington, *Political Power: USA/USSR*, New York: Viking, 1964, ch. II. For recent work see David E. Powell, "The Making of the New Soviet Man: An Analysis of Socializing Institutions," paper read at the 1970 Annual Meeting of the American Political Science Association, Los Angeles; and Charles D. Carey, "Political Socialization of Soviet Youth and the Building of Communism," paper read at the 1971 Annual Meeting of the American Political Science Association, Chicago.

4. Statements made in this essay about the family draw upon the following sources: F. M. Atakhodzhaev, *Vozniknovenie i razvitie sovetskogo zakonodatel'stva o zakliuchenii i rastorzhenii braka v Uzbekistane*, Tashkent: Izd. SamGu, 1963;

"Changes in Marriage and Family Law Are Discussed," *Current Digest of the Soviet Press*, XIX, no. 6 (1967), 14–16; H. Kent Geiger, *The Family in Soviet Russia*, Cambridge, Mass.: Harvard University Press, 1968; Peter H. Juviler, "Family Reforms on the Road to Communism," in Peter H. Juviler and Henry W. Morton, eds., *Soviet Policy-Making*, New York: Praeger, 1967, pp. 29–60; A. S. Makarenko, *The Collective Family: A Handbook for Russian Parents*, Garden City, N.Y.: Doubleday, 1967; Gregory J. Massell, "Law as an Instrument of Revolutionary Change in a Traditional Milieu: The Case of Soviet Central Asia" (paper read at the 1967 Annual Meeting of the American Political Science Association, Chicago); Rudolf Schlesinger, *Changing Attitudes in Soviet Russia: The Family*, London: Routledge & Kegan Paul, 1949; and G. M. Sverdlov, *Sovetskoe semeinoe pravo*, Moscow: Gosiurizdat, 1958.

5. Statements made in this essay about the educational system draw upon the following sources: Jeremy R. Azrael, "Soviet Union," in James S. Coleman, ed., *Education and Political Development*, Princeton: Princeton University Press, 1965, pp. 233–71; James Bowen, *Soviet Education: Anton Makarenko and the Years of Experiment*, Madison, Wis.: University of Wisconsin Press, 1962; Urie Bronfenbrenner, "Soviet Methods of Character Education," *American Psychologist*, XVII, no. 8 (1962), 550–64; Nicholas DeWitt, *Education and Professional Employment in the USSR*, Washington, D.C.: U.S. Gov't. Printing Office, 1961; U.S. Department of Health, Education, and Welfare, *Education in the USSR*, Washington, D.C.: U.S. Gov't. Printing Office, 1957; William K. Medlin, "Historical Perspectives on Social Change: Education in Central Asia" (paper read at the 1966 Midwest Slavic Conference, Colum-

bus, Ohio); *O kommunisticheskom vospitanii i ukreplenie sviazi shkoly s zhizn'iu: Sbornik dokumentov,* Moscow: Izd. Prosveshchenie, 1964; and "Entering the School Year— Interview with M. A. Prokofyev, USSR Minister of Education," *Current Digest of the Soviet Press,* XIX, no. 34 (1967), 25–26.

6. Statements made on peer groups in this essay primarily draw upon the following sources: Harold J. Berman and James W. Spindler, "Soviet Comrades' Courts," *Washington Law Review,* XXXVIII, no. 4 (1963), 842–910; *Druzhinniku: Sbornik zakonodatel'nykh i inykh materialov,* Moscow: Gosiurizdat, 1963; Darrell P. Hammer, "Law Enforcement, Social Control and the Withering of the State: Recent Soviet Experience," *Soviet Studies,* XIV, no. 4 (1963), 379–97; K. S. Iudel'son, *Polozhenie o tovarishcheskikh sudakh,* Moscow: Gosiurizdat, 1962; Klaus Mehnert, *Soviet Man and His World,* New York: Praeger, 1961; Joseph Novak, *No Third Path,* Garden City, N.Y.: Doubleday, 1962; Robert Sharlet, "Russia's Courts of Public Pressure," *The Nation,* CC, no. 3, (January 1965), 55–57, 68; Dennis M. O'Connor, "Soviet People's Guards: An Experiment with Civic Police," *New York University Law Review,* XXXIX, no. 4 (1964), 579–614.

7. Statements made about occupational groups in this essay draw upon the following sources: Arvid Broderson, *The Soviet Worker,* New York: Random House, 1966; Alex Inkeles and Raymond A. Bauer, *The Soviet Citizen,* Cambridge, Mass.: Harvard University Press, 1959; Robert E. Lane and David O. Sears, *Public Opinion,* Englewood Cliffs, N.J.: Prentice-Hall, 1964, ch. 4; Joseph Novak, *The Future Is Ours, Comrade,* New York: Dutton, 1960; and N. G. Valentinova, "Vliianie vzaimootnoshenii v proizvodstvennom kollektive na povyshenie interesa k tru-

du," in *Sotsiologiia v SSSR,* Moscow: Izd. Mysl', 1966, I, 440–56.

8. Statements made about intermediate groups in this essay draw upon the following sources: Emily C. Brown, *Soviet Trade Unions and Labor Relations,* Cambridge, Mass.: Harvard University Press, 1966; Margaret Dewar, *Labour Policy in the USSR, 1917–1928,* London: The Royal Institute of International Affairs, 1956; Ralph T. Fisher, Jr., *Pattern for Soviet Youth: A Study of the Congresses of the Komosomol, 1918–1954,* New York: Columbia University Press, 1959; Allen Kassof, *The Soviet Youth Program,* Cambridge, Mass.: Harvard University Press, 1965; A. I. Lepeshkin, *Mestnye organy vlasti sovetskogo gosudarstva, 1921–1936,* Moscow: Gosiurizdat, 1959; T. Nikolaeva, *Vospitatel'naia rabota profsoiuzov,* Moscow: Profizdat, 1966; and Howard R. Swearer, "The Functions of Soviet Local Elections," *Midwest Journal of Political Science,* V, no. 2 (1961), 129–49.

9. Statements made about the mass political socialization machinery of the Communist party in this essay draw upon the following sources: John A. Armstrong, *The Politics of Totalitarianism: The Communist Party of the Soviet Union from 1934 to the Present,* New York: Random House, 1961; Merle Fainsod, *How Russia is Ruled,* rev. ed., Cambridge, Mass.: Harvard University Press, 1964; Alfred G. Meyer, "The Functions of Ideology in the Soviet Political System," *Soviet Studies,* XVII, no. 3 (1966), 273–85; Ellen P. Mickiewicz, *Soviet Political Schools: The Communist Party Adult Instruction System,* New Haven: Yale University Press, 1967.

10. Statements made about the communications media in this essay draw upon the following sources: Gabriel A. Almond and G. Bingham Powell, Jr., *Comparative Politics: A De-*

velopmental Approach, Boston: Little, Brown, 1966, ch. VII; Richard R. Fagen, *Politics and Communications*, Boston: Little, Brown, 1966; Gayle D. Hollander, "Recent Developments in Soviet Radio and Television News Reporting," *Public Opinion Quarterly*, XXXI (Fall, 1967), 359–65; Alex Inkeles, *Public Opinion in Soviet Russia: A Study in Mass Persuasion*, Cambridge, Mass.: Harvard University Press, 1950, 1958; Ithiel de Sola Pool, "The Mass Media and Politics in the Modernization Process," in Lucian W. Pye, ed., *Communications and Political Development*, Princeton: Princeton University Press, 1963, pp. 234–53; and N. D. Psurtsev, ed., *Razvitie sviazi v SSSR, 1917–1967*, Moscow: Izd. Sviaz', 1967.

11. Statements made about the arts in this essay draw mainly upon the following sources: Edward J. Brown, *Russian Literature Since the Revolution*, New York: Collier Books, 1963; Central Statistical Board of the USSR, *Cultural Progress in the USSR: Statistical Returns*, Moscow: Foreign Language Publishing House, 1958; Paul Hollander, "Models of Behavior in Stalinist Literature: A Case Study of Totalitarian Values and Controls," *American Sociological Review*, XXXI, no. 3 (1966), 352–64; Abram Tertz, *On Socialist Realism*, New York: Vintage Books, 1960; and Avraham Yarmolinsky, *Literature Under Communism*, Bloomington, Ind.: Russian and East European Institute, 1960.

12. Statements about the mass political socialization function of the judiciary in this essay draw mainly

from the following sources: Harold J. Berman, *Justice in the U.S.S.R.*, rev. ed., New York: Vintage Books, 1963; George Feifer, *Justice in Moscow*, New York: Simon and Schuster, 1964; M. V. Kozhevnikov, *Istoriia sovetskogo suda, 1917–1956*, Moscow: Gosiurizdat, 1957; Samuel Kucherov, "The Jury of Tsarist Russia and the People's Assessors of the Soviet Union," *Ost Europa Recht*, no. 3 (September 1966), esp. pp. 178–87; M.Iu. Raginskii, *Vospitatel'naia rol' sovetskogo suda*, Moscow: Gosiurizdat, 1959; and Robert Sharlet, "The Trial of Ushakova," in the series "The Russia We Know" (Mark Hopkins ed.), *Milwaukee Journal*, Feb. 8, 1965, p. 12.

13. Statements made about the mass political socialization function of the military in this essay draw upon the following sources: Merle Fainsod, *How Russia Is Ruled*, rev. ed., Cambridge, Mass.: Harvard University Press, 1964, ch. 14; M. I. Kalinin, *O kommunisticheskom vospitanii i voinskom dolge*, Moscow: Voennoe Izd. Ministerstva Oborony SSSR, 1967; Roman Kolkowicz, *The Soviet Military and the Communist Party*, Princeton: Princeton University Press, 1967, ch. IV; the section on "Education in and for the Red Army," in Lucy L.W. Wilson, *The New Schools of New Russia*, New York: Vanguard, 1928, pp. 129–36; and Zigurds L. Zile, trans. and ed., *The World of the Soviet Serviceman*, Madison, Wis.: University of Wisconsin Law School mimeograph, 1959.

14. On the sports societies, see Henry W. Morton, *Soviet Sport*, New York: Collier Books, 1963.

4

NICHOLAS DeWITT
Indiana University

THE OCTOBER REVOLUTION
AND SOVIET EDUCATION

World historians may forever disagree, as far as means are concerned, as to whether the October 1917 upheaval in Russia was actually a popular revolution or a conspiratorial coup d'état. The upheaval was brutal and disruptive, and its human costs were high. However, the fact remains that it had lasting results in modernizing Russian society. The end result of the 1917 uprising, the protracted civil war, and the construction of socialism in one country was the introduction of a radical change in governmental, political, social, economic, and cultural conditions in a major Eurasian power.

For fifty years, using various means, Communist leaders have struggled to sustain socio-political change and to deepen its impact by developing different institutions which could establish and perpetuate the new practices of the socialist state. Education served one of the most crucial functions of blending the new goals of Communist society with the unique history, institutions, and traditions the Soviet state had inherited from the tsarist past. One of the major goals of the Revolution was to reeducate all toilers in the spirit of the supreme socialist consciousness and to provide them with skills for productive work—a task to be accomplished by a new system of mass education. This system was indeed created and is functioning today by providing diverse types of education to some 73 million people, almost one-third of the entire Soviet population. The quantitative achievements of this system are impressive indeed. Almost universal literacy, some 25 million persons in the ranks of the new Soviet intelligentsia, almost 7 million persons with secondary specialized training, over 5 million persons with higher professional and university education—these are visible achievements of that system.

In appraising the impact of the October Revolution upon education in the Soviet Union over the last five decades, one must recognize the following factors. Education, as one of the most complex societal institutions, derives its foundations, its strengths, and its weaknesses from the society it is called upon to serve. The purpose of education according to the Soviet press appears disarmingly simple: "to build communism."[1] The apocalyptic vision of the Communist millenium to come which fixed the imagination of those who led the Revolution is still with their heirs and continues to be the major item of faith urged on all Soviet children. The Soviet state, which came in on a wave of idealism about the potential for transforming society and the nature of man, is, more than five decades later, still struggling with the problem of educating the "new Soviet man" according to these ideals.

The vexing problem of educating the new Soviet man at the threshold of the era of "scientific communism" is a reflection of difficult interactions between Soviet society, with its changing objectives, and education, with its effects upon the development of the individual, his character, and his talent. The major underlying difficulty in examining these interactions is the very dualism which permeates every aspect of life in Soviet society—the dichotomy of the ideal and the real forms.

The first involves the professed aims of education as stated by Communist leaders, echoed by educators, proclaimed in the Soviet Constitution and various directives of the Communist party and the Soviet government. All of these are a mixture of ideology, good intentions, and apocalyptic visions of the ideal Communist society as an ultimate social good. The other involves the individual as he is subjected to the actual educational practices in the system itself. These include the instructional programs and processes of schooling, educational opportunities, choices, and the motivation of an individual to learn and to develop his personal abilities for his private gain. The two aspects—what the state expects from the individual as a citizen and as a producer and what the individual wants out of society as a beneficiary of the education he receives—are by no means in harmony. It is difficult to disentangle the two in examining the efforts of the Communist state to modernize the traditional society it aimed to replace.

The first problem relates to the goals of society as they are currently promulgated by the ruling elite—what kind and how much education should be minimally offered by the state in order to foster a sufficient productive contribution from each citizen at any given stage of the national development. Essentially, this problem is to determine what the state wants out of the individual in making him a "productive resource" by offering him functional education at a minimum cost to society.

The second problem deals with the personal motivation of the individual for the betterment of his lot through education. He seeks education at no cost to himself. Be it for self-enlightenment or for personal gain, individuals in Soviet society are seeking out educational opportunities of their own choosing. Since Soviet citizens do not pay tuition and receive monthly stipends to enable them to go to school, the private costs of education in the USSR are exceedingly small. The rewards for completing education, however, are remarkably high, for most salaries are differentiated by level of education and an individual performing job functions similar to another but having a higher level of educational attainment receives higher pay. Thus, whatever the level of education, there is in a sense a "pay-off" to the individual who has a better educational background.

The evolution of education in the postrevolutionary period and the Soviet school reforms of the late 1950s are attempts to change the school system from above so as to make it more responsive to pressing national needs. The basic assumption is that the state—the national government and its arms—knows and can predict what kind and how much education individuals ought to have. In the USSR, as anywhere else, the "demand" for education is no doubt largely a reflection of the continuous rise of educational aspiration of parents for their children. These private aspirations are fostered further by the regime's system of motivations and incentives, which bestow monetary rewards and prestige upon the highly educated elite.

However, these educational aspirations of parents and youth represent only the potential and what Soviet authorities often call the "subjective demand." On top of this potential demand, the state planning bodies superimpose upon all educational institutions, and particularly on upper secondary and higher education, a somewhat different "demand function." It is claimed that it is an "objective" or *derived* demand which establishes actual needs and requirements through a complex method of nationwide projections for personnel with given occupational skills and derived educational specializations.

The major pillars of the Soviet system of national and centralized planning are so-called balances. There are three such national "balances": (1) material, or allocation of commodity flows, (2) financial, or allocation of monetary flows, and (3) labor, or allocation of human resource flows. In essence, the "labor balance" consists of a checkerboard method of ascertaining, for each occupation and industry sector, where people are presently employed and where new additions can be obtained and with which specific qualifications—that is, education, training, and experience. The "source of supply" in this labor balance is determined by detailed tabulations of occupation, education, and place of future employment of the *new* accessions to the labor force. The majority of these new accessions are youth aged fifteen to twenty. Their assimilation into the labor force simply means the termination of their formal education. This in turn means that all educational institutions on the secondary school level and beyond are given annual admission quotas. Each educational establishment determines how to fill its respective quota in order to assure the proper "output" of educated manpower several years hence. This type of educational planning, based on manpower projections, was initiated in 1927 and continues to be the main tool of decision-making of the Soviet government concerning educational policy and practice.

The ideal aim of Soviet education was stipulated by *Pravda* in the following manner:

> The Soviet school is called upon to prepare well-rounded, educated individuals who have mastered the foundations of knowledge and who at the same time are capable of systematic physical labor; to instill in the young the desire to be useful to society and to take an active part in producing the values society needs.[2]

However, it is the availability of educational opportunities and the types of training, both of which are determined by the national labor requirements plan, which decide the extent to which these aims can be fulfilled by the individual.

POLYTECHNICAL EDUCATION—FIRST PHASE

No aspect of Soviet education, past or present, has aroused as much controversy as polytechnical training.[3] Yet no phase of Soviet educational policy has been so neglected and so frequently misinterpreted. Neither extensive theoretical studies[4] nor brief surveys of the practices of Soviet "polytechnical" education[5] have done full justice to this important and extremely complex topic. As interpreted by Communist educators, "polytechnism" is a concept of so many dimensions that it is difficult to avoid slighting some of them. However, the numerous educational reforms of the last decades have elevated polytechnism to a position of key importance in Soviet educational policy,[6] although the ideal of integrated training has been present for a long time in the Soviet Union.

Polytechnical education is an essential ingredient of the Marxian theory of education.[7] It forms the central pillar of Marxist educational philosophy founded upon a utopian conception of human nature and of the future Communist society. Marx envisaged that the individual under communism would enjoy the opportunity to achieve the all-sided development of his capabilities—a condition which, Marx claimed, was unattainable under capitalism because of the division of labor. Communism was expected to eliminate this division of labor. In the Communist society, distinctions between different forms of labor would vanish, the unification of mental and physical labor would be realized, and education would give every individual uniform, integrated training in both the theory and the practice of all branches of production. It is this concept of integrated training which is the basis of polytechnism. To Marx, polytechnical education was one of the three basic ingredients of Communist education along with physical and aesthetic training. Marx believed that the individual, provided this opportunity, would seize it and thus free himself from the fetters of narrow, specialized development.[8]

Lenin was clearly in basic theoretical agreement with Marx on the role of polytechnical education in the Soviet system.[9] Soviet legislation concerning public education in the wake of the 1917 Revolution invariably emphasized Lenin's ideas of "free, universal and compulsory general and polytechnical education, familiarizing in theory and practice all youths of both sexes up to the age of sixteen with all major branches of production" and assuring "close unity of education and socially productive work."[10]

On October 16, 1918, the Soviet government issued a decree on the "unified labor school," in which the polytechnical principle was designated as the basis of Soviet education. In March 1919, the Eighth Congress of the Communist party adopted a policy directive calling for "universal and compulsory general and polytechnical education" for all youths up to age seventeen.[11] In December 1920, there was a special party conference on public education which devoted most of its attention to problems of a "unified labor school" and polytechnical instruction. In 1921, the Soviet government was obliged to retreat somewhat from the Eighth Congress policy by lowering the educational age limit from seventeen to fifteen, but it reaffirmed the principle of universal general and polytechnical education.[12] These policies were continued until the end of 1931.

This first period of Soviet educational development was marked by grandiose plans, sweeping pronouncements, lofty slogans—and meager results. Until about 1926–27, there was much talk of applying Marx's concepts of polytechnical instruction, but neither the facilities, teaching staff, nor a comprehensive instruction program could be provided. When one reads the directives and regulations of the *Narkompros* (People's Commissariat of Education) for the early and mid-1920s, one is immediately struck by their preoccupation with financial and material problems—where to get money to pay the teachers and how to scrape together enough resources to avoid having to close down the schools altogether. During this period the very concepts of organized learning were ambiguous and uncertain. Often the so-called proletarization of education—i.e., giving preferential treatment to workers and their children regardless of intellectual capacity—was regarded as enough to implement the aims of polytechnism. Nevertheless, labor and laboring activity were the center of polytechnical education as interpreted in the 1920s.

This period of Soviet educational evolution was unique in other respects as well. From the Revolution up until 1931, the educational system was highly experimental and permissive.[13] In fact, there was a great deal of pluralism in educational policy-making. The 1920s have been described by some observers as a phase of Soviet education marked by courageous and brilliant experimentation with the ideas of Western liberal educators. But even if it were true that this period was marked by greater willingness to experiment with the ideas of Western liberal educators, the fact remains that these ideas did not find fertile soil, and that there was no real understanding of the fundamental philosophical basis of Western educational precepts. Soviet attempts to transplant vulgarized versions of progressive educational ideals to "proletarian soil," and to apply them in the late 1920s largely in the arena of productive labor education, resulted in the downgrading of the entire educational process.

One frequent subject of controversy during this period was the notion of the "withering away of the school."[14] Although the *Narkompros* claimed that it had worked out a nationwide "complex educational program,"[15] some of these experimental ventures lacked any specification whatever of the actual content of educational instruction. "Learning through doing" was considered applicable to anything from scrubbing floors and building roads to composing "collective poems." Collectivism was practiced to such an extreme that individual learning was replaced by group practice, and individual grading by amorphous group performance criteria. Social and political participation overshadowed all other pursuits. The teachers' authority was nonexistent. Parental authority was likewise rejected and castigated as a "capitalist survival," and the family was sentenced to "wither away" along with the school and the state.[16] This stage of educational chaos, later described in Soviet pronouncements as a period which exposed "the importance of the educational theories of pseudoreformers,"[17] finally came to a close in 1931.

In the evolution of the Soviet system of education the most radical change took place in 1931 with the restoration of traditional schooling, which despite recent modifications has lasted to this day. In September 1931, the Central Committee of the Communist party declared:

> The fundamental shortcoming of the school is that it does not provide a sufficient amount of general education and handles unsatisfactorily the task of preparing fully literate persons for *technicums* and higher educational establishments, persons who have acquired the fundamentals of knowledge (physics, chemistry, mathematics, languages, geography, etc.). Because of this, polytechnical education in many instances acquires a formalistic character and does not prepare builders of socialism, who can combine theory with practice and who have mastered technology.[18]

The same resolution directed that polytechnization and the amalgamation of education and productive labor should be carried out in such a way that "all socially productive labor performed by students is directly subordinated to study and the educational objectives of the school."[19] Later in 1931, the People's Commissariat of Education and thereafter the Communist party Central Committee and the Soviet government issued a series of decrees which put an end to all the earlier extreme experimental projects in Soviet education. Soviet educators, armed with party and government policy pronouncements, proceeded to shape the new concept of polytechnical education. From that time until the late 1950s, polytechnical education was considered to mean the firm acquisition of applied knowledge through learning of the natural sciences, physics, chemistry, and mathematics.

The reaction against innovation was evident in other aspects of Soviet schooling as well. Soviet education went back to the time-tested traditional methods of instruction. Emphasis was again placed upon discipline and obedience, individual learning and grading, and the mastery of basic academic knowledge. Directed study and training once more took precedence over haphazard observation of environmental facts. Individual performance became a yardstick of educational success. Social and political participation were pushed into the realm of extracurricular activity; student interference with teaching was drastically curtailed; and the authority of the teacher was restored. The family was again considered a useful element of socialist society, and parents were called upon to aid the school.[20] From 1931, the state demanded technically educated but obedient individuals, and the educational system was revised to produce them. This change in educational policy may have been a by-product of an overall adjustment in ideological and doctrinaire orientation reflecting the restoration of traditional symbols of authority and foreshadowing the emergence of inequality in Soviet society. It is apparent, nevertheless, that the most important motivating factor for the change was the pressing need for an educational system capable of producing the kind of young people required by the emergent industrial society—young people with training in science and technology and with habits of work and disciplined obedience. Emerging industrialization called for greater specialization and division of labor quite contrary to Marxist prophecies. The series of educational decrees issued in 1931 embodied these aims and redefined Soviet elementary and secondary education as general education with stress on literacy, general knowledge, and especially basic scientific knowledge.

The establishment of this new pattern marked the beginning of a prolonged period in which polytechnical instruction ceased to be actively discussed. The majority of the experimental pedagogues of the 1920s were purged or silenced in the "pedology" purge of 1936.

From 1936 until the 1950s, the orthodox interpretation of Lenin's educational principle of the "unity of theory and practice" prevailed; classroom instruction in the fundamentals of science came first, supplemented by the "practical application of science in the formation of work habits."[21] For two decades, until 1952, there seems to have been unanimous contempt for what was called naked technicism or applied vocational training without theoretical foundation. It was not the task of general education schools to provide vocational and specialized training, and these undertakings were delegated to separate educational institutions (vocational, trade, and semiprofessional schools). The policy of instruction—fundamentals first and application thereafter —has been carried over into the recent stage of educational reforms.

By design the Stalinist educational system was geared to the development of a "learned elite," persons who devoted themselves almost exclusively to higher specialized learning and never worked with their hands. Although social ethos and Marxist disquisitions about unity of mental and physical work demanded that academic studies be related to "production" and to "labor," neither of these concepts was adequately defined at any time. While the number of educated persons was relatively small and in 1930 there were only some three hundred thousand persons with higher education in the USSR, they could be provided with white-collar supervisory jobs. Consequently, until the 1950s the training of a technocratic elite caused little trouble. But as the output of the Soviet educational system increased and it became no longer possible to give white-collar and supervisory jobs to all these educated specialists, difficult problems began to emerge.

THE KHRUSHCHEV REFORMS—POLYTECHNISM IN THE SECOND PHASE

Controversy surrounding the reintroduction of polytechnical education in the 1950s relates basically to the issues of output and employment of the educated elite. For some three decades the Soviet regime had been promising to its citizens the introduction of universal secondary education. In 1961, the Twenty-second Communist party Congress reiterated that by 1970, eleven-year education should become a reality for all Soviet children.[22] So far this promise has not been fulfilled. Obviously, parents and pupils alike want this opportunity; but from the state's point of view, this unfulfilled goal presents certain complications, as upward mobility and education would be in conflict. If there is to be universal secondary schooling, the very content of education has to be defined in such a way that it is *not* education itself, but socially productive labor which thereafter should become the source of upward mobility.

The educational reforms of the 1960s are the results of the very success of the Soviet instructional policies which had been in existence since 1931–1932. In the 1950s Soviet secondary schooling was expanding more rapidly than other components of the educational system. The annual number of secondary school graduates increased from 100,000 to over 1,700,000 in 1967.[23] This rapid expansion of secondary schooling was responsible in part for the educational reforms—adjustment of the initial academic curriculum to the needs of some diversified and vocationally oriented training. Polytechnical education was redefined as productive labor training. In the late 1950s, first through a process of piecemeal adjustment and then by radical institutional reform in 1958, primary-secondary schools became institutions for turning out students who, in addition to having academic preparation, were trained in labor skills and thus ready for employment. The 1958 reforms changed the school grade structure from 4-3-3 to a 4-4-3 system, with the addition of mandatory vocational training in the three upper grades of secondary school. The meaning of these educational reforms, because of their complexity, was at least a controversial one, not only among Western students of Soviet society but also among the Soviet planners, educationalists, and parents. In the early 1960s, as the reform progressed, most of the official Soviet press was singing the praises of its successful fulfillment by 1965. Occasionally, however, slightly skeptical voices were heard about its purpose and effectiveness.

Most teachers, and especially the members of the Academy of Pedagogical Sciences who were ordered to design the polytechnical courses, did not have the slightest idea about practical laboring activity in industry, agriculture, construction, or business. As the reforms progressed, it became obvious that: (1) the teachers themselves didn't know how to teach applied subjects; (2) the skilled workers hired to supervise pupil training neither understood nor cared much about theoretical subjects and the fundamentals of production; (3) the pupils had such a low cognitive perception of what they were doing that they could imitate the job functions mechanically but could not comprehend the fundamentals of the technological processes involved; (4) the general theoretical courses on the "fundamentals of production" were simply watered-down science courses; (5) though the pupils were taught work skills, they never had enough exposure for mastering such skills; and (6) those trained in a particular skill often did not take employment, upon graduation, which would utilize the learned skill.[24] What the students received was not genuine polytechnical instruction but a poor version of apprenticeship training thrust upon them in an academic setting and in addition to academic subjects.

Just as the deadline of its full implementation was approaching in the summer of 1964, the Soviet government abruptly decreed the elimination of certain major features of Khrushchev's education program. The timing of the reform and some of its features were measures designed to speed up additions to the Soviet labor force of young people with skill qualifications who were needed to alleviate the shortages caused by demographic trends. The sharp drop in the birth rate caused by wartime losses affected the Soviet school age population throughout the 1950s and curtailed the availability of new entrants to the work force in the early 1960s. The reform was aimed at alleviating this situation; and as the emergency eased, the reform lost its meaning and consequently some of its labor-channeling features were scrapped by the Soviet government in 1964.

In August 1964, the Central Committee of the Communist party of the Soviet Union and the Council of Ministers of the USSR decreed a cutback from eleven years of primary-secondary school to ten years— the length it had been in the first place, before the reform. The change transformed schools to a new 4-4-2 grade structure, eliminating vocational training (and part-time employment) in the upper secondary schools.

This shift was not entirely surprising, for Khrushchev's school reform was based on short-run considerations. The solution had been to superimpose on the standard general education curriculum a localized system of supplemental labor training shaped in accordance with local economic needs and the availability of skilled training outlets; this solution did not produce the desired results. The reform's emphasis on vocational-technical training in the general education schools and part-time employment of upper secondary school students resulted in a considerable deterioration of standards and quality of instruction. This had an adverse effect not only in primary-secondary general education, but also in semiprofessional and professional training programs, which were forced to absorb the graduates of general education schools, now with worse preparation than before. Finally, the separate network of Soviet vocational-technical schools, which had been specifically geared to apprenticeship-training in economic enterprises, was handicapped in recruiting students.

In recent years there has been a considerable shift in priorities for specialized secondary education. In the summer of 1963, the USSR Council of Ministers reviewed the status of specialized manpower training and decreed one very significant measure.[25] It stipulated that the tempo of secondary semiprofessional (*technicum*) education should be speeded up over that of higher education. This was a new departure. The Soviet planners decreed a radically new target for the output of semiprofessional graduates and stipulated that the Soviet economy should have a ratio of 3 to 4 semiprofessionals to 1 professional (higher education) graduate. They claimed that objective fac-

tors—new technology and new organization of economic activity—
were responsible for the shift in these ratios from the prior ratio of
about 3 semiprofessionals to 2 professionals.

This means that the output of graduates from *technicums* should
eventually increase to about 2 to 2½ times that of institutions of higher
education. By 1969 total graduates from *technicums* had already risen
to 1,035,000 (from 510,700 in 1963) compared with 565,000 graduates
of institutions of higher education (up from 331,700 in 1963). This is
largely the result of a significant increase in *technicum* admissions
(from 955,000 in 1963 to 1,312,000) which helped to siphon off some of
the applicants pressing for admission to higher education, where admissions increased from only 722,400 to 895,000 during the same period.[26]

The piecemeal undoing of certain provisions of Khrushchev's
educational reform really began with higher and secondary specialized
education. In May 1964 (while Khrushchev was traveling in Egypt),
the Central Committee of the Communist party of the Soviet Union
and the USSR Council of Ministers adopted a decree concerning the
"further improvement" of specialized education.[27] It ordered a curtail-
ment in the length of training in higher education and secondary
specialized schools by anywhere from six to eighteen months, thus
restoring the prereform length of training in higher education to 4 to
5½ years (depending upon specialty) and in *technicums* to 3 to 4 years.
Thus, in 1964–1965, all types of specialized training establishments
began to follow the path set for pedagogical training, which was cut
from 5 to 4 years in May of 1963.[28]

RECENT CHANGES IN EDUCATION

The reason given for this wholesale conversion and accelerating
training schedules was that the year to year and a half devoted to
applied and on-the-job experience, introduced as a reform measure,
was "no longer necessary," for the majority of those entering higher
educational institutions either had two or more years of employment
experience or else had already acquired a working specialty while in
secondary school.

In view of the cut in the length of study, the Ministry of Higher
and Secondary Specialized Education further decreed a complete review of all curricula and syllabi in specialized fields in order to eliminate the duplication of instructional material and in order to transfer
not "absolutely essential courses" from the category of "required" to
"optimal overload electives." The motto now is: "Save and make the

most efficient use of the student's time." Since industrial practice and work experience are to be concentrated in the upper courses, present indications are that the curricular revision will affect the more advanced and highly specialized courses in the upper years of study.

The recent expansion of professional and semiprofessional training was brought about by increasing extension-correspondence and evening education. Part-time higher and secondary specialized education, though introduced in the late 1930s, is really a postwar development in the Soviet Union. It gained particular impetus from Khrushchev's school reforms. In April 1964, the Central Committee of the Communist party and the Council of Ministers of the USSR decreed the further expansion of evening and extension-correspondence education and called for its qualitative improvement.[29] Although the quality of part-time specialized education remains poor in comparison with day-time instruction programs, its quantitative gains over the last fifteen years have been spectacular.

Admissions and enrollments in part-time programs have multiplied four times, outstripping day programs by a substantial margin. By the fall of 1968, over 50 percent of all students in Soviet higher and secondary specialized schools were in evening or extension-correspondence programs. This enormous expansion of part-time education was due to a variety of factors. First, it is convenient and cheap, for it does not require additional capital outlays for instructional and residential facilities. It permits more intensive utilization of existing staffs. And above all, it uses the student's leisure time without withdrawing him from his current employment position in the economy. But all of these considerations apparently were not enough to give it a clear advantage. The quality of training was abysmally bad and again persons who allegedly trained in part-time programs to improve their present occupational proficiency were actually retraining themselves for other and totally unrelated occupations.

In September 1966, the USSR Council of Ministers and the Central Committee of the Communist party decided to curtail part-time education. It decreed that "as the practical experience of the last few years has demonstrated, the training of specialists in day programs has indisputable superiority not only as far as the quality of education is concerned, but also in terms of lesser economic wastefulness."[30] It decreed that future expansion of higher education should proceed for most professional occupations in the day divisions.

Since Khrushchev's brand of "polytechnism" did not work, in the summer of 1964, the government of the USSR created a mammoth commission to revise curricular contents for primary and secondary education. General directions were clear. Diversification of secondary education, creation of programs to suit differential abilities of students, and strengthening of political indoctrination based on principles of what is called now "scientific communism"—were all unresolved issues of the recent school reforms.[31] The new curricula were to be implemented by an entirely new administrative setup.

For several decades the Soviet Union had the pretense of having a decentralized system of primary-secondary education. Under this system various union and autonomous national republics had their own separate Ministries of Education. The Russian Republic had in a sense a primacy, and, with its research arm—the Academy of Pedagogical Sciences—set the pace for curricular contents and teaching practices in the entire USSR. Through its Administration on Instruction and Methodology *(Uchebno-Metodicheskoe Upravlenie)* and the RSFSR Academy of Pedagogical Sciences *(Adademiia Pedagogicheskikh Nauk RSFSR)*, the RSFSR Ministry of Education played a key role in formulating model standards for school curricula, textbooks, teaching methods, examinations, etc. THE RSFSR Academy of Pedagogical Sciences was also the major curricular research center of the USSR. Several (though not all) Ministries of Education in *other* Union republics have pedagogical research institutes, which adapt centrally prescribed programs of instruction to local conditions, primarily adjusting programs to the linguistic (and/or geographical) peculiarities of a given republic. The Ministries of Education of the other republics followed the pattern of the RSFSR Ministry of Education, making only minor modifications to suit local conditions.

This is all past history now. In August 1966, the USSR Supreme Soviet modified the Soviet Constitution and decreed the establishment of an All-Union Ministry of Public Education, which was to develop a unified and standard system of primary-secondary education for the entire country. Among other things, this new central Ministry of Education was to see that the speedy "eradication" of the "past educational policies and practices"—namely Khrushchev's reform measures—was undertaken.[32] The new ministry is in charge of all phases of the prospective (i.e., long-range) planning of education, including not only the contents of general education but polytechnic and labor vocational training as well. It determines not only *what* is to be taught, but how many ought to be taught.

"Education for what?" is a major question in Soviet society. There are many views of the functions of education in a society and judgment and values determine which are selected for emphasis. However, the multiplicity of attitudes about the roles education can play may be grouped into four major areas. These are: (1) education as a human right and as an individual good *per se;* (2) education as an instrument of thought-control and mass regimentation; (3) education as a means for the creation of elites for leadership roles in society; and (4) education as a tool for developing differentiation and specialization of human inputs into the productive process. It is implicitly assumed that the process of education is based on the transmission of knowledge which is manipulated toward these ends. In the Soviet Union, education was consciously utilized for all four ends. The state used it to achieve categories two and four; Soviet citizens viewed it as serving the ends of the first and third categories.

In conclusion, then, Soviet educational policy has been, for decades in the past, and will continue to be, for decades in the future, confronted by two interacting forces. The first is the role education must play as a weapon in the hands of the government in the social, political, and, particularly, the economic transformation of Soviet society. The second is the end product of that education: the Soviet citizen as an individual—his self-growth and the development of his knowledge, intellect, and skill, and his desire for education of his own choosing.

Most of the ideological disquisitions and verbal exercises with the scriptural utterings of Marxism-Leninism have limited bearing upon the actual practices of developing the trained manpower potential of the Soviet Union. Lenin and Stalin denounced the prerevolutionary past, Khrushchev denounced Stalin's era, and now Khrushchev's heirs denounce Khrushchev's era by relying upon the same basic ideological preconceptions and by quoting virtually the same passages from the Marxist-Leninist scriptures about what the ideal education should accomplish in training the ideal individual for the ideal Communist society. The study of the theory and philosophy of Soviet education explains some of the ideological precepts, but it provides little clue to action and practical solutions.

Over the last few decades Soviet planners have intensified their drive to implant, through formal education as much as possible and as early as possible, some kind of basic functional skill or specialty which would enable the state to integrate an individual into productive employment and which would help to retain him in that employment. This policy continues.

Either for self-enlightenment or for personal gain, the individual seeks out educational opportunities which will advance his status in Soviet society. Fundamentally, the individual is seeking what he can get from the state by partaking of as much education as possible at the least cost to himself. The Soviet citizen outwardly embraces character traits which are expected of him and in a formal way passes educational requirements imposed upon him. In both cases, the internalization of values and the quality of learning may be openly questioned.

By looking at these two problems and their interaction, we find clues to recent changes in Soviet educational policies and practices. The Soviet individual and the Soviet state are engaged in a highly pragmatic game—who gets what out of whom. Essentially, the problems of Soviet education are not significantly different from those anywhere else. Pragmatic tests of education have been a guide to change in Soviet education policy over the last five decades. And as a guide to his actions, the Soviet citizen asks himself the basic question: "What is an education good for, anyway?"

NOTES

1. See the message of the Central Committee of the Communist Party of the Soviet Union and the Council of Ministers of the USSR to the Soviet people concerning the Fiftieth Anniversary of the Revolution, *Pravda,* November 5, 1967.
2. *Pravda,* November 16, 1958.
3. For a survey of recent polytechnical instruction, see W. K. Medlin, C. B. Lindquist, and M. L. Schmitt, *Soviet Education Programs,* Bulletin 1960, no. 17, Washington, D.C.: U.S. Department of Health, Education and Welfare, Office of Education, 1960.
4. M. J. Shore, *Soviet Education: Its Psychology and Philosophy,* New York: Philosophical Library, 1947, *passim.*
5. N. DeWitt, *Soviet Professional Manpower: Its Education, Training and Supply,* Washington, D.C.: National Science Foundation, 1955, pp. 34–37; A. Korol, *Soviet Education, for Science and Technology,* Cambridge: The Technology Press of the Massachusetts Institute of Technology, and New York: Wiley and Sons, 1957, pp. 27–32. See also I. Nikodimov, *O politekhnicheskom obrazovanii v SSSR,* Munich: Institute for the Study of the USSR, 1957; H. Wittig, "Marx on Education: Philosophical Origins of Communist Pedagogy," *Soviet Survey,* no. 30 (October–December 1959), pp. 77–81, and the same author's "Die Marx'sche Bildungskonzeption und die zweite 'Polytechnisierung' der Sowjetschule," *Das Parlament,* December 10, 1958, as well as R. V. Rapacz, "Polytechnical Education and the New Soviet School Reforms," in G. Z. F. Bereday and J. Pennar, eds., *The Politics of Soviet Education,* New York: Praeger, 1960, pp. 28–44.
6. *Uchitel'skaia gazeta,* November 4 and 5, 1967. The appeals of the Fiftieth Anniversary and L. I. Brezhnev's speech reiterate original statements and slogans about unity of physical and mental labor through polytechnical education.
7. For an extensive discussion of the

origins, development, and ideological implications of this concept, see Shore, *op. cit.*, esp. pp. 146–50, 227–40. It is interesting to note that Marx, in developing the concept of polytechnical education, was profoundly influenced by the British factory school system and the ideas of the utopian socialists, especially Robert Owen.

8. K. Marx and F. Engels, *Sochineniia,* 2nd. ed., V, Moscow, 1955, 265–70, 318–20.

9. See, for example, Lenin's article on Marx in the *Granat Entsiklopedicheskii Slovar'*, St. Petersburg, 1914–16; and a convenient summary of Lenin's views on polytechnical education in *Uchitel'skaia gazeta,* April 23, 1955. See also V. I. Lenin, *Stat'i i otryvki po voprosam narodnogo prosveshcheniia i shkoly,* Moscow, 1938.

10. A photoreproduction and transcript of Lenin's theses of the Communist party program for public education may be found in *Narodnoe obrazovanie,* no. 11 (November 1957), pp. 7–8.

11. MP RSFSR, N. I. Boldyrev, comp., *Direktivy VKP(b) i postanovleniia sovetskogo pravitel'stva o narodnom obrazovanii: sbornik dokumentov za 1917–1947 gody,* I, Moscow, 1947, 8.

12. *Ibid.,* p. 26.

13. R. A. Bauer, *The New Man in Soviet Psychology,* Cambridge: Harvard University Press, 1952.

14. Z. I. Ravkin, *Sovetskaia shkola v period vosstanovleniia narodnogo khoziaistva, 1921–1925,* Moscow, 1959, esp. pp. 188–90.

15. Akademiia Pedagogicheskikh Nauk RSFSR, I. A. Kairov *et al.*, eds., *Narodnoe obrazovanie v SSSR,* Moscow, 1957, p. 42. This program described study areas of human knowledge in their relationship to the revolutionary transformation of the world and were based on the principle of learning through active participation. For an extensive discussion, see also Ravkin, *op. cit., passim.*

16. For a most interesting interpretation of this stage of Soviet education, see F. M. Hechinger, *The Big Red Schoolhouse,* New York: Doubleday, 1959. He is inclined to believe, quite reasonably, that in order to consolidate its power and authority, the Communist dictatorship had to undertake a massive destruction of the prevailing social order, including all educational institutions. This is, in effect, what was accomplished during the first phase of Soviet educational development, whether by folly or deliberate intent.

17. Akademiia Pedagogicheskikh Nauk RSFSR, Kairov, *op. cit.,* p. 44.

18. Ministerstvo Prosveshcheniia RSFSR, M. M. Deineko, comp., *Spravochnik direktora shkoly: sbornik postanovlenii, prikazov, instruktsii i drugikh rukovodiashchikh materialov o shkole,* Moscow, 1st ed., 1954, 2d ed., 1955, this quote from 2d ed., p. 18.

19. *Ibid,* p. 20.

20. A governmental decree or regulation of the Commissariat (Ministry) of Education was issued to enforce each and every one of these changes (*ibid., passim*).

21. M. N. Skatin, *O politekhnicheskom obrazovanii v obshcheobrazovatel'noi shkole,* Moscow, 1953, p. 13. Of course many other articles on this subject have appeared recently, but this particular reference is cited because its author is a member of the Research Institute on Methods of Instruction of the Academy of Pedagogical Sciences of the RSFSR.

22. *Vestnik vysshei shkoly,* no. 11, 1961, p. 4.

23. Nicholas DeWitt, *Education and Professional Employment in the USSR,* Washington, D.C.: National Science Foundation, 1961, p. 153. The figure for 1967 is graduates from general secondary schools. U.S. Congress, Joint Economic Committee, *Soviet Economic Per-*

formance 1966–67, Washington, D.C., 1968, pp. 83, 86.

24. *Sovetskaia pedagogika*, no. 6, 1964, pp. 36–43; no. 7, 1964, pp. 25–32; no. 9, 1964, pp. 3–13.
25. *Biuleten' MVSSO*, August 1963, pp. 4–13.
26. U.S. Congress, Joint Economic Committee, *Economic Performance and the Military Burden in the Soviet Union*, Washington, D.C., 1970, p. 89.
27. *Vestnik vysshei shkoly*, no. 6, 1964, pp. 3–6; *Biuleten' MVSSO*, no. 1. 1965, pp. 1–6; *Ekonomicheskaia gazeta*, July 18, 1964, p. 39.
28. Note that the idea of training multi-specialty teachers was abandoned, and the majority of Soviet teachers will be trained in just one specialty.
29. *Biuleten' MVSSO*, June 1964, pp. 13–17.
30. *Uchitel'skaia gazeta*, September 10, 1966 (Decree of the Council of Ministers of the USSR and Central Committee of the CPSU concerning improvement of higher and secondary education).
31. *Uchitel'skaia gazeta*, November 21, 1967.
32. *Uchitel'skaia gazeta*, August 6, 1966.

5

WILL ADAMS

William Jewell College

CAPITAL PUNISHMENT IN SOVIET CRIMINAL LEGISLATION, 1922-1965: A CODE CONTENT ANALYSIS AND GRAPHIC REPRESENTATION

The history of capital punishment in Russia, and of the struggle against it, provides a unique combination of extremes: bloody excesses by governments, implacable hostility to the death penalty, and startling reversals by former opponents once they were in power. The present study is concerned with the period beginning June 1, 1922, when the first Criminal Code of the Russian Soviet Federated Socialist Republic (RSFSR) came into force. But a word of background will put some events of the Soviet period in perspective.

PROLOGUE[1]

The Russian Tradition

As long ago as A.D. 1020, Article 1 of the *Russkaia Pravda*, Russia's first law code, limited vengeance for murder. At the end of the reign of Iaroslav "the Wise" in 1054, such vengeance was forbidden alto-

Part of the paper has been reprinted, with permission, from *American Journal of Comparative Law*, XVIII (1970), 575–94.

gether, constituting what later Russian historians often regarded as the first *de jure* abolition of legislatively authorized execution.[2]

The budding tradition of Russian hostility to the death penalty was strengthened by an oft-quoted passage in the Testament of the Grand Prince of Kiev, Vladimir Monomakh, in 1125: "Do not kill anyone, either guilty or not, nor do you order to kill. Do not destroy a Christian soul, even in case death is well deserved."[3] Capital punishment did not reappear in Russian codes until the end of the fourteenth century, although the Mongols had brought the institution with them in the interim.[4] The Moscow *Sudebniki* of 1497, 1550, and 1589 steadily increased the list of capital offenses, although they also increased the circumstances under which a noncapital alternative was provided.[5]

When Michael Romanov was elected tsar in 1613, he won the support of the aristocracy by promising them immunity from death sentences.[6] But the *Ulozhenie* of 1649 resumed the upward trend in capital punishment, listing some sixty capital offenses.[7] Combined with the military code of Peter "the Great" in 1715, over two hundred legislative articles now prescribed execution, including sixty-nine which provided no alternative to the death penalty.[8]

When Elizabeth Petrovna was contending for succession to the throne in 1741, however, she reportedly promised God that if she were successful, she would take no life.[9] Upon gaining power she exiled rather than executed her opponents, and in a series of decrees between 1742 and 1754 abolished the death penalty *de jure*.[10] On this basis Russia could claim to be the first European country in the modern era to abolish capital punishment, although abolition was never complete *de facto*.[11] Catherine "the Great" added to the record of officially expressed hostility to capital punishment in her famous Instructions to the Legislative Commission in 1767.[12]

Although sporadic executions continued, the death penalty did not reappear in Russia's ordinary criminal legislation until the Speransky codification of 1833.[13] But many "ordinary" offenses which were often capital in other countries (such as murder and rape) remained noncapital. Moreover, the bloody repressions of Nicholas II, especially after 1905, did not utilize the criminal code or the civil courts. They depended entirely on military courts and codes, "extraordinary" decrees, even punitive expeditions and pogroms.

But the heritage of Monomakh, Iaroslav, Elizabeth, and Catherine, to say nothing of such literary figures as Radishchev, Dostoevsky, and Tolstoy, made it possible for Russian opponents of capital punishment to speak of a Russian tradition hostile to the death penalty.[14]

The Duma Period

The Revolution of 1905 had two opposite effects on the history of capital punishment in Russia. On the one hand, it resulted in widespread executions by the government. On the other, it brought concessions which included establishment of a Duma and, consequently, political parties and groupings.

In the years from 1905 to 1910, capital punishment received a great deal of attention from a wide variety of interest groups, parties and party presses, and the Duma.[15] The First Duma's first bill was an unsuccessful attempt to abolish the death penalty, adopted unanimously on June 19, 1906.[16] Similar bills were introduced into the Second and Third Dumas, but the government succeeded in preventing their passage.[17]

The effect of prolonged controversy, however, was to keep the issue of capital punishment alive in the public mind. And statistics indicated a tendency for the pace of executions to slow when the Duma was in session, and to quicken when it was not, at least into 1908.[18] Moreover, the image emerged of a center and left united in implacable opposition to the death penalty, with support coming only from the government, the reactionaries, and some conservatives. There were occasional suggestions from the extreme left, notably certain peasant deputies and Lenin, of a kind of double standard—that executions of the masses by the oppressors are reprehensible, but executions of those who prey on the masses might be acceptable. And both Bolsheviks and Mensheviks had refused in 1903 to incorporate a demand for abolition of capital punishment into their program.[19]

At any rate, the legislative, political, and literary history of capital punishment in Russia prior to 1917 left an ambivalent heritage, ranging all the way from the bloodiest of repressions to the most vigorous attacks on such practices.

The Socialist Tradition

The socialist heritage on capital punishment was also an ambivalent one. On at least one occasion Marx scathingly denounced capital punishment.[20] On the other hand, he endorsed revolutionary terror against the "class enemy," at least to the extent necessary for the proletariat to seize and maintain power.[21]

Despite their revolutionary predilections, European socialist parties generally pressed for abolition of the death penalty in many countries, including Russia.[22] The leading party, the German Social

Democrats, demanded abolition in the Erfurt and Manheim Congresses, 1891 and 1906 respectively.[23] And the 1910 Copenhagen Congress of the Second International unanimously condemned capital punishment.[24]

Both as Russians and as socialists, therefore, the revolutionaries of 1917 were familiar with the distinctions between judicial death sentences and terror, between political and nonpolitical executions, and between absolute and conditional opposition to capital punishment. And the Soviet government would soon learn what the tsarist regime had known for a long time—the distinction between *de facto* and *de jure* abolition.

The Provisional Government

Ten days after the February Revolution, the Provisional Government abolished the death penalty.[25] The move was greeted with unanimous approval by press organs ranging from conservative to radical, except for the silence of *Pravda* and *Izvestia*.[26]

But as Russian military forces disintegrated, especially after the collapse of the July offensive, military leaders on the right and even leftist political commissars pressed for restoration.[27] On July 12, 1917 (Old Style), the Provisional Government restored the death penalty at the front.[28]

Where the March abolition met with virtually unanimous approval, the July restoration fragmented public opinion. Only the Bolsheviks, through their refusal to participate in the Provisional Government, remained untainted as a party with responsibility for this return to "tsarist methods." Together with the growing Left Socialist Revolutionaries (SR's), they agitated for a new abolition.[29]

Lenin explained Bolshevik support of an SR resolution of condemnation in the Petrograd soviet with a comment stressing the double standard. The resolution, he wrote, "contains the true and splendid thought . . . that capital punishment is a weapon against the *masses* [his emphasis] (it would be different if it were a question of a weapon against the landowners and capitalists)."[30] But during 1917 Lenin often qualified his readiness to resort to executions with repeated assurances that such measures would probably not be needed.[31] And Bolsheviks continued to agitate against the death penalty.[32]

The Pre-Code Soviet Period, 1917–1922

After ratifying the October Revolution, the very first act of the Second Congress of Soviets on November 7, 1917 (New Style) was a new abolition of capital punishment.[33] Lenin was not present, and according to Trotsky he was considerably agitated upon learning of the move.[34] But to most Bolsheviks, Left SR's, and other factions which remained in the Soviet government, it seemed the logical culmination of the determined and consistent socialist campaign against the death penalty.

The exigencies of civil war and foreign intervention led to restoration of capital punishment in mid-1918.[35] On January 17, 1920, the death penalty was again abolished,[36] although unlike the earlier abolition this one seemed to be motivated by tactical consideration—the encouragement of desertion.[37] In any case, with Baron Wrangel still active in the Crimea and the Poles advancing into the Ukraine in early May, capital punishment was restored on May 4, 1920.[38]

Thus ended the last Soviet experiment with abolition until 1947. But the issue remained alive. In early 1922 the Central Executive Committee (CEC) was preparing the first RSFSR Criminal Code. On May 17 Lenin wrote to Commissar of Justice D. I. Kurskii urging retention of the death penalty for political offenses.[39]

The draft of the Judicial Commission of the CEC simply included death as the first of several possible punishments in Article 32 of the General Part. But in the CEC debates, Riazanov led a protest which succeeded in removing it from Article 32 and devoting a separate Article 33 to the subject.[40] Most important, Article 33 provided for capital punishment "pending its abolition by VTsIK"—a clear expectation that a new abolition was anticipated by many leading Bolsheviks.[41]

The abolition was a long time in coming, and was not permanent when it did come. But the history of capital provisions in Soviet criminal legislation from the RSFSR Criminal Code of 1922 (which came into force on June 1) to mid-1965 shows some interesting evidence of the continued ambivalence of the Russian and Socialist traditions, and some curious departures from them.

SOVIET CRIMINAL LEGISLATION, 1922–1965

Like the old imperial and other continental civil law systems, Soviet criminal codes are divided into a General Part and a Special Part. The former deals with basic principles (definition of crime, types of punishment, mitigating and aggravating circumstances, etc.), while the latter defines specific offenses and prescribes penalties.

Soviet federalism has meant that comprehensive criminal codes exist only at the republic level.[42] The Russian Republic (RSFSR) adopted comprehensive criminal codes in 1922, 1926, and 1960. The All-Union government (USSR) has adopted "statutes" *(polozhenie, zakon)* of three types: (1) Principles of Criminal Legislation of the USSR and Union Republics (1924, 1959) which, like the RSFSR Principles statute of 1919, generally corresponded to the General Part

TABLE 1

MAJOR RSFSR AND USSR CRIMINAL LEGISLATION, 1922–1965

Effective Date	Legislation: *USSR, italic* RSFSR, roman
Dec. 12, 1919	Basic Principles for the Criminal Law of the RSFSR, *SU* No. 66, item 590, Dec. 28, 1919, pp. 589–92 [630–33].
June 1, 1922	Criminal Code of the RSFSR, *SU* No. 15, item 153, 1922.
Oct. 31, 1924	*Basic Principles of the Criminal Legislation of the USSR and the Union Republics, SZ No. 24, item 205, 1924.*
Oct. 31, 1924	*Statute on Military Crimes, SZ No. 24, item 207, 1924.*
Jan. 1, 1927	Criminal Code of the RSFSR, *SU* No. 80, item 600, Nov. 22, 1926.
Feb. 27, 1927	*Statute on State Crimes, SZ No. 12, item 123, Feb. 25, 1927;* incorporated into RSFSR Code, *SU* No. 49, item 330, June 6, 1927.
Aug. 27, 1927	*Statute on Military Crimes, SZ No. 50, item 505, July 27, 1927;* incorporated into RSFSR Code, *SU* No. 12, item 108, Jan. 9, 1928.
Jan. 1, 1959	*Basic Principles of the Criminal Legislation of the USSR and the Union Republics, Dec. 25, 1958, Ved. SSSR No. 1, 1959.*
Jan. 1, 1959	*Statute on State Crimes, Dec. 25, 1958, Ved. SSSR No. 1, 1959.*
Jan. 1, 1959	*Statute on Military Crimes, Dec. 25, 1958, Ved. SSSR No. 1, 1959.*
Jan. 1, 1961	Criminal Code of the RSFSR, not published in *Vedomosti RSFSR* but available in various editions.

of the republic codes. (2) Statutes on State Crimes (1927, 1959), corresponding to the Chapters on State Crimes in republic codes. (3) Statutes on Military Crimes (1924, 1927, 1959), corresponding to republic chapters on the same subject. In addition, (4) periodic USSR decrees superseded conflicting provisions in republic codes. Usually, but not invariably, the republics amended their codes to conform to the changes. Table 1 recapitulates these landmarks of Soviet criminal legislation.[43]

The 1919 RSFSR Principles listed death by shooting as the last of several possible penalties (Art. 25), adding a note that People's Courts might not impose death sentences.[44] The aforementioned characterization of capital punishment as temporary in the General Part of the 1922 RSFSR Code was repeated in both of the other codes and in both USSR Principles. All but the 1924 Principles devoted a separate article to the death penalty, and all since 1926 have labeled death an "exceptional" punishment.[45]

There have also been fluctuations in such matters as exemption from the death penalty (minors, pregnant women) and the statute of limitations. But it is the penalty clauses in the Special Part of the RSFSR Criminal Codes and USSR legislation which can best be quantified.

Two opposing extreme views of the significance of Soviet law are rejected here: (1) that Soviet codes reveal nothing, since the regime may ignore them with impunity; (2) that Soviet codes accurately portray juridical reality. Rather, legislation reflects changes in penal policy (else why change it?), but correlations between these changes and executions, extra-legal executions, or developing legal theory must await examination or compilation of criminal statistics, jurisprudence, court decisions, press reports and commentary, and other data.

Methodology

A code content analysis might be expected to show: (1) Variations in the number of capital crimes and in availability of alternative penalties in the code as a whole; (2) similar variations within different categories of crimes (State Crimes, Military Crimes, Personal Crimes, etc.); and (3) relative trends between these different categories of offenses.

Besides simply counting capital crimes, this study attempts to quantify the degree of compulsion which the legislator assigned to the death penalty. The wording of the penalty clauses is the main indicator. A rating scale (Table 2) recognizes a spectrum ranging from a

TABLE 2

RATING SCALE: DEGREE OF COMPULSION TO IMPOSE DEATH PENALTY

Rating	Definition

Unqualified Death Penalty (No special circumstances required):

9   Death mandatory, no alternative.

8   Death normally mandatory, with noncapital alternative under extenuating circumstances.

7   Death listed as first of two or more alternative penalties.

6   Noncapital alternative precedes death penalty; or clause prescribes punishment "up to death."

Qualified Death Penalty (Special circumstances required):

5   Death mandatory, no alternative, in presence of specified special circumstances (e.g., wartime, mercenary motives, especially harmful consequences, etc.).

4   Death normally mandatory under such special circumstances, with noncapital alternative under extenuating circumstances.

3   Death listed as first of two or more alternative penalties, under such special circumstances.

2   Noncapital alternative precedes death penalty, or clause prescribes punishment "up to death," under such special circumstances.

1   Double aggravation: Capital only under two sets of special circumstances (e.g., committed in wartime from mercenary motives).

No Death Penalty (Capital punishment not applicable):

0   Noncapital offense.

X   Not an offense; not in criminal codes.

mandatory death sentence (9) to a noncapital penalty (0). The scale is subdivided into two main groups. Unqualified death penalties (ratings 6–9) represent offenses for which simple violation may entail death. Qualified death penalties (1–5) are normally noncapital, but may be subject to a death sentence in the presence of certain aggravating circumstances.[46]

The three RSFSR Criminal Codes with all amendments prescribed death for seventy-two offenses,[47] although no more than fifty-one were capital at any one time. Twenty-two were military crimes, seventeen were serious state crimes, and fourteen were other state crimes. The other nineteen were scattered among various chapters of the codes. Table 3 lists all capital offenses with citations, grouped insofar as possible in accordance with the classification of Soviet codifiers.[48]

The penalty clause of each capital provision in each criminal enactment of the RSFSR and the USSR has been assigned an appropriate rating on the scale described in Table 2. This makes it possible to portray on the charts below the history of Soviet penal policy on capital punishment for each category of crime as classified in Table 3. For each category of crime, ratings have been totaled for each quarter year in which there was any change.[49] The result is a series of fluctuating rating totals which have been plotted on graphs. These graphs indicate the variations in penal policy and the comparative trends which we are seeking.

Limitations of the Methodology

The significance of these results should be understood in the light of what they show. This requires an understanding of what they cannot show.

1) The rating scale is merely ordinal; it is not interval. Thus higher or lower ratings and rating totals indicate only greater or lesser degree of compulsion of the death penalty. There is no precise mathematical relationship between them.[50]

2) Data deal only with the death penalty, not other punishments. Maximum terms of deprivation of freedom, for example, may not parallel changes in capital punishment, as witness the increase of the maximum from ten to twenty-five years in conjunction with the peacetime abolition of the death penalty in 1947.[51]

3) Since the analysis is based upon penalty clauses, it cannot reflect changes in the definition of an offense.[52] An amendment to a particular clause might broaden or narrow the scope of activity rendered criminal without changing the rating.[53]

4) Data deal with legislative prescription of the death penalty, not death sentences or executions. Unfortunately, reliable Soviet criminal statistics are generally unavailable. Actual death sentences and executions no doubt fluctuated within periods appearing on graphs as a straight line.

TABLE 3
CAPITAL CRIMES IN 1922, 1926 & 1960 RSFSR CRIMINAL CODES

Crime No.	Capital Offenses by Type of Crime	Average Ratings	1922	1926	1960
I-1: Especially Dangerous (Counterrevolutionary) State Crimes					
1	Sabotage (*diversiia;* cf. wrecking)	6.7	65	58/9	68
2	Terrorist act against government official	6.3	64	58/8	66
3	Treason; Treason by serviceman	(7.6) 5.5	---	58/1a,b	64
4	Participation in counterrevolutionary organization	5.4	60, 62	58/11	72
5	Armed uprising, secession	(5.8) 5.0	58	58/2	---
6	Aiding foreign government against USSR	(5.8) 5.0	59	58/3	---
7	Undermining state institutions	(5.8) 5.0	63	58/7	---
8	Counterrevolution by tsarist official	(5.8) 5.0	67	58/13	---
9	These crimes committed against another workers' state	(4.8) 4.3	---	58/1	73
10	Inducing foreign attack	(5.5) 4.1	---	58/5	---
11	Espionage	3.7	66	58/6	65
12	Antisoviet propaganda and agitation [3.1]	2.6	69	58/6	65
13	Aiding international bourgeoisie	(3.0) 2.6	61	58/4	---
14	Wrecking (*sabotazh*) [3.5]	(2.7) 2.6	63	58/14	69
15	Unauthorized return from banishment abroad	(9.0) 1.1	71	---	---
16	Terrorist act against foreign official	(6.0) .9	---	---	67
17	Using religious prejudice to overthrow the government	(5.0) .6	119	---	---
I-1, Supplement: USSR Decrees Never Incorporated into RSFSR Code					
A	Defection abroad	(7.4) 5.2	SZ No. 76, 1929.		

TABLE 3—continued

Crime No.	Capital Offenses by Type of Crime		Average Ratings		Article Numbers	
				1922	1926	1960
B	Theft of socialist property, in transit or from collective farms ___		(6.2) 3.9	SZ No. 62, 1932.		

I-2: Other State Crimes (against Administrative Order)

Crime No.	Capital Offenses by Type of Crime		Average Ratings		Article Numbers	
18	Counterfeiting ___		(6.6) 6.3	85	59/8	87
19	Banditry ___		4.4	76	59/3	77
20	Wartime tax evasion ___ [5.0]		(4.2) 3.7	___	59/6	82
21	Mass disorders (Leaders) ___ [4.1]		3.5	75	59/2	79
22	Smuggling ___ [3.7]		3.2	97	59/9	76
23	Destruction or damage of railways or communications ___ [3.4]		(2.8) 2.4	___	59/3b	86
24	Breach of labor discipline by transport workers ___		(3.3) 2.1	___	59/3c	___
25	Breach of civil aviation duty ___		(2.9) 1.6	___	59/3d	___
26	Wartime agitation for national, religious, or racial dissension ___ [1.2]		1.0	83	59/7	74, 227
27	Evading wartime mobilization ___ [1.2]		(1.1) 1.0	81c	67; 193/10a	81
28	Speculation (in currency) ___ [3.5]		.7	97	59/12	88
29	Disrupting corrective labor institutions ___		(6.0) .6	___	___	77/1
30	Aiding illegal entry, exit (an official, as a business) ___ [5.0]		(.5) .5	98	55/10	83
31	Stealing military arms, ammunition ___ [1.0]		(.5) .4	___	59/3a	USSR

II: Crimes by Public Officials

Crime No.	Capital Offenses by Type of Crime		Average Ratings		Article Numbers	
32	Provocation to bribery _ [6.0]		(.8) .7	115	119	___
33	Abuse of authority ___ [4.5]		(.7) .6	110	112	___
34	Unjust sentence (by a judge) ___ [5.0]		.6	111	114	177

TABLE 3—continued

Crime No.	Capital Offenses by Type of Crime	Average Ratings		Article Numbers		
				1922	1926	1960
35	Bribe taking _____ [1.2]		.3	114	117	173
36	Embezzlement (*rastrata*) _____ [1.0]		.1	113	116	92
37	Exceeding authority ___ [1.0]		.1	106	110	171
38	Bribe giving; intermediary _____ [1.0]		.1	114; a	118, 174	174,/1

III: (Other) Crimes against Administration

39	Foreign registry, revelation, of a secret defense invention _____	(7.1)	2.6	____	84b	____
40	Resisting, coercing public official _____	(8.0)	.9	86	73; /1	191,/1
41	Speculation (in goods) _____ [5.0]		.6	97	107	154
42	Encroachment on life of militiaman or people's guard (*druzhinik*) _____	(5.0)	.4	____	____	191/2

IV: Economic Crimes

43	Official conspiring to make contract disadvantageous to state _____ [8.0] (.8)		.7	128a	129	____
44	Maladministration of state institution with waste or damage _____	(8.0)	.7	128	____	____
45	Breach state contract, bad faith _____	(2.0)	.2	130	____	____
46	Certain economic crimes, wartime _____ [1.0] (.1)		.1	131	132	____

V: Crimes against Socialist Property

47	Stealing (*khishchenie*) _____ [5.5] (1.1)		1.0	180h; a	162e	93/1

VI: Crimes against Personal Property

48	Robbery (*razboi*) _____ [4.8]		2.8	184	167	146

TABLE 3—continued

Crime No.	Capital Offenses by Type of Crime	Average Ratings	Article Numbers 1922	1926	1960
	VII: Crimes against the Person				
49	Murder (aggravated) _ [3.3]	2.4	142	136	102
50	Rape (aggravated) ___ [2.0]	.1	169	153	117
	VIII: Military Crimes				
51	Abandonment of sinking warship ____ (7.3)	6.4	___	193/23	262
52	Unwarranted abandonment of battle ____	4.7	211	193/22	263
53	Voluntary surrender ___ (4.6)	4.5	211	193/22	264
54	Evading duty by maiming, malingering _	4.4	206	193/12	249
55	Abusing, exceeding authority; neglect of duty ____ [4.4]	4.3	209	193/17	260
56	Desertion ____	4.2	204; 205c	193/7	247
57	Unwarranted abandonment of duty, post ____ [4.8]	3.8	205; 204	193/8	246
58	Military espionage ____ (4.4)	3.6	213	193/24	___
59	Unwarranted abandonment of unit in combat (4.1)	3.4	___	193/9	248
60	Unwarranted absence _ [4.0]	3.2	204	193/10	245
61	Commander surrendering, abandoning materiel ____	2.8	210	193/20	261
62	Insubordination ____	2.6	202	193/2	238
63	Unwarranted departure from battle orders by commander ____ (3.0)	2.5	210	193/21	___
64	Revealing military secret ____ [5.0] (2.7)	2.4	___	193/25	259
65	Resisting, coercing superior officer ____	2.0	203	193/3, 193/4	240
66	Pillaging (stealing from battlefield dead) ____	1.5	214	193/27	266
67	Violating guard duty regulations ____	1.4	208	193/15	255

TABLE 3—continued

Crime No.	Capital Offenses by Type of Crime	Average Ratings	Article Numbers 1922	1926	1960
68	Violence against population of area of military operations _____	1.3	214	193/28	267
69	Dissipation, loss of military property _____	1.3	207	193/14	251
70	Refusing military duty due to religious or other beliefs _____	(1.0) .7	____	193/13	____
71	Force against superior officer _____	(3.0) .4	____	____	242
72	Violating rules on combat lookout _____ [3.0]	(2.3) .4	____	____	257

Notes to Table 3

Crime numbers assigned here are used throughout this study.

For an explanation of average ratings, see note 48.

Where two article numbers cited for the same crime in the same code are separated by a semicolon, it indicates an amendment with the latter article superseding the former (crime nos. 27, 38, 40, 47, 56, 57). Where they are separated by a comma, two articles were in effect simultaneously (crime nos. 3, 4, 26, 38, 40, 65).

Space limits have required omission of a basic article number in crimes 38, 40, and 47. Thus "114; a" means that a new Art. 114a superseded 114; "191,/1" means that Arts. 191 and 191/1 were both relevant and in effect simultaneously.

5) Similarly, fluctuations in extra-legal executions are not depicted here.

Despite these limitations, the graphs show some patterns which do correlate with known facts of Soviet history, and suggest other hypotheses not heretofore apparent.

A CODE CONTENT ANALYSIS

I-1. *Especially Dangerous (Counterrevolutionary) State Crimes.*[54]

Chart I-1 indicates the fluctuations in death penalties for each of the seventeen offenses in this category (see Table 3 above for names of crimes). Graph I-1 portrays these variations in the number of capital crimes and rating totals. Several patterns emerge.

The 1922 RSFSR Criminal Code was written with fresh memories of the recent Civil War. It is not surprising, therefore, that most of the

Chart I-1:
Especially Dangerous (Counterrevolutionary) State Crimes

Crime No.	1922[3]	25[3]	27[1]	29[4]	1930	32[3]	34[3]	1940	47[2]	1950	50[1]	54[2]	59[1]	1960
1	8	8	7				7		3		7	7	6	
2	8	8	7				7		3		3	7	6	
3	X	X	X				8.5		4.5		8.5	8.5	6	
4	8	8	5.5				6		2.5		3.5	4	6	
5	8	8	7				7		3		3	3	X	
6	8	8	7				7		3		3	3	X	
7	8	8	7				7		3		3	3	X	
8	8	8	7				7		3		3	3	X	
9	X	X	5.5				5.5		2.5		3.5	3.5	6	
10	X	X	7				7		3		3	3	X	
11	8	5	3				3		1		3	3	6	
12	3.5	3.5	3				3		3		3	3	0	
13	8	8	3				3		1		1	1	X	
14	X	0	5				5		1		1	1	0	
15	9	9	X				X		X		X	X	X	
16	X	X	X				X		X		X	X	6	
17	5	5	X				X		X		X	X	X	

Subtotals

	1922[3]	25[3]	27[1]	29[4]		32[3]	34[3]		47[2]		50[1]	54[2]	59[1]	
Year	1922[3]	25[3]	27[1]	29[4]		32[3]	34[3]		47[2]		50[1]	54[2]	59[1]	
Ratings	89.5	86.5	74				83		36.5		48.5	53	42	
Crimes	12	12	13				14		14		14	14	7	
Average	7.5	7.2	5.7				5.9		2.6		3.5	3.8	6	

Chart I-1, Supplement:
USSR Decrees Never Incorporated into RSFSR Criminal Code

	1922[3]	25[3]	27[1]	29[4]	1930	32[3]	34[3]	1940	47[2]	1950	50[1]	54[2]	59[1]	1960
A	X			9		9			5				X	
B	X			X		8			0				X	

Subtotals

	1922[3]	25[3]	27[1]	29[4]		32[3]	34[3]		47[2]		50[1]	54[2]	59[1]	
Year	1922[3]	25[3]	27[1]	29[4]		32[3]	34[3]		47[2]		50[1]	54[2]	59[1]	
Ratings	X			9		17			5				X	
Crimes	X			1		2			1				X	
Average				9		8.5			5					

Grand Totals

	1922[3]	25[3]	27[1]	29[4]	32[3]	34[3]	47[2]	50[1]	54[2]	59[1]
Year	1922[3]	25[3]	27[1]	29[4]	32[3]	34[3]	47[2]	50[1]	54[2]	59[1]
Ratings	89.5	86.5	74	83	91	100	41.5	53.5	58	42
Crimes	12	12	13	14	15	16	15	15	15	7
Average	7.5	7.2	5.7	5.9	6.1	6.3	2.8	3.6	3.9	6

GRAPH I-1
ESPECIALLY DANGEROUS (COUNTERREVOLUTIONARY) STATE CRIMES

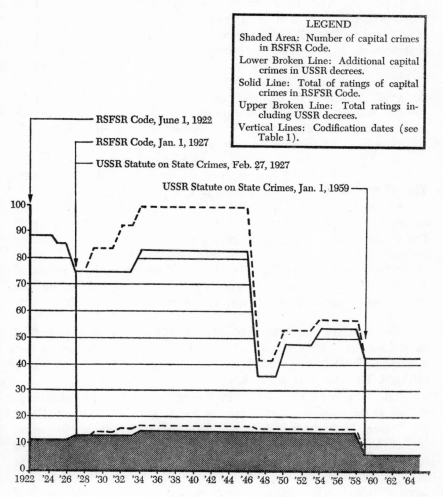

dozen capital counterrevolutionary offenses entailed mandatory death sentences except under extenuating circumstances. A 1925 All-Union decree on espionage (crime no. 11), superseding the provision remaining in the Russian Republic code, was the only change before the new code of 1926. Three years became the normal penalty, but death was mandatory if the espionage risked or caused especially serious consequences.[55]

The 1926 code reshuffled capital offenses,[56] increasing the number of capital crimes by one but reducing the degree of compulsion of the death penalty. The rise of Stalin, however, portended both a rise in the degree of compulsion (and thus a rise in ratings) and a centralizing trend as two All-Union decrees opened the floodgates for death sentences although neither was incorporated in the RSFSR code (Chart I-1, Supplement; dotted lines on Graph I-1). In November 1929, a USSR decree branded Soviet officials defecting abroad "outlaws" and declared them subject to execution within twenty-four hours after identity was established.[57] On August 7, 1932, another All-Union decree rendered capital the theft *(khishchenie)* of goods in transit and of collective farm or cooperative property.[58]

An All-Union decree of 1934 which was incorporated into the RSFSR code introduced treason *(izmena rodine)* for the first time.[59] This all-time peak persisted through the purges and the war.[60]

The peacetime abolition of the death penalty in May 1947 vastly reduced the degree of compulsion for imposing capital punishment.[61] But growing cold war tensions were accompanied in January 1950 by restoration for traitors, spies, and saboteurs as "an exception" to the abolition.[62] And on May 21, 1954, the USSR Supreme Court extended a recent USSR act, making aggravated murder capital, to include murder stemming from a terrorist act against a public official (crime no. 2).[63]

The legislation of 1958–1960, like the 1926 code, again reshuffled capital offenses. Six disappeared. One was new—terrorist act against a foreign official (crime no. 16). Only espionage (no. 11) had a higher rating.[64] The rest were either lower or became noncapital.

The net effect is a marked reduction in the number of total ratings. A look at the *average* rating, however, suggests a qualification (Chart I-1, bottom line). It is now higher than at any time since 1947, even higher than in the 1927–1932 period. In a limited sense, therefore, one might argue that penal policy has become "more severe."[65] This change is partly editorial; the variety of wording in the old penalty clauses has been standardized to provide death as the second alternative (a 6 rating). But it also represents increased use of unqualified death sentences, a noteworthy development.

In sum, these patterns correlate with many facts of Soviet political history. The first peak coincides with apprehension over capitalists and kulaks during the New Economic Policy, and with the early succession struggle after Lenin's death. The drop in the new code of 1926 suggests mitigating influences of the jurists who wrote it and perhaps increasing confidence as Stalin won out. Use of USSR decrees not incorporated into Republic codes indicates growing centralization. The purges and the war coincide with the all-time peak. Victory and renewed loyalty were cited as the basis for the 1947 abolition, and the cold war was in high gear at the 1950 restoration. "Thaw," de-Stalinization, and renewed emphasis on legality by jurists accompany the new 1959 statute. The end of USSR decrees standing alone coincides with Khrushchev's talk of the strengthened role of the Republics. The rise in unqualified death penalties will be explored later.

I-2. *Other State Crimes.*[66]

The totals from Chart I-2 are plotted on Graph I-2. Trends generally parallel those of the more serious state crimes, but on a lower level. The main differences are the absence of a post-1950 build-up, and the presence of a rise after 1961.

Mass disorders, smuggling, damaging railways or communications,

CHART I-2
OTHER STATE CRIMES (AGAINST ADMINISTRATIVE ORDER)

Crime No.	1922^3	23^3	27^1	27^2	29^1	29^2	1930	30^3	31^1	36^1	1940	47^2	47^3	1950	59^1	1960	61^2
18	8	8	8	8	8	8		8	8	8		4	4		0		6
19	8	8	5	5	5	5		5	5	5		1	1		6		6
20	X	X	5	5	5	5		5	5	5		5	5		0		0
21	8	8	5	5	5	5		5	5	5		1	1		0		0
22	5	5	5	5	5	5		5	5	5		1	1		0		0
23	X	X	X	X	X	5		5	5	5		1	1		0		0
24	X	X	X	X	X	X		X	5	5		1	1		X		X
25	X	X	X	X	X	X		X	X	5		1	1		X		X
26	2	2	5	1	1	1		1	1	1		1	1		0		0
27	X	0	X	X	X	X		1	1	1		1	1		2		2
28	0	5	0	0	0	0		0	0	0		0	0		0		2
29	X	X	X	X	X	X		X	X	X		X	X		X		6
30	X	5	0	0	0	0		0	0	0		0	0		0		0
31	X	X	X	X	1	1		1	1	1		1	0		0		0
TOTALS																	
Year	1922^3	23^3	27^1	27^2	29^1	29^2		30^3	31^1	36^1		47^2	47^3		59^1		61^2
Ratings	31	41	33	29	30	35		36	41	46		18	17		8		22
Crimes	5	7	6	6	7	8		9	10	11		11	10		2		5
Average	6.2	5.8	5.5	4.8	4.2	4.5		4	4.1	4.2		1.6	1.7		4		4.4

GRAPH I-2
OTHER STATE CRIMES (AGAINST ADMINISTRATIVE ORDER)

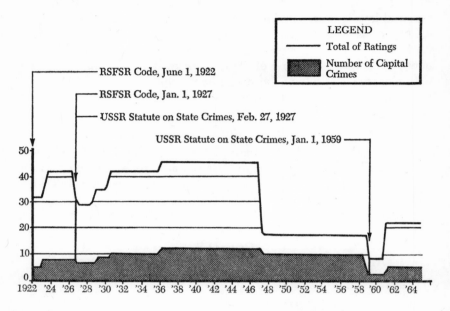

and certain other offenses have become noncapital. The rise in rating for banditry (no. 19)[67] might simply be an editorial change of the type already described. But introduction of similar penalties for counterfeiting (no. 18, previously noncapital) and disruption of correctional labor institutions (no. 29, a new offense) in 1961 amendments suggests that these were responses to real problems. The same is true of currency speculation (no. 28) which became capital for the first time since 1927.

As before, average ratings show a somewhat but not markedly different pattern. And codification periods produce declines, while present legislation makes increased use of unqualified death penalties.

II. *Official Crimes.*
III. *Crimes against Administration.*[68]

These two groups show markedly similar patterns. The lone exception is foreign registry of a vital defense invention (no. 39), which had a 7 rating through its 1931–1947 tenure. Otherwise, both sets of crimes peak during NEP. This suggests distrust of officials (bribery,

CHART II:
CRIMES BY PUBLIC OFFICIALS

Crime No.	1922[3]	22[4]	27[1]	27[4]	28[2]	1930 1960	62[1]
32	6	6	0	0	0		X
33	5	5	2	2	0		X
34	5	5	5	0	0		0
35	2	1	2	0	0		1
36	1	1	1	0	0		0
37	1	1	1	0	0		0
38	0	1	0	0	0		0
TOTALS							
Year	1922[3]	22[4]	27[1]	27[4]	28[2]		62[1]
Ratings	20	20	11	2	0		1
Crimes	6	7	5	1	0		1
Average	3.3	2.9	2.2	2	0		1

GRAPH II
CRIMES BY PUBLIC OFFICIALS

32. Provocation to Bribery
33. Abuse of Authority Disorganizing Administration
34. Unjust Sentence (by a Judge)
35. Bribe Taking (1922-1926, 1962-   )
36. Embezzlement
37. Exceeding Authority
38. Bribe Giving; Acting as an Intermediary

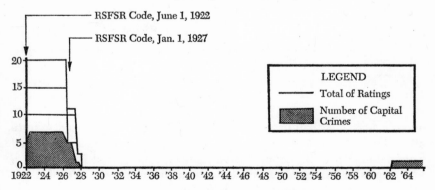

embezzlement, etc.), some of whom had worked for the tsar, and of
capitalists (speculation in goods).

Administrative crimes became entirely noncapital in the 1926 code,

Chart III:
(Other) Crimes against Administration

Crime No.	1922³	27¹	1930	31³	1940	47²	47³	1950 1960	62¹
39	X	X		7		3	X		X
40	8	0		0		0	0		0
41	5	0		0		0	0		0
42	X	X		X		X	X		5
Totals									
Year	1922³	27¹		31³		47²	47³		62¹
Ratings	13	0		7		3	0		5
Crimes	2	0		1		1	0		1
Average	6.5	0		7		3	0		5

Graph III
(Other) Crimes against Administration

39. Foreign Registry or Revelation of a Secret
    Defense Invention (1931-1947)
40. Resisting, Coercing, Public Authority (1922-1926)
41. Speculation (in Goods) (1922-1926)
42. Encroachment on Life of Militiaman or People's
    Guard (*Druzhinik*) (1962-   )

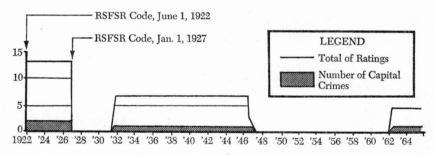

and official crimes had become so by mid-1928. They remained so until
after the 1958–1960 revisions. But 1962 amendments again rendered
bribe-taking (no. 35) capital among official crimes, and introduced a
new capital administrative crime—encroachment on the life of a militiaman or people's guard (*druzhinik*) (no. 42).[69]

These last increases coincided with those among less serious state
crimes, while the "especially dangerous" state crimes remained at an
all-time low. These patterns indicate that in the early 1960s the Soviet

regime was far more concerned about crimes which threatened the regular operation of the system than by those which might threaten to overturn it.

IV. *Economic Crimes.*
V. *Crimes against Socialist Property.*[70]

These two groups show patterns which are basically similar to those of groups II and III above—greatest provision for capital punish-

CHART IV:
ECONOMIC CRIMES

Crime No.	1922[3]	23[3]	27[1]	27[4]	1930 1960	61[1]
43	X	8	0	0		X
44	X	8	X	X		X
45	2	2	X	X		X
46	1	1	1	0		X
TOTALS						
Year	1922[3]	23[3]	27[1]	27[4]		61[1]
Ratings	3	19	1	0		X
Crimes	2	4	1	0		X
Average	1.5	4.8	1	0		

GRAPH IV
ECONOMIC CRIMES

43. Official Conspiring to Make Disadvantageous Contract
44. Maladministration of State Institution, with Waste or Damage
45. Breach of Contract with State Institution in Bad Faith
46. Certain Economic Crimes Committed in Wartime

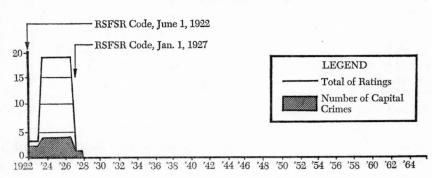

CHART V:
CRIMES AGAINST SOCIALIST PROPERTY

Crime No.	1922[3]	23[3]	27[1]	1930 1960	61[2]
47	6	5	0	‖‖	6
TOTALS					
Year	1922[3]	23[3]	27[1]		61[2]
Ratings	6	5	0		6
Crimes	1	1	0		1
Average	6	5	0		6

GRAPH V
CRIMES AGAINST SOCIALIST PROPERTY

47. Stealing (*Khishchenie*, large scale)

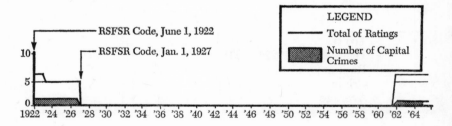

LEGEND
—— Total of Ratings
▨ Number of Capital Crimes

—— RSFSR Code, June 1, 1922
—— RSFSR Code, Jan. 1, 1927

1922 '24 '26 '28 '30 '32 '34 '36 '38 '40 '42 '44 '46 '48 '50 '52 '54 '56 '58 '60 '62 '64

ment in the 1920s, less in the 1960s, and noncapital in between. There are, of course, certain exceptions to this general pattern.

When Western commentators speak of economic crimes in the Soviet Union, they often refer to such offenses as speculation, theft of socialist property, counterfeiting, and bribe-taking.[71] But to Soviet code writers, economic crimes have concerned more mundane abuses by capitalists or state officials which harm operation of the economy.[72]

Official conspiracy to make a contract disadvantageous to the state (no. 43) and maladministration of a state institution resulting in waste or damage (no. 44) first appeared by amendment in 1923 with a mandatory death sentence except under mitigating circumstances. Breach of a contract with the state in bad faith (no. 45) and certain economic crimes committed in wartime (no. 46) permitted death sentences under aggravating circumstances in the original 1922 code. But two of these crimes disappeared from the 1926 code while the other two became noncapital then and likewise disappeared from the 1960 code.

This peculiar pattern is rather easily explained. The early peak illustrates the regime's anxiety over harboring class enemies during the the New Economic Policy. Abandonment of such repression coincides with abandonment of NEP and anticipates the "attainment of social-ism." After all, how can a private entrepreneur breach a state contract or conspire with a state official if there are no private entrepreneurs?

Large-scale theft[73] of socialist property is the only crime against socialist property which has ever been capital. It reveals the capital-early-and-late pattern previously noted. But during the middle period when it was noncapital, death might have been imposed on such acts under the USSR decree of August 7, 1932 (I-1, Supplement, crime B). That edict cast the offense in terms of a state crime, however, while the RSFSR code continued to describe it as a noncapital property crime.

CHART VI:
CRIMES AGAINST PERSONAL PROPERTY

Crime No.	1922[3]	27[1]	29[3]	1930 1940	47[2]	47[3]	1950	54[2]	59[1]	1960
48	6.5	1	5		1	0		3	0	
TOTALS										
Year	1922[3]	27[1]	29[3]		47[2]	47[3]		54[2]	59[1]	
Ratings	6.5	1	5		1	0		3	0	
Crimes	1	1	1		1	0		1	0	
Average	6.5	1	5		1	0		3	0	

GRAPH VI
CRIMES AGAINST PERSONAL PROPERTY

48. Robbery

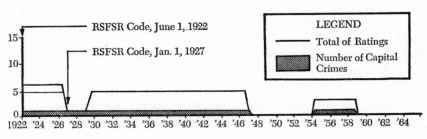

VI. *Crimes against Personal Property.*

Again there has been only one capital crime in this group. Robbery[74] was subject to a death sentence until the 1947 abolition. The USSR Supreme Court's decree of May 21, 1954 (note 63), made it capital again when combined with murder, but it became noncapital in the present code.

This pattern may indicate a decline in the incidence of robbery. NEP, the purges, and the war may have produced conditions more hospitable to the offense than those now prevailing. Its continuing noncapital status while speculation became capital suggests that the Soviet underworld may have turned to more refined methods. Or perhaps this trend signifies an effort by the regime to discourage too great attachment to "petty bourgeois" values—the amassing of personal property. In any case, the patterns for socialist property above and crimes against the person below provide interesting contrasts.

VII. *Crimes against the Person.*

Aggravated murder and rape are the only offenses ever capital in this category. Yet neither was so before 1934. In that year an amendment required mandatory death for aggravated murder by military personnel.[75] Unless there were a great many unruly servicemen running around, most murder remained noncapital.[76] But on April 30, 1954, a USSR decree "On increasing criminal responsibility for premeditated murder" extended the 1950 restoration of the death penalty to those convicted of aggravated murder.[77]

The 1958 reforms created an anomalous legal situation. The 1954 decree was repealed effective January 1, 1959.[78] Article 136 of the 1926 RSFSR code, noncapital except for the military, remained the only Russian Republic legislation which both defined the offense and prescribed punishment. Article 22 of the new USSR Principles Statute did provide that death, as an "exceptional measure," might be applied for aggravated murder as set forth in "the criminal laws of the USSR and the Union Republics, establishing responsibility for premeditated murder. . . ." But there was now no USSR statute, and no new RSFSR statute on murder came into force until the new code took effect on January 1, 1961 (see Article 102). Case reports, however, seem to indicate that civilian murder did sometimes entail death between 1959 and 1961.

Rape was also rather lightly punished under earlier codes. But a USSR decree in early 1949, though still treating it as noncapital, began

CHART VII:
CRIMES AGAINST THE PERSON

Crime No.	1922[3]	1930	34[3]	1940	47[2]	1950	54[2]	1960	62[1]
49	0		2.5		.5		6		6
50	0		0		0		0		2
TOTALS									
Year	1922[3]		34[3]		47[2]		54[2]		62[1]
Ratings	0		2.5		.5		6		8
Crimes	0		1		1		1		2
Average	0		2.5		.5		6		4

GRAPH VII
CRIMES AGAINST THE PERSON

49. Murder
50. Rape (1962-   )

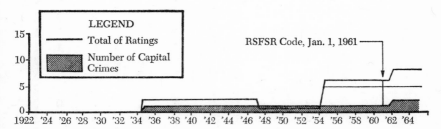

a trend toward greater severity.[79] Somewhat lower noncapital penalties appeared in the 1960 code (Article 117), but a 1962 amendment prescribed death as second alternative for aggravated rape,[80] rendering that offense capital for the first time in Soviet history.

These developments suggest an increase in such crimes, as have certain Soviet sources.[81] But another Soviet explanation is interesting.

In 1963 Professor Kerimov of the Leningrad law faculty explained to the present writer that as a people becomes more civilized it comes to hold human life and personal security in higher esteem. Thus prescribing death for aggravated murder and rape is a sign of advancing civilization. He did not mention civilization's attitude toward the offender's life. The Soviet apologist may therefore interpret whatever happens next as an advance. If death penalties for personal crimes increase, this shows respect for the person (the victims); if they decrease, this too shows respect for the person (the offender).

It should also be noted that these trends represent a great departure from the traditional Soviet justification of capital punishment. Even contemporary Soviet treatises explain it in the same terms in which Marx and Lenin justified terror—as a legitimate weapon against enemies of the system.[82] Increased prescription of death for nonpolitical "ordinary" crimes can hardly be so justified. The death penalty is still labeled "exceptional" in the codes,[83] but there would seem to be a trend toward "normalization" of capital punishment.

CHART VIII:
MILITARY CRIMES

Crime No.	1922³	22⁴	23³	24⁴	26²	27³	29²	34³	40³	47²	47³	57¹	59¹
51	X	X	X	X	X	9	9	9	9	5	5	5	3
52	4	4	4	5	5	5	5	5	5	5	5	5	3
53	X	X	4	5	5	5	5	5	5	5	5	4	3
54	3	3	3	4	4	4	4	5	5	5	5	5	3
55	0	0	5	5	5	5	5	5	5	5	5	5	1
56	5	6	6	6	6	3	3	3	5	5	5	4	3
57	0	4	4	4	4	3	5	5	5	5	5	0	0
58	8	8	8	9	9	5	5	5	5	1	1	X	X
59	X	X	X	X	X	4	4	4	4	4	4	4	3
60	0	4	4	4	4	4	4	4	4	4	4	0	0
61	4	4	4	3	3	3	3	3	3	3	3	1	2
62	2	2	2	2	2	1	1	3	3	3	3	3	3
63	4	4	4	3	3	3	3	3	3	3	3	1	X
64	X	X	X	X	5	5	5	5	5	1	0	0	0
65	6	6	6	7	7	1	1	1	1	1	1	1	3
66	4	4	4	4	4	1	1	1	1	1	1	1	2
67	4	4	4	4	4	1	1	1	1	1	1	1	1
68	4	4	4	1	1	1	1	1	1	1	1	1	2
69	2	2	2	2	2	1	1	1	1	1	1	1	2
70	X	X	X	X	X	1	1	1	1	1	1	1	X
71	X	X	X	X	X	X	X	X	X	X	X	X	3
72	X	X	X	X	X	X	X	X	X	X	X	0	3
TOTALS													
Year	1922³	22⁴	23³	24⁴	26²	27³	29²	34³	40³	47²	47³	57¹	59¹
Ratings	50	59	68	68	73	65	67	70	72	60	59	43	40
Crimes	12	14	16	16	17	20	20	20	20	20	19	16	16
Average	4.2	4.2	4.3	4.3	4.3	3.3	3.4	3.5	3.6	3	3.1	2.7	2.5

GRAPH VIII
MILITARY CRIMES

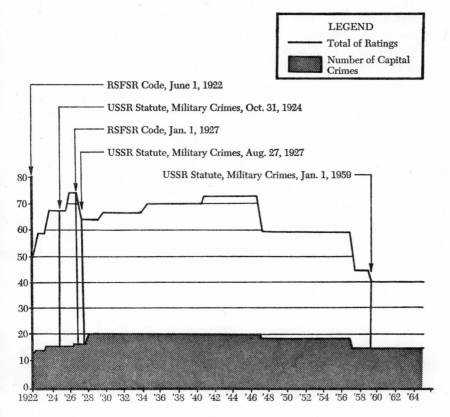

LEGEND
—— Total of Ratings
▨ Number of Capital Crimes

RSFSR Code, June 1, 1922

USSR Statute, Military Crimes, Oct. 31, 1924

RSFSR Code, Jan. 1, 1927

USSR Statute, Military Crimes, Aug. 27, 1927

USSR Statute, Military Crimes, Jan. 1, 1959

1922 '24 '26 '28 '30 '32 '34 '36 '38 '40 '42 '44 '46 '48 '50 '52 '54 '56 '58 '60 '62 '64

VIII. *Military Crimes.*

Military crimes constitute the largest single block of capital offenses. In mid-1922 there were twelve, the same number as those falling within most serious state crimes (I-1 above). But capital military offenses began to climb, and the number has never been equaled by any other group of crimes since that time.

On the other hand, most military crimes have been capital only in wartime or under "battle conditions," i.e., qualified death penalties (1–5 ratings). Thus rating totals generally hover below those of the less numerous serious state crimes. The only exception, following 1947, is explained by the fact that peacetime abolition had less impact on military crimes (mostly noncapital in peacetime already).

The need for establishing a well-disciplined army out of a motley assortment of "toilers," often commanded by distrusted former tsarist officers, explains the rise under the first RSFSR code—a development somewhat similar to the July 1917 restoration by the Provisional Government over strenuous Bolshevik objections. Fortuitously, the 1924 USSR Statute on Military Crimes left totals unaffected, although it shuffled ratings. But the all-time peak in both total and average rating was reached on the eve of the 1927 codification.

The new All-Union statute in mid-1927 established the peak number of capital military crimes, which remained until 1947. But total and average ratings dropped, the average to a record low thus far. From here on all indices present the closest approximation to a bell-shaped curve in this entire study. Rating increases accompany the rise of Stalin, the purges, and the war. The first two parallel the pattern for serious state crimes (I-1); the last rendered desertion more subject to death, as fighting already raged in Europe.

From the wartime peak, the 1947 peacetime abolition brought the first marked decline. And military crimes were the first to be affected by the post-Stalin ferment. Penalties were reduced in 1957,[84] two years before the new statute reduced them still further.[85]

IX. *Grand Totals.*

Chart IX gives grand totals of all capital crimes and ratings, and these are plotted on Graph IX. The overall pattern is a dialectically downward movement in both number and ratings of capital crimes over four time periods: 1922–1927, 1927–1947, 1947–1959, and 1959–1965.

It seems significant that three of the four valleys—1922, 1927, and 1959—correspond to codification periods. The other, of course, was the 1947 peacetime abolition. Such a pattern supports a recurrent theme in Western literature—that of tension between Soviet jurists and politicians.[86] When politicians decide to enact such macabre measures as those following Kirov's assassination, any half-literate peasant can write them up. But codification requires expertise, which means calling in the jurists. Each time, the result was a level of prescription for the death penalty below that which the politicians would long tolerate.

A critical scholar wrote of the 1961 rise that "the Party Central Committee has decided to change its policy and revert to Stalinist methods in dealing with offenders. It is at present [1961] too early to say to what extent the new decrees will be enforced, but it may already be assumed that the 'thaw' in the Party's policy in this sphere is over."[87] The average ratings in Chart IX show that they have hovered around

3.8 since 1959, somewhat higher than during the peacetime abolition period 1947–1959. But even this current average has never exceeded that for any period before 1947, the number of capital offenses remains lower than any time before 1959, and the total of ratings is lower than any earlier period except for the 1947–1959 valley. This is hardly a reversion to "Stalinist methods."

X. *Qualified and Unqualified Death Penalties*

Another interesting pattern emerges when separate totals are secured for unqualified death penalties, under which simple violation could entail death (ratings 6–9); and qualified ones, normally non-capital, requiring aggravating circumstances for a death sentence (ratings 1–5). Chart X presents these data; rating totals of both categories (but not total number of crimes) are plotted on Graph X.

The NEP period showed higher provision for death without qualification, but the 1926–1927 legislation reversed this pattern. The 1947 abolition eliminated unqualified death penalties, but even qualified ones dropped slightly. In 1950 the latter dropped again as some un-

CHART IX:
CAPITAL PUNISHMENT IN SOVIET CRIMINAL CODES, 1922–1965

Year	1922[3]	22[4]	23[3]	25[3]	26[2]	27[1]	27[2]	27[3]	27[4]	28[2]
GRAND TOTALS										
Ratings	219	228	262	259	264	193	188	181	171	169
Crimes	41	44	50	50	51	43	43	46	41	40
Average	5.3	5.2	5.2	5.2	5.2	4.5	4.4	3.9	4.2	4.2

Year	1929[1]	29[2]	29[3]	29[4]	*1930*	30[3]	31[1]	31[3]	32[3]	34[3]	36[1]	*1940*
GRAND TOTALS												
Ratings	170	177	181	190		191	196	203	211	225.5	230.5	
Crimes	41	42	42	43		44	45	46	47	49	50	
Average	4.1	4.2	4.3	4.4		4.3	4.4	4.4	4.5	4.6	4.6	

Year	1940[3]	47[2]	47[3]	*1950*	50[1]	54[2]	57[1]	59[1]	*1960*	61[2]	62[1]–65
GRAND TOTALS											
Ratings	232.5	124	118		130	143	127	96		116	124
Crimes	50	49	45		45	46	43	26		30	33
Average	4.7	2.3	2.6		2.9	3.1	3.0	3.7		3.9	3.8

GRAPH IX
CAPITAL PUNISHMENT IN SOVIET CRIMINAL CODES, 1922-1965

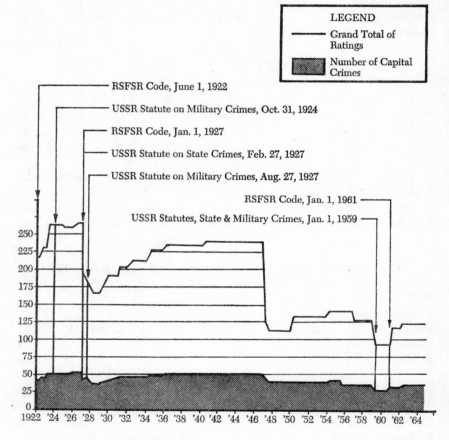

LEGEND
— Grand Total of Ratings
▨ Number of Capital Crimes

RSFSR Code, June 1, 1922

USSR Statute on Military Crimes, Oct. 31, 1924

RSFSR Code, Jan. 1, 1927

USSR Statute on State Crimes, Feb. 27, 1927

USSR Statute on Military Crimes, Aug. 27, 1927

RSFSR Code, Jan. 1, 1961

USSR Statutes, State & Military Crimes, Jan. 1, 1959

qualified penalties reappeared. Finally, legislation since 1958 has restored the pattern of the 1920s, with unqualified death penalties again exceeding those for which aggravating circumstances are required, but at a much lower level than in the pre-1927 period.

SUMMARY AND CONCLUSIONS

Russian and socialist history before 1917, and precode Soviet history to 1922, show ambivalent attitudes toward capital punishment. Abolition and restoration by the tsars and the Provisional Government recurred under the Soviets. In all three situations, jurists played a major role in the campaign against the death penalty.

This code content analysis suggests a continuing incipient struggle after 1922. Each new code reduced capital provisions. Moreover, the struggle appears to have passed through four stages, each with its own distinctive tactics.

(1) In 1923 efforts to limit the death penalty took the form of amendments to the General Part of the RSFSR Criminal Code to restrict the circumstances (pregnancy), persons (minors), and time (statute of limitations) for imposing a death sentence (see note 45).

CHART X:
QUALIFIED AND UNQUALIFIED DEATH PENALTIES IN SOVIET CRIMINAL
CODES, 1922–1965

Year	1922[3]	22[4]	23[8]	25[3]	26[2]	27[1]	27[2]	27[3]	27[4]	28[2]
UNQUALIFIED DEATH PENALTIES (Ratings 6–9 only):										
Ratings	145.5	151.5	161.5	155.5	79		66			
Crimes	19	20	21	20	11		9			
QUALIFIED DEATH PENALTIES (Ratings 1–5 only):										
Ratings	73.5	76.5	100.5	103.5	108.5	114	110	115	105	103
Crimes	22	24	29	30	31	32	32	37	32	31

Year	1929[1]	29[2]	29[3]	29[4]	1930	30[3]	31[1]	31[3]	32[3]	34[3]	36[1]	1940
UNQUALIFIED DEATH PENALTIES (Ratings 6–9 only):												
Ratings				75				82	90	104.5		
Crimes				10				11	12	14		
QUALIFIED DEATH PENALTIES (Ratings 1–5 only):												
Ratings	104	111	115			116	121			121	126	
Crimes	32	33	33			34	35			35	36	

Year	1940[3]	47[2]	47[3]	1950	50[1]	54[2]	57[1]	59[1]	1960	61[2]	62[1]-65
UNQUALIFIED DEATH PENALTIES (Ratings 6–9 only):											
Ratings		0			15.5	28.5		54		72	
Crimes		0			2	4		9		12	
QUALIFIED DEATH PENALTIES (Ratings 1–5 only):											
Ratings	128	124	118		114.5	114.5	98.5	42		44	52
Crimes	36	49	45		43	42	39	17		18	21

GRAPH X
QUALIFIED AND UNQUALIFIED DEATH PENALTIES
IN SOVIET CRIMINAL CODES, 1922-1965

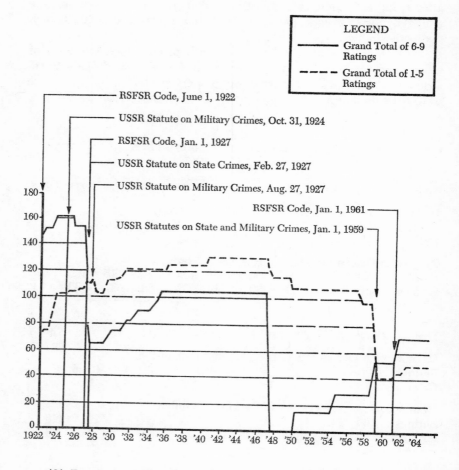

LEGEND

——— Grand Total of 6-9 Ratings

---- Grand Total of 1-5 Ratings

RSFSR Code, June 1, 1922

USSR Statute on Military Crimes, Oct. 31, 1924

RSFSR Code, Jan. 1, 1927

USSR Statute on State Crimes, Feb. 27, 1927

USSR Statute on Military Crimes, Aug. 27, 1927

RSFSR Code, Jan. 1, 1961

USSR Statutes on State and Military Crimes, Jan. 1, 1959

(2) Between 1927 and 1947 the struggle took the form of hedging about capital provisions in the Special Part, as indicated by greater use of qualified penalty clauses (1–5 ratings; see Graph X).

(3) In the 1947–1958 period, those seeking to limit capital punishment relied upon the 1947 peacetime abolition. Piecemeal restoration in 1950 and 1954, however, showed it to be a losing battle.

These findings for the second and third periods reveal a remarkable insight not previously apparent. In regard to formal legal provisions, there was considerable substance during the entire Stalin period to the Soviet claim that capital punishment was an "exceptional" measure of punishment—however unexceptional execution may have been in practice—as qualified ratings consistently exceeded unqualified ones.

(4) Finally, efforts to reduce the death penalty under present Soviet criminal legislation have taken the form of reducing the number of capital offenses. At the same time, there has been a trend toward what might be called the "normalization" of capital punishment.

Normalization is indicated by two main developments. (a) Increased use of unqualified 6 ratings has heralded a return to the pattern, though not the level, of the 1922 code (Khrushchev's "return to Leninism"?), as unqualified rating totals again exceed qualified ones.[88] (b) The new emphasis on capital punishment for crimes against the person, and its revival for the first time since the 1920s for certain administrative and official crimes which hamper administration,[89] make current provisions for the death penalty look more normal than "exceptional." Nevertheless Soviet codes still describe "the supreme measure of punishment" as an "exceptional measure of punishment, pending its total abolition. . . ."[90]

Regarding the temporary aspect of the death penalty, there is of course no deadline suggested. And some Soviet spokesmen see no inconsistency between an expectation of ultimate abolition and continued use at present. "We favor establishing a life without crime and punishment, but we must reckon with actual reality, in whose conditions the world lives."[91] Even so, the dialectical postponement of abolition does not resolve an anomaly arising out of normalization.

Soviet jurists still justify retention of capital punishment in the same terms as did Lenin, confusing terror with the juridical death sentence.[92] Yet the propriety of executing "class enemies" who endanger the regime of the toilers becomes of increasingly questionable relevance as the death penalty is turned toward personal, official, and administrative crimes and away from state crimes.

Does this mean that further reduction, or even a new abolition, is unlikely? Against normalization and postponement other factors must be balanced. The 1947 abolition while Stalin yet lived may have been tactical to encourage guerrillas and bandits to resume normal life, as did the 1920 abolition. But it may also have reflected continuing pressure against the death penalty. Moreover, some contemporary Soviet jurists can remember the campaigns against tsarist and Kornilov executions. And they still quote Marx about how "a society glorying in its civilization" would find it difficult to justify capital punishment.[93] If these factors do not insure an early abolition, they do suggest that any effort to return to Stalinist proportions would encounter vigorous and influential resistance.

This study has afforded a glimpse of various patterns which emerge from the history of capital punishment in Soviet criminal legislation, 1922–1965. Of course, legal codes provide only one window on reality. But the view through that window is an intriguing one, and carries implications far beyond the formalities of statutory law.

NOTES

1. The Prologue is a synopsis, omitting criminological and jurisprudential material, of William W. Adams, Jr., "Capital Punishment and the Russian Revolution," unpublished Ph.D. dissertation, Columbia University, 1968.

2. George Vernadsky, *Medieval Russian Laws*, New York., 1947, pp. 26, 35. The original provision constituted Article 1 of both the "Short Version" (1020) and the "Long Version" (the next century) of the *Russkaia Pravda*. Article 2 of the "Long Version" noted the abolition. Cf. A. A. Zimin, *Pamiatniki russkogo prava*, Moscow, 1952, I, 108.

3. Quoted by N. S. Tagantsev, *Smertnaia kazn'* (henceforth cited as *Sm. Kazn'*), St. Petersburg, 1913, p. 57n; "ni prava, ni kriva ne ubivaite, ne povelievaite ubiti ego, asche budet povinen smerti,—*dusha ne pogubliaite nikakaia zhe krest'iany*" (Taganstev's emphasis). Cf. N. P. Zagoskin, *Ocherk istorii smertnoi kazni v Rossii*, Kazan, 1892, pp. 26, 102.

4. On the Mongol Yasa, see V. Riasanovsky, *Fundamental Principles of Mongol Law*, Tientsin, 1937, esp. pp. 83, 85. The 1397 Charters of Dvina Land and Pskov were the first Russian codes to prescribe death; Vernadsky, *op. cit.*, pp. 58, 63. This is not to suggest that there were no executions by Russian authorities between Iaroslav's death and 1397, only that there was no Russian legislation on the subject.

5. V. D. Grekov, ed., *Sudebniki XV–XVI vekov*, Moscow-Leningrad, 1952, *passim*. The commentaries are especially valuable for those not familiar with medieval Russian.

6. V. O. Kliuchevsky, *A History of Russia*, trans. C. J. Hogarth, New York, 1911–1926, III, 74.

7. Tagantsev, *op. cit.*, pp. 59, 59n; Zagoskin, *op. cit.*, p. 43.

8. Tagantsev, *loc. cit.*; n. 2 cites another source giving the total as 122, a figure given also by Zagoskin, *op. cit.*, p. 63. The legislation of this period also witnessed a rapid growth in imaginative means for dispatching those sentenced to death. Hanging was usual, but blasphemy and arson entailed burning, counterfeiters were to have molten metal poured down the throat, and the wife who murdered her husband was to be buried alive up to the neck. Other crimes entailed decapitation, drowning, quartering, impaling, and breaking on the wheel. Peter added burning on a slow fire, tearing the flesh with pincers before quartering, and, for the first time, shooting, by firing squad. Zagoskin, *op. cit.*, pp. 53–58, 64, *et passim*.

9. Zagoskin, *ibid.*, p. 75; Tagantsev,

op. cit., p. 65, refers to this story as a legend.

10. Tagantsev, *op. cit.,* pp. 66–67; Mikhail Gubskii, "Smertnaia kazn'," *Entsiklopedicheskii slovar',* St. Petersburg, 1900, XXX, 495, and the 1956 *Bol'shaia sovetskaia entsiklopediia,* XXXIX, 392, both refer to these decrees as constituting an abolition of capital punishment, while Tagantsev, "Otmiena smertnoi kazni," *Zhurnal ministerstva iustitsii,* no. 3 (March 1917), p. 11 (henceforth cited as "Otmiena") and N. Rostov, "Smertnaia kazn," *Malaia sovetskaia entsiklopediia,* Moscow, 1930, VIII, 47, both regard the abolition as purely formal.

11. Brutal corporal punishment continued under Elizabeth, and the knout was introduced during her reign. Flailing with the knout, and running the gauntlet for military crimes, often constituted disguised death sentences. Many military crimes continued to be capital, and military courts might try civilians under certain circumstances, especially for political offenses.

12. *Nakaz Ekateriny Vtoroi,* St. Petersburg, 1893. Article 209 suggested that capital punishment was unnecessary in peacetime. "Wartime" included not only international conflict but domestic unrest. Cf. Arts. 79, 210. Catherine allowed executions during the Pugachëv rebellion in the 1770s. But in 1790 she commuted Radishchev's death sentence.

13. *Svod Zakonnov,* XV, ch. 2, Art. 17.

14. Zagoskin, *op. cit.,* p. 102, observed in 1892 that "in the matter of capital punishment, at least for the last 150 years, we are not only not behind other civilized peoples of Europe, but far in advance of them" and that "Russia is on the high road to the complete abolition of that form of punishment."

15. Public protests by medical, legal, academic, and other professional associations, trade unions, peasant organizations, etc., are collected in the following sources: Saul Ushero-vich, *Smertnye kazni v tsarskoi Rossii,* Kharkov, 1933, esp. pp. 232–46 *et passim;* S. I. Viktorskii, *Istoriia smertnoi kazni v Rossii,* vol. XLI of *Uchënyia zapiski imperatorskago moskovskago universiteta, otdiel iuridicheskii,* Moscow, 1912, pp. 367–68, 372; M. N. Gernet, *Smertnaia kazn',* Moscow, 1913, pp. 30–33; S. S. Ostroumov, *Prestupnost' i eë prichiny v dorevoliutsionnoi Rossii,* Moscow, 1960, p. 324.

16. *Stenograficheskii otchët: Gosudarstvennaia Duma,* 126 vols., St. Petersburg, 1906–1916 (henceforth cited *Sten. ot.*), First Duma II, 1503. The bill read: "Article 1. Capital punishment is abolished. Article 2. In all cases for which the laws in force (the criminal code, the code on criminal and corrective punishments, military and naval regulations on punishment) prescribe the death penalty, it shall be replaced by the next most severe punishment." The death penalty, executions, amnesty, and related matters had been frequently discussed prior to June 19; see *ibid.,* I, 27, 31, 34, 421–44, 639–62, and II, 1469–1504.

Taganstev defended the bill in the State Council on June 27, 1906; see Taganstev, *Sm. kazn',* pp. 141–50, for his speech. In the fifteen member committee considering the bill, two spoke in favor and four against; *ibid.,* p. 152. But on July 8 the tsar dissolved the Duma and the State Council ceased to meet. On March 14, 1907, with the Second Duma in session, the State Council decided that the bill had lapsed with the dissolution of the First Duma; Viktorskii, *op. cit.,* p. 368.

17. For the Second Duma, see *Sten. ot.,* 1907, I, 748, 980, and II, 1146–64; also Alfred Levin, *The Second Duma,* 2nd ed., Hamden, Conn., 1966, pp. 106–07; 245–55, 258–78, *et passim.* For the Third Duma, see *Sten. ot.,* 1908, first session, III, 3640, second session, I, 3129–32.

The bill was introduced June 19, 1908, signed by 103 Duma members embracing nearly all leftists and centrists, several conservatives and nationality representatives, and even one rightist. For the bill, names of sponsors, and explanatory notes, see *Prilozheniia k stenograficheskim otchëtam, 1907–1908*, II, no. 636; party affiliations and other data on members of the first three Dumas are found in N. A. Granat, *Entsiklopedicheskii slovar'*, 40 vols., Moscow, 1890–1917, XVII, "Supplement." The Duma Committee on Judicial Reform substituted a weak call for limiting capital punishment in its report of May 1, 1910; *Prilozheniia . . .*, 1909–1910, II, no. 382. Even this proposal died when the Duma refused to place it on the agenda, November 12, 1910; Viktorskii, *op. cit.*, p. 369.

18. D. N. Zhbankov, "Smertnye prigovory i kazni v 1905–1910 godakh," *Sovremennyi mir*, St. Petersburg, 1911, no. 4, p. 296; cf. Viktorskii, *op. cit.*, p. 370.

19. During the debate, which took place at the Second RSDLP Congress of 1903, someone inquired, "And for Nicholas II?" Lenin, "Kak burzhuaziia ispol'zuet renagatov," *Sochineniia*, 4th ed., Moscow, 1950, XXX, 9.

20. "[I]t would be very difficult, if not altogether impossible, to establish any principle upon which the justice or expediency of capital punishment could be founded in a society glorying in its civilization." Karl Marx, "Capital Punishment," in Lewis S. Feuer, ed., *Marx & Engels: Basic Writings on Politics & Philosophy*, Garden City, N.Y., 1959, p. 487.

21. Remarks by Marx, Engels, and Lenin are cited with approval in M. D. Shargorodskii, *Nakazanie po sovetskomu ugolovnomu pravu*, Moscow, 1958, ch. 4.

22. Gernet, *op. cit.*, pp. 20–28.

23. *Ibid.*, p. 33.

24. E. H. Carr, *The Bolshevik Revolution 1917–1923*, 3 vols., London, 1953, I, 154n. The declaration was signed, among others, by Lenin, Zinoviev, Trotsky, Kamenev, Radek, and Lunacharskii; Iu. Martov, *Doloi smertnuiu kazn'!*, Berlin, 1923, p. 12.

25. *Sbornik ukazov i postanovlenii vremennago pravitel'stva*, Petrograd, 1917; henceforth cited *SUVP*, February 27–May 5, 1917 (O.S.), I, item 16, p. 37; cf. Robert Browder and Alexander Kerensky, *The Russian Provisional Government, 1917*, Stanford, 1961, I. 199–200.

26. Conservatives and radicals generally hailed the idea of bloodless revolution; liberals saw abolition as fulfillment of the Russian cultural tradition, socialists as fulfillment of one of their demands. Browder and Kerensky, *op. cit.*, I, 200–04; cf. A. A. Gertsenzon, "Karatel'naia politika i ugolovnoe zakonodatel'stvo vremennogo pravitel'stva," *Sovetskoe gosudarstvo i pravo*, no. 2 (1941), p. 75. Tagantsev exulted that nothing could hold back "the sovereign will of the people, and on March 12, 1917, the command of the people's representatives . . . rang out with all its absolute power: 'Capital punishment is abolished!' " Tagantsev, "Otmiena," *op. cit.*, p. 14. *Isvestia*, the Soviet organ, was then edited by Bolshevik sympathizer and later party member Steklov.

27. Browder and Kerensky, *op. cit.*, II, 891, 981–84, 998, *et passim;* Frank A. Golder, *Documents of Russian History, 1914–1917*, New York, 1927, p. 429; Alexander F. Kerensky, *The Catastrophe*, New York, 1927, pp. 302–03.

28. "Fully conscious of the grave responsibility it bears for the fate of the homeland, the Provisional Government deems it necessary: (1) to restore the death penalty in wartime for military personnel convicted of certain heinous crimes;

(2) to establish military-revolutionary courts consisting of soldiers and officers to try such crimes immediately." *SUVP*, I, item 2, no. 974, trans. in Browder and Kerensky, *op. cit.*, II, 982; cf. Golder, *op. cit.*, pp. 429–30.

29. A leading spokesman for the Left SR's on the subject was Maria Spiridonova, once sentenced to death by a tsarist court and later doomed to live out her life in Soviet prisons and exile; Oliver H. Radkey, *The Agrarian Foes of Bolshevism*, New York, 1958, pp. 348–49, 370–71. On July 24 the Moscow city government, controlled by Right SR's, condemned the move; on August 10 the Petrograd soviet followed suit; *ibid.*, pp. 372, 380; cf. Browder and Kerensky, *op. cit.*, II, 985n, 986.

30. *Rabochii*, September 8, 1917, trans. in Lenin, "Paper Resolutions," *Collected Works of V. I. Lenin*, New York, 1932, XXI, 115. *Rabochii* was a disguised *Pravda*, which had been suppressed after the July uprising.

31. For example, Lenin told the First Congress of Soviets on June 17, 1917, that his party was ready to take power, adding: "Our program in relation to the economic crisis is this—to demand the publication of all those unheard-of profits . . . on war orders; to arrest 50 or 100 . . . capitalists, and in this way break all the threads of intrigue." *Izvestia*, June 19, 1917, trans. in Golder, *op. cit.*, p. 365. Cf. Lenin's article in *Pravda:* "The twentieth century 'Jacobins' would not guillotine the capitalists. . . . It would be enough to arrest 50–100 magnates . . . for a few weeks to *expose their intrigues* [his emphasis] and to show all the exploited 'who needs the war.'" Lenin, *Soch.*, 2nd ed., Moscow, 1932, XX, 505, quoted in N. V. Krylenko, *Lenin o sude k desiatiletiiu so dnia smerti*, Moscow, 1934, p. 164.

32. An army intelligence report a month before the October Revolution noted the effectiveness of Bolshevik propaganda. Their argument "is quite simple and comprehensible to the masses . . . the government introduced the death penalty with the view of exterminating the soldiers, workers, and peasants." James Bunyan and H. H. Fisher, *The Bolshevik Revolution 1917–1918*, Stanford, 1934, p. 25.

33. "Capital punishment, restored by Kerensky at the front, is abolished. Full freedom of agitation at the front is restored. All soldiers and officer-revolutionaries now under arrest for so-called 'political crimes' are to be released immediately." *Sobranie Uzakoneii i Rasporiazhenii Robachago i Krest'ianskago Pravitel'stva RSFSR* (henceforth cited *SU RSFSR*), Moscow, 1917, no. 1, item 10, Dec. 1, 1917, p. 12.

34. "'This is madness,' he repeated. 'How can we accomplish a revolution without shooting? Do you think you can settle with your enemies if you disarm? What repressive measures have you then? Imprisonment? Who pays any attention to that in a time of bourgeois war when every party hopes for victory? . . . It is a mistake . . . an inadmissible weakness. Pacifist illusion. . . .'" Leon Trotzky, *Lenin*, New York., 1925, pp. 133–34; cf. G. P. Maximoff, *The Guillotine at Work*, Chicago, 1940, pp. 28–29.

35. The decrees, orders, and instructions which sprayed forth from the Sovnarkom and from individual commissars during 1918 were often imprecise, sometimes contradictory. It is not possible to cite any one decree, therefore, as restoring capital punishment. But the first judicial death sentence (as distinct from Cheka or other extra-legal executions) was passed by the Supreme Revolutionary Tribunal on Admiral A. M. Shchastnyi on June 21, 1918; *Pravda*, June 21, 1918, p. 3, and June 22, p. 3; *Izvestia*, June 21, p. 5, and June 22, p. 6.

The *Izvestia* account is more complete.

36. *SU RSFSR* no. 4–5, item 22, Jan. 28, 1920, p. 16. The preamble noted the rout of white armies and the extensive military gains, the capture of Admiral Kolchak, and the consolidation of Soviet authority. These create "new conditions" which "give the worker-peasant government an opportunity at present to renounce" the death penalty "with respect to the enemies of Soviet authority." Capital punishment is abolished "both by sentences of the [Cheka] and by sentences of . . . tribunals under the All-Russian Central Executive Committee."

37. The tactical motivation is suggested by the fact that, unlike 1917, executions continued. The decree included no amnesty, so those already under death sentence did not escape. Many were hastily shot on the eve of the decree; others were shipped to areas of martial law (not covered by the decree) so their executions could be carried out without violating it. And some observers contend that secret executions by the Cheka never let up. Maximoff, *op. cit.*, pp. 119–22.

38. *SU RSFSR* no. 54 (1920).

39. Lenin, "Pis'mo D. I. Kurskomu po voprosu o terrore," *Soch.*, 3rd ed., Moscow-Leningrad, 1937, XXVII, 296. As usual Lenin confused terror with the judicial death sentence, but he made it clear that he expected the code to include capital punishment.

40. D. B. Riazanov helped organize the Communist Academy and the Marx-Engels-Lenin Institute in Moscow, but was exiled in 1931. During these 1922 debates, he argued that capital punishment "is in the sharpest contradiction with all the principles and bases of scientific socialism and our communist program. . . . I consider it necessary to exclude absolutely any deprivation of life, any extermination,

from the criminal code so long as it is intended not for a year but for a more permanent and extended period of time. . . ." *III sessiia Vserossiiskogo Tsentral'nogo Ispolnitel'nogo Komiteta* [RSFSR], *IX sozyva, biulleten'*, Moscow, 1922, no. 9, May 25, 1922, p. 4.

41. The full text of the revised Article 33 read: "In cases heard by the revolutionary tribunals, pending its abolition by VTsIk [CEC], in cases when the supreme measure of punishment is prescribed by the articles of the criminal code, death by shooting shall be applied."

42. The 1924 USSR Constitution, Art. I (o), authorized the All-Union government to "establish principles of the judicial organization and procedure, as well as civil and criminal legislation for the Union." The "Stalin" Constitution of December 1936, Art. 14 (u), gave the All-Union level jurisdiction over "[l]egislation concerning the judicial system and judicial procedure; criminal and civil codes." James H. Meisel and Edward S. Kozera, eds., *Materials for the Study of the Soviet System*, 2nd ed., Ann Arbor, 1953, nos. 79 and 107. The new provision seemed to herald new comprehensive All-Union codes, perhaps displacing the republic codes, but none were forthcoming. So the de facto situation remained as before, and in February 1957 Art. 14 was amended to restore de jure the earlier relationship.

43. In the study which follows, a legislative change initiated at the All-Union level is regarded as taking effect when the USSR decree takes effect, even though not yet incorporated into republic codes. Changes originating at the republic level are regarded as taking effect in accordance with the provisions of the relevant RSFSR decrees.

44. In this respect Soviet practice resembled late imperial practice. After 1890 tsarist civil courts handed down no death sentences. Military

and special tribunals ordered execution of civilians and soldiers alike, as did Soviet Revolutionary and Military Revolutionary Tribunals during the Civil War.

45. For the 1919 provision, see Art. 25 (o); in 1922, Art. 33; 1924, Art. 13, n. 2; 1926, Art. 21; 1959 Principles, Art. 22; 1961 Code, Art. 23. The 1924 Principles did not describe execution as "exceptional," but did confine it to especially serious crimes.

That pressure continued into the 1920s for limitation of the death penalty is evidenced by the fact that Art. 33 of the 1922 Code was amended no less than five times in the first thirteen months it was in effect. Three restricted the application of death sentences to minors and pregnant women, one imposed a statute of limitations; see respectively *SU RSFSR* nos. 47, 58, 72–73 (1922), and 48 (1923). The fifth, *SU RSFSR* no. 15 (1923), was necessitated by the abolition of the Revolutionary Tribunals on November 11, 1922; *SU RSFSR* no. 62, item 902 (1922); cf. John N. Hazard, *Settling Disputes in Soviet Society*, New York, 1960, pp. 342–43, 480. It thus became necessary for the first time to confer on regular civil courts the power to impose death sentences.

46. Criminological historians often use the term "qualified death penalty" to refer to death sentences entailing some sort of punishment (e.g., torture, quartering) beside simple execution. This is not the sense in which the term is used here.

47. In addition, two All-Union decrees were never incorporated into Republic codes. These pertained to offenses against the state and are treated along with the seventeen serious state crimes. See Crimes A and B in Table 3.

48. Within each group, crimes are listed in descending order by average rating for the entire 1922–65 period. Each rating is multiplied

by the number of years it was in effect, products are added, and the sum is divided by 43 (total number of years). When an offense was not in the code (an X rating) for part of the period, the total is also divided by the number of years it was in effect. These figures appear in parentheses. When an offense was noncapital (a rating of 0) for part of the period, the total is also divided by the number of years the crime was capital. These figures appear in brackets.

49. Only those amendments which changed a rating can be detected on the charts. Occasionally, an amendment left a rating unaltered. Quarter years were divided December–February, March–May, June–August, September–November; e.g., 27^1 means December 1926–February 1927. When a USSR decree was later incorporated into the RSFSR Criminal Code, the change is regarded as having taken place on the date of the USSR enactment.

50. In an interval scale all similar intervals are equal; i.e., the difference between 9 and 8 equals the difference between 6 and 5 equals the difference between 3 and 2; the difference between 7 and 5 equals that between 4 and 2; etc. The same is true of a ratio scale, except that there is also an absolute zero; thus 8 is double 4, 9 is triple 3, 1 half of 2, etc. None of this is true of an ordinal scale. In such a scale it can be said only that 8 is more than 4, 6 is in between, etc.

51. "The historic victory of the Soviet people . . . has demonstrated not only the mature might of the Soviet state but also, most of all, the exceptional loyalty of the entire population of the Soviet Union . . .

"Moreover, the international situation . . . since the surrender of Germany and Japan shows that the cause of peace may be considered secure for a long time, despite attempts of aggressive elements to provoke war.

"Considering these circumstances and in accordance with the wishes of the unions of workers, service personnel, and other authoritative organizations expressing the opinion of broad public circles, the Presidium of the Supreme Soviet of the USSR believes that application of capital punishment is no longer necessary in peacetime.

"The Presidium of the Supreme Soviet of the USSR decrees: 1. To abolish in peacetime the death penalty provided for crimes under laws now in effect in the USSR. 2. To apply in peacetime confinement in corrective labor camps for a term of 25 years for crimes punishable by death under laws now in effect. 3. In the case of death sentences not yet carried out prior to promulgation of the present decree, upon decision of the Supreme Court, to replace the death penalty with the penalties provided for by Article 2 of the present decree." *Ved. SSSR* no. 17, May 31, 1947.

52. Reference is to the *sostav prestupleniia*, the "substance of the crime," or *corpus delicti*.
53. Indeed, before 1958 courts might impose death for an offense not capital in the codes by applying the doctrine of analogy.
54. Chapter I of all three RSFSR codes concerned "State Crimes." It was divided into two parts. Part 1 in the two earlier codes dealt with "counterrevolutionary crimes"; the current code calls them "especially dangerous state crimes." Part 2 contained the less serious state crimes. Thus the designations "I-1" and "I-2."
55. USSR decree "On espionage and the collecting and transmission of economic information not to be made public," *Sobranie zakonov i rasporiazhenii raboche-krest'ianskago pravitel'stva SSSR* (henceforth cited SZ *SSSR*) Moscow, 1925, no. 52, item 390, August 14, 1925. The new provision prescribed depriva-

tion of freedom for at least three years, but made death mandatory "when the espionage caused or could have caused especially serious consequences for the interests of the state. . . ."
56. Two disappeared as separate code provisions. Unauthorized return from banishment abroad (*izgnanie*; crime no. 15) disappeared entirely as an offense—perhaps because the Bolsheviks stopped doing their enemies such favors—although *izgnanie* continued to be listed as a possible penalty; cf. Arts. 32 (a) (1922) and 20 (a) (1926); it is not in the present code, Art. 22 (1960). *Vysylka* means banishment from parts of the USSR, not deportation; Art. 26 (1960); cf. *udalenie* in the earlier codes. The other disappearing offense (crime no. 17) did not actually cease to be punishable, but was simply incorporated into another article (crime no. 14).

Two offenses (nos. 9 and 10) appeared for the first time, and wrecking became capital for the first time (called *sabotazh* in early codes, *vreditel'stvo* now; first introduced as an amendment July 10, 1923, *SU RSFSR* no. 48, item 479; "sabotage" is better rendered in Russian as *diversiia*, q. v.).
57. *SZ SSSR* no. 76, item 732, Nov. 21, 1929. Its provisions were retroactive, and death was mandatory (9).
58. *SZ SSSR* no. 62, item 360, 1932. The rating was 8. Neither of these last two USSR decrees was formally repealed until January 1, 1959. "List of acts which have lost force . . . ," nos. 27 and 42, *Ved. SSSR* no. 15, April 13, 1959. But whereas the 1929 decree had continued to appear in collections of criminal legislation, the 1932 edict had given way to a decree of June 4, 1947, which accompanied the peacetime abolition of capital punishment and substituted heavy prison sentences for the 1932 penalties; *Ved. SSSR* no. 19, June 4, 1947.

59. *SZ SSSR* no. 33, item 255, 1934. When committed by military personnel it involved an automatic death sentence (9), while civilians might be imprisoned under extenuating circumstances (8); thus the combined 8.5 rating. The double standard for civilian and military offenders was eliminated in the 1958–60 revisions (Art. 64, 1960). The new rating was a 6. The old tsarist crime of "betrayal of the motherland" was abandoned in the early Soviet period. But certain Civil War decrees spoke of treason to the toilers; e.g., deserters "who fail to appear within the [grace] period . . . shall be considered enemies and traitors *[predateliami]* to the toiling people. . . ." *SU RSFSR* no. 25, item 287, 1919. Art. 69 of the 1922 code forbade agitation to overthrow the Soviets "by violent or treasonous *[izmennicheskikh]* acts. . . ." The 1929 decree on defection declared such an act "to fall under the heading of treason" (*kvalifitsirovat' kak izmenu*).

60. While this study deals with the substantive law, the temper of the purge period is well illustrated by two procedural decrees. On the evening of the Kirov assassination, December 1, 1934, a decree limited investigation of terrorist acts or organizations to ten days, gave defendants twenty-four hours' notice of the results, forbade appearance by them or their attorneys at the trial, forbade appeals and mercy pleas, and ordered that death sentences be carried out at once; *SZ SSSR* no. 64, item 459, 1934, incorporated into RSFSR Code of Criminal Procedure *SU RSFSR* no. 2, item 8, 1935. On September 14, 1937, a similar decree appeared on wrecking and sabotage. Defendants had twenty-four hours' notice, appeal was forbidden, and execution was to be immediate if a mercy plea was rejected; *SZ SSSR* no. 61, item 266, 1937, into RSFSR procedural code *SU RSFSR* no. 3, item 38, 1938. These two acts were repealed only after Stalin's death on April 19, 1956. *Ved. SSSR* no. 8, item 193, 1956.

61. It is a distortion to criticize the abolition on the ground that many were now sentenced to twenty-five years who previously could have received only ten; Yurii P. Mironenko, "Penal Policy Becomes More Severe" (henceforth cited, "Penal Policy"), *Bulletin of the Institute for the Study of the USSR* (henceforth cited *Bulletin*) VIII, no. 7, (July 1961), 32. One might as easily say that many received twenty-five years who previously would have been shot—and thus unavailable to celebrate the amnesties of the mid-1950s which freed most or all of them long before their terms expired!

62. *Ved. SSSR* no. 3, p. 1, 1950. Both the 1947 abolition and this decree restoring the death penalty were repealed in 1959; "List of acts which have lost force . . . ," nos. 92 and 100, *loc. cit.*

63. *Sovetskoe ugolovnoe pravo: Chast' osobennaya*, Moscow, 1957, pp. 172–73, cited in Mironenko, "The Campaign to Extend the Death Penalty" (henceforth cited "Campaign"), *Bulletin*, VI, no. 1, (January 1959) 28. The other affected crimes were banditry, murder, and armed robbery.

64. That the codifiers intended to increase punishment and not just create editorial uniformity where espionage is concerned is evidenced by the fact that the noncapital penalties were also increased from a minimum three years to a minimum seven years, deprivation of freedom. See crime no. 11.

   Two other crimes (nos. 4 and 9) also show a rise in rating in 1959. But these articles prescribed punishment as set forth in various other articles of the code, so their rating becomes the average of the articles referred to.

65. Mironenko, "Penal Policy."

66. These offenses were called "crimes against administrative order" in the two earlier codes.

67. Cf. "Decree of the Plenum of the USSR Supreme Court," May 28, 1954, sec. 7, *Ugolovnyi kodeks RSFSR*, Moscow, 1926, pp. 112–13.

68. Note that the vertical scale on Graphs II–VII is half that on I-1, I-2, and VIII, in order to magnify the lower totals.

69. One might inquire whether this renewed use of the death penalty for these types of offenses was part of Khrushchev's "return to Leninist norms." Cf. Staff Study, "Economic Crimes in the Soviet Union" (henceforth cited Staff Study), *Journal of the International Commission of Jurists*, V, no. 1 (Summer 1964), 11: "As used in . . . the 1961–62 period, the death penalty clearly represents a partial return to the penal policies of the early years of the Stalinist period."

70. In the first two RSFSR Criminal Codes, a chapter on "Crimes against Property" included both collective and private property. The present code separates them, and they are separated in this study so that the varying patterns in provision for the death penalty will be clearly visible.

71. Staff Study, pp. 8–9.

72. Speculation in goods (no. 41) presently appears in chapter six, Economic Crimes (Art. 154). But in the 1922 code it was classed as a lesser state crime (I-2), and in 1926 it was a crime against administration (III)—the classification used here. Speculation in currency was and is a state crime (no. 28). All other offenses mentioned in Staff Study, *ibid.*, appear in other chapters of the code, and the present chapter six is entirely noncapital.

73. *Khishchenie* in the 1922 and 1960 codes. The 1926 code attempted to eliminate distinctions in tsarist law between *krazha* (secret stealing), *grabëzh* (open stealing), *khishchenie* (grand larceny), etc. They were grouped (Art. 162) under *pokhishchenie*, a general term for stealing.

74. *Razboi*, sometimes translated armed robbery, or assault with intent to rob.

75. *SU RSFSR* no. 34, item 206, Sept. 1, 1934, incorporating an earlier USSR decree.

76. The 1947 peacetime abolition reduced the rating of the capital clause from 5 to 1 (double aggravation). When averaged with the noncapital clause the rating totals were thus 2.5 before and .5 after 1947, giving the peculiar pattern on Graph VII in which rating totals are lower than number of capital crimes between 1947 and 1954.

77. *Ved. SSSR* no. 11, 1954. Since the 1950 decree permitted rather than demanded death, and since RSFSR Article 136 on aggravated murder was noncapital (except for military offenders), the combination of the two provisions may be regarded as authorizing death as a second alternative—a 6 rating.

78. "List of acts which have lost force . . . ," no. 101, *loc. cit.*

79. *Ugolovnyi kodeks RSFSR*, Moscow, 1956, p. 127, citing *Moskovskii bol'shevik* no. 4, Jan. 6, 1949. Apparently the decree did not appear in *Vedomosti*. The previous maximum of eight years' deprivation of freedom gave way to ten to fifteen years or, under aggravating circumstances, fifteen to twenty.

80. USSR decree, Feb. 15, 1962, *Ved. SSSR* no. 8; incorporated into RSFSR code July 25, 1962, *Ved. RSFSR* no. 29. The aggravating circumstances were: Rape by a group, by a recidivist, entailing especially serious consequences, or of a minor.

81. On the high incidence of hooliganism and crimes against the person, see A. Piontkovsky, "Guarantees of Justice," *Izvestia*, Aug. 28, 1965, Eng. trans. in *Current Digest of the Soviet Press* (henceforth

cited *CD*), XVII, no. 35 (Sept. 22, 1965), 31–32. And a militia chief has revealed that hooligan murders as a percent of all homicides increased from 25 percent to 33 percent between 1962 and 1964; Yu. Inkyanov, "Punish Hooligans Severely," *Izvestia*, Oct. 23, 1965, Eng. trans. in *CD*, XVII, no. 43 (Nov. 17, 1965), 29–30.

82. See, e.g., M. D. Shargorodskii, *Nakazanie po sovetskomy ugolovnomu pravu*, Moscow, 1958, ch. 4.

83. Art. 22, 1958 USSR Statute on State Crimes; Art. 23, 1960 RSFSR Criminal Code. Cf. Boris S. Nikiforov, *Kommentarii U. K. RSFSR*, 2nd ed., Moscow, 1964, p. 58.

84. *Ved SSSR* no. 5, item 100, Feb. 15, 1957.

85. It would be interesting to run a similar analysis on the *U.S. Uniform Code of Military Justice* and compare results.

86. See, e.g., D. Barry, "The Specialist in Soviet Policy Making: The Adoption of a Law," *Soviet Studies*, XVI (1964), 152–66; Harold J. Berman, "The Struggle of Soviet Jurists against a Return to Stalinist Terror," *Slavic Review*, no. 2 (June 1963), pp. 314–20; John N. Hazard, *Settling Disputes in Soviet Society*, New York, 1960, *passim*.

87. Mironenko, "Penal Policy," p. 37.

88. Of course, the reversal of the ratio between 6–9 and 1–5 ratings and the resulting increased average ratings are as much due to the reduced number of capital offenses as to the greater use of the unqualified death penalty.

89. There are other similarities between the 1922 and 1960 codes. Both spoke of "punishment," though in somewhat different terminology *(kara, nakazanie)*, while the 1926 code spoke of "measures of social defense." And both retained the distinction, which had existed in imperial Russian law, between various sorts of stealing *(krazha, grabëzh, khishchenie)*, while the 1926 code sought to combine them under a general stealing statute *(pokhishchenie)*. Incidentally, the failure of this latter effort brings to mind Justice Holmes's famous dictum regarding legislative efforts to simplify common law pleading: "The forms of action are dead, but they rule us from their graves."

90. USSR 1958 Statute on Principles . . . , Art. 22; RSFSR 1960 Criminal Code, Art. 23; citations in Table 1, above.

91. N. Gribachev, "Contrary to Logic," *Izvestia*, Feb. 19, 1967, p. 5, Eng. trans. in *CD*, XIX, no. 7 (March 8, 1967), 19. The article was a reply to A. Sharov's critical review in *Novyi mir* (no. 10, 1966) of Gribachev's story, "Execution at dawn."

92. Shargorodskii, *op. cit.*, pp. 63–68.

93. *Ibid.*, p. 63.

6

GEORGE M. ENTEEN
The Pennsylvania
State University

SOVIET HISTORIANS
REVIEW THEIR OWN PAST:
THE REHABILITATION OF
M. N. POKROVSKII

Historians arrived at a post-Stalin interpretation of Pokrovskii before the party publicly took up the matter of his standing. Pokrovskii's name was bruited about in the flurry of disputation surrounding the Twentieth Party Congress. If there was favorable reference to him in 1956,[1] then there was at least one reversion to the formula anti-Leninist in 1957.[2] But by that time even those who stood against a favorable evaluation of him had thrown out the old catchwords. In 1959, with the publication of Volume VII of the third edition of the *Small Encyclopedia*,[3] Pokrovskii was brought back into the Marxist fold despite his "vulgar errors" and "economic materialism." Praise of his energy, his devotion, and his practical leadership coupled with warnings against a revival of ideas long ago transcended might be considered the essence of the official interpretation. The formula included remarks about the harmful consequences of the cult of personality. Such pronouncements, praising Pokrovskii and abusing Stalin, are to be found in all the authoritative writings—party statements, the preface to

This paper is reprinted with permission from *Soviet Studies*, XX (1969), 306–20.

Pokrovskii's republished works, and the writings of Academician Nechkina's Council on Historical Scholarship. Even though one might take issue with this official interpretation or deem it shallow, undeniably it is reasonable in its sobriety and based on facts. Most noteworthy, it is sufficiently general to let disagreements that are more than trivial arise in the context of it.

If the official interpretation does little more for the foreigner than arouse a sigh and a nod of approval, the literature on the subject is a fit object of study. Historiography has come to be a major preoccupation of Soviet historians, and they have already written a few hundred books and articles about their own professional past. A study of Pokrovskii's rehabilitation should narrate the debate while indicating the major characteristics of the scholarship that has grown out of it. Working through the literature can bring one to some conclusions about how Soviet historians work—how they use sources, how they handle abstractions, and how they reconcile differences. It can also shed light on the norms of the profession—show how the historians' self-consciousness affects their traditions and their responses to directives from above. The literature can also show how one sector of the intellectual life is pushed and pulled by one of the great moving forces of Soviet society—the legacy of Joseph Stalin.

In 1958, the Pokrovskii problem ceased to be a search for the proper adjectives when S. M. Dubrovskii, a student, friend, and critic of Pokrovskii, brought facts to the issue and initiated the ongoing reevaluation. Dubrovskii is given credit for being one of the first Marxists, at least one of the first who grew up in Pokrovskii's own circle, the Institute of Red Professors, to criticize adversely his teacher's overall interpretation of Russian history. After challenging him in seminar he polemicized against the concept of merchant capitalism in print in 1929–1934.[4] To his credit he remained silent the following year, when Pokrovskii, on his deathbed, found himself in a storm of controversy. Dubrovskii was one of the first to speak out against his former teacher when the official campaign got underway in 1936. Subsequent banishment spared him from participating in the campaign when it rose to its peak of deformity and rudeness. It may have been that Dubrovskii's sound pedigree as a critic of Pokrovskii helped save Dubrovskii's life and limited his punishment to two periods of exile. He is now a professor at the Institute of History.

Dubrovskii first presented his 1958 report at the Institute of History; he apparently caused such a stir that the Museum of the Revolution invited him to repeat it.[5] Only after the Twenty-second Congress did the authorities let it be published; it appeared in *Voprosy Istorii*[6] together with an edited version of a discussion of it. Then part of it was republished as a chapter in the third volume of *Outlines of the History of Soviet Historical Scholarship*.[7]

What draws one's attention to Dubrovskii's article is not its conclusions or particular formulations. Its style and technique, its solid professionalism, are noteworthy. Dubrovskii is the first historian since 1924[8] to assess Pokrovskii without nihilism or apologetics. Because the article was genuinely historical, it sought to illuminate the milieu in which Pokrovskii worked and lived, thereby casting light on a host of problems concerning the evolution of Soviet scholarship. The discussion brought out new information about the ideological battles that raged in the early 1930s and about Stalin's direct intervention through his notorious letter to the editors of *Proletarskaia Revoliutsiia*.[9]

That Dubrovskii wrote objectively about Pokrovskii does not signify absence of passion on his part nor that he kept apart from polemics. According to Dubrovskii, the temper of Pokrovskii's denigration created

> a tendency to restore certain erroneous historical ideas, to reduce the role of the masses of people, and to idealize the activities of certain princes, tsars, and their subordinates. The objectives of national liberation in the pre-revolutionary period were frequently depicted in a manner that disregarded class interests; national interests were counterposed to class interests; true patriotism was confused with pseudo-patriotism. The military art of the past was frequently pictured only as an art, with silence as to which classes and whose interests it served.[10]

Such trends, Dubrovskii points out, were evident in the popular arts as well as scholarship; their danger lay in the fact that they inhibited the study of Marxism-Leninism; they nurtured dogmatism and sustained Stalin's ideological deviations.[11]

This polemic was just one of a multitude leveled by Dubrovskii against Stalin and the national school of historiography.[12] The latter are the aging students and spiritual heirs of the old masters of the Imperial Academy of Sciences, those referred to as "bourgeois professors" in the 1920s. They had been restored to places of honor in the 1930s, while the denigration of Pokrovskii physically destroyed the most prominent and talented members of what in the 1920s had been known as the Marxist camp. The years since 1958 have been marked by the ascendancy of Dubrovskii, along with Academicians Nechkina and Mints, erstwhile Red Professors. The rehabilitation of Pokrovskii, then, inevitably affected leadership and influence in the historical profession.

Presentation of some of the arguments makes it evident that Pokrovskii was again the object of controversy, and that a variety of motives, which reside both in the traditions of Soviet historiography and in reasons of state, were at work. To keep to the old interpretation of Pokrovskii—to call him an anti-Marxist, an anti-Leninist, to accuse him of moral disarmament of the Russian people, and even to go so far as to speak of a *pokrovshchina*[13]—would sustain a void in Soviet historiography. The old interpretation was so obviously at variance with the facts of Pokrovskii's life and the nature of his commitment that it embarrassed Soviet historians, professionally and personally. It helped make Soviet historiography vulnerable to its critics by taking attention away from its achievements. The cynicism that no doubt resulted from the Stalinist interpretation separated practicing historians in all fields from the designated leaders of the craft and thereby diluted their authority. Moreover, taking a stand for Pokrovskii provided an opportune occasion for de-Stalinization. His legacy could be championed both as an attack on the former leader and as the restoration of the good name of an old Bolshevik, a militant Marxist whom Lenin praised.

Rehabilitating Pokrovskii was, of course, likely to bring unwanted consequences. The reevaluation of his legacy raises a host of interlocking questions that many would like to consider answered for all time. It poses problems about the October Revolution, about what Lenin had expected, and perhaps most troublesome, about what Bukharin had proposed. The rehabilitation of Pokrovskii carries with it the need for Soviet historians to work out an interpretation that explains how Pokrovskii could arrive at conclusions so greatly at variance with current ones and yet be Marxist-Leninist. Does this imply that there is more than one Marxism? Are there, instead of the single block of steel aspired to by Lenin, various interpretations of Marxism that have varying measures of validity? If not, according to what principle does one decide that one interpretation reflects the interest of the proletariat, while all others are bourgeois distortions?

Thus the rehabilitation foretells rewards even as it reveals dangers. But it touches different individuals and groups of historians differently —both their intellectual dispositions and their material interests.

In 1958, Academician Nechkina became head of the Research Council on the Problem of the History of Historical Scholarship, a body designed to coordinate work in that field on a nationwide scale. One of her first initiatives was an invitation to her colleagues to discuss the periodization of Soviet historiography.[14] Their acute self-consciousness assured a lively response to her challenge, and a wide-ranging, thought-provoking debate ensued; nonspecialists joined the discussion and even nonhistorians attended, making it remarkable in our age of specialization. Only fifteen contributions were approved for publication and appeared between 1960 and 1962, but fifty historians participated.[15] The discussion constitutes the next chapter in the reevaluation of Pokrovskii.

The published works give evidence that divergent trends persisted among specialists in historiography. It proved impossible for the historical leadership to discard the Stalinist interpretation of Pokrovskii and induce all the historians to close ranks behind a new one. One author reported the opinions of some "skeptics" who opposed holding the discussion on grounds that it would impede practical work. "Because there are so many opinions, so many historians . . . any discussion of these problems would be fruitless." The author himself disagreed, affirming that "the unity of views required for practical work can be achieved only in the course of broad, creative discussion."[16] But his statement of the problem reflects a malaise about public expression of disagreements. In construing it a temporary state of affairs, he implicitly rejects the normality of public debate of dissenting views.

Not all the critics kept silent. It is noteworthy that the Institute's antagonists did not uphold the Stalinist view, but rather abandoned it by 1957 in favor of their own interpretation of Soviet historiography. It was close in spirit to the Stalinist one but employed the rhetoric fashionable after the Twentieth Congress.

The main architect of what might be called, without too much distortion, the conservative interpretation is Mikhail Emilianovich Naidenov, a professor at Moscow University. He first expounded his views in two articles on the historiography of the October Revolution, both published in 1957. One of the articles, published in a collection commemorating the fortieth anniversary of the Revolution,[17] is a masterpiece. It is perhaps the best single work on Soviet historiography; moreover, it should form part of any bibliography on the Russian Revolution and be made required reading for anyone interested in the latter-day interpretation of Leninism. The work shows a rare sensitivity to the essay form. The second article appeared in *Vosprosy*

Istorii.[18] It is at once a disheartening work of research and a bold, clever polemic. Naidenov commends Pokrovskii as a "major historian" (*krupnyi istorik*)[19] and praises his efforts as a pedagogue and editor, but he argues that Pokrovskii, like most Marxists in the 1920s, based his conclusions on personal impressions of the Revolution, not on genuine research. Most importantly, Pokrovskii failed, in Naidenov's view, to comprehend Lenin's teachings on imperialism, and he never even mentioned Lenin's theory of growing-over.[20] At the same time Naidenov praises a work of Pokrovskii's arch rival, Emelian Iaroslavskii, who was closely associated with Stalin, and who presided over the liquidation of the so-called school of Pokrovskii in the years of the great purge.

Whereas Dubrovskii had stressed the harmful consequences of Stalin's direct intervention into historical affairs—setting it in the context of the creation of the cult of personality—Naidenov stresses its educational value—setting it in the context of class conflict. As concerns Stalin's letter to the editors of *Proletarskaia Revoliutsiia* in 1931, Naidenov argues that it

> rendered great positive influence on the makeup of the entire ideological front, including historical scholarship. It uplifted the feeling of Bolshevik *partiinost'* on the part of historians, [increased their] intolerance [*neterpimost'*] to any sort of departure from Leninism and intensified [their] interest in Marxist-Leninist theory. Our scholars began to study the classical works of Marxism-Leninism more broadly and deeply.[21]

Completely out of keeping with the new evaluation of the 1920s fostered by the Institute of History, Naidenov asserted that the Leninist conception of the October Revolution was set forth for the first time "fully and systematically" only in 1936 in Volume I of the *History of the Civil War*. "This important victory was consolidated in Chapter VII" of Stalin's *Short Course*.[22] This is Naidenov's most controversial point: It was the criticism of Pokrovskii and his school that brought Soviet historians to the Leninist understanding of the Russian historical process.[23]

In the periodization debate, Professor Naidenov turned out to be Nechkina's principal antagonist. She devoted much of her final summary article[24] to polemics with him, seeking to prove that his dating the Leninist stage in the 1930s involved him in a series of contradictions. The entire matter—whether Pokrovskii's works and other writings of the 1920s can be considered truly Leninist—evokes a deeply emotional response among Soviet historians. Unfortunately, even if one accepts Nechkina's points about Naidenov's contradictions, it does not take away Naidenov's central thesis that important differences stand between Pokrovskii's works and those that followed—with respect to both their philosophies of history and their understanding of Russian history. We might feel that greater clarification results from calling the latter system of views Stalinist instead of Leninist, but both terms have polemical overtones, and the name is less important than the distinction itself. The works of the 1930s differed so significantly from Pokrovskii's, I think, that one cannot without loss of clarity apply the same adjective to both periods. Even though Naidenov uses this distinction didactically, to discredit Pokrovskii and most work done in the 1920s, it happens to be too well founded to be discarded. Glossing over it compelled Nechkina and like-minded scholars to minimize Pokrovskii's significance and to hold up other lesser historians and even some political figures as major historians. But running through all the sources is the fact that Pokrovskii was the leader of an organized, hierarchical arrangement of Marxist scholars, and the others, in varying degrees, shared his major concepts. One feels that Nechkina uses sleight of hand in suggesting that Naidenov tends to create a cult of personality around Pokrovskii.[25] Even one sympathetic to the anti-Stalinist thrust of her interpretation must acknowledge that she has misrepresented her opponent's views.

In addition to the intellectual side of the debate and the ideological overtones, it is evident that there is a dimension of personal animosity and rivalry. It shows up in Naidenov's singling out a historiographical work written by Nechkina in 1919–1920[26] as an example of the low level of Marxist scholarship of the period. Surely he struck foul in censuring a book she wrote as a second-year student in Kazan University, especially since she had disavowed it in print as long ago as 1929.[27] We can agree with the following summary by Nechkina: "The concept advanced by our critics clearly displays an undeserved underevaluation of the young Marxist scholars and an unfounded overestimation of the Marxism of the 'old professors.' "[28] The words, which are Nechkina's, make explicit Naidenov's assumption: the young Marxists of the 1920s, who now govern the profession, are Leninist Marxists only owing to the criticism of Pokrovskii carried out under the auspices of Stalin.

Over and above polemics, the periodization discussion brought out an abundance of facts tied together by a variety of themes, which is their most important feature for a foreign specialist. Historians known previously only by their initials and surnames gained biographies, and leading figures, like Pokrovskii, were endowed with personal qualities; early scholarly institutions also became increasingly distinctive. Yet, had one been able to study the sources in sequence, i.e., to hear Dubrovskii's report in 1958 with its implicit promise to clarify the major events on the historical front, he would have felt disappointed in the periodization debate. Despite the increasing verisimilitude of the reader's picture of the young Soviet scholarly community, the historians' descriptions of the crucial events remained guarded and veiled. Dubrovskii's promise was not fulfilled but merely reiterated.

Soviet historians failed in the debate to come up with a unified schema of periodization; yet their discussions interest the reader as an application of historical materialism to the study of historiography. It is one example of how they treat the history of ideas. Numerous schemata were introduced in quest of a principle capable of showing the distinctive qualities of facts and of governing judgments about their separation into different periods. Once again, at the poles of the discussion stood Nechkina and Naidenov. All agreed that the principle would have to bring out the relationship between historical ideas and the economic substructure and should also reveal the law-governed autonomy of ideas. Nechkina proposed, in effect, that assertions about the past provided the basis for the necessary distinctions: the character of statements about the historical process itself and related factual problems reveals the unity of a stage and the movement from one to another.[29]

In defending herself against Naidenov's criticism that her formulation ignored class conflict—the chief characteristic of Soviet historiography[30]—she pointed to the impossibility of employing class conflict as a principle of development in a classless society.[31] We can say that in this instance Nechkina offered more persuasive arguments. By defining historiography in terms of its purpose, i.e., making assertions about the past, she casts the problem of class conflict on an empirical level. Her approach lets one examine the bearing of class conflict in successive periods and distinguishes between changes that result from the internal needs of the discipline and changes that come about in response to events without. Naidenov's approach reduces historiography wholly to an epiphenomenon of class conflict—a search for reflection within the discipline of exterior phenomena. Even if we were to agree momentarily with Naidenov that class conflict is the force governing history, we could assert that Nechkina's approach provides a better context for perceiving its operation.

The literature about Pokrovskii, we see, brought up thorny problems of definition in what Soviets frequently call theory of historiography. In the course of time, it led to a quite formal and rigorous statement that sought to refine prevailing notions about science and social phenomena. The author of the statement, A. M. Sakharov,[32] a junior professor at Moscow University and a member of Academician Nechkina's Council on Historiography, sought to define the subject matter of historiography by indicating elements in the discipline of history additional to assertions about the past. He also sought to specify elements in the historian's milieu that bear upon his assertions about the past. He urges the historiographer to reveal the influence of these elements on the historian's conclusions, while at the same time taking note of the social consequences of the conclusions. We might say that he has proposed a feedback model of explanation, though the metaphor is not his. He advises historians to show how the consequences of a certain state of affairs (the conclusions as affected by the milieu) in turn affect the original condition. This is just part of the historiographer's task.

Sakharov urges him to lay bare the *zakonomernost'* (the inner tendencies or logical relationships) inhering in the ideas themselves. We take this to mean a relationship of ideas analogous to that obtaining between the theory of Kepler about planetary motion, the theory of Galileo about terrestrial motion, and Newton's law of gravity: each set of statements containing an unconfirmed prediction that serves as a point of departure for later theorizing. Although Sakharov discusses this concept in connection with the researcher's tasks, the reader waits in vain for advice on how to identify such patterns, and how to decide whether a given event is a manifestation of such a pattern or a reflection of external processes. But it would be idle to dwell on this shortcoming. A body of theory valuable to the researcher does exist; he need not approach his subject matter wholly intuitively.

In 1961–1962 political events impinged sharply on historical research, and the party leadership explicitly joined the respective legacies of Pokrovskii and Stalin. The Central Committee prepared its case even a year or two before the Twenty-second Congress when it solicited reports from one or more of the senior historians about the standing of Pokrovskii. Then Ilyichev, head of the Agitprop Department, set forth the official position in a speech on the cult of personality. He delivered it to the Twenty-second Congress and it was reproduced in *Pravda*.[33] The message was reiterated by Suslov to a meeting of University Chairmen of Departments of Social Science, and reproduced in *Pravda*[34] and *Kommunist*.[35] Suslov devoted just a small portion of his speech to Pokrovskii, upholding the interpretation associated with Nechkina and Dubrovskii. Ilyichev gave slightly more attention to the matter by quoting in full Lenin's letter to Pokrovskii on the occasion of the publication of the *Brief History of Russia*. The letter, which had long been misrepresented, congratulated the author and commented on the merits of the work.

Party intervention thus affirmed the majority opinion among historians and served to uphold the leadership. Shortly thereafter a host of works appeared; some of them, like Dubrovskii's, were written before the Twenty-second Congress.[36] A decision was taken, moreover, to republish some of Pokrovskii's own writings.[37] But even the official statement did not result in uniformity of opinion. The disposition of historians to resist the new interpretation is one instance of an irony widespread in the Communist world in the post-Stalin decade. In upholding the Stalinist legacy, some historians found themselves in a position of dissent. This very circumstance reflected a norm they were out of sympathy with. In fact, a large part of their dissent was for the sake of a tradition intolerant to this norm. A situation resulted that could itself be considered a classical illustration of dialectics.

Still another irony is reflected in the means employed by the leadership to combat their Stalinist opponents. In 1962, A. P. Nosov, a *dotsent* in the *kafedra* of the History of the CPSU at Moscow University, and A. N. Zakharikov, a student of Nosov, published a book entitled *Some Problems in the Struggle of the CPSU for the Marxist Treatment of the History of Bolshevism*.[38] It bore the imprimatur of the Higher Party School. The book is a model of Stalinist scholarship in both its conclusions and mode of presentation. It is a haphazard medley of didactically selected facts and arbitrary interpretations tied together only by the authors' prejudices. Yet it is invaluable for the foreign specialist to whom archives are closed. The book takes up the historical struggles of the 1920s and early 1930s in greater detail than any other work, and its broad range of references includes extracts from the Central Party Archives. Just as the anti-Stalin campaign swelled in crescendo, the authors completed their work. Consequently, it was subjected to harsh criticism at the All-Union Congress of Historians of 1962 by Academicians Ponomarev, Pospelov, and Mints.[39] The last, a participant in the events treated by the authors, was especially severe, but justifiably so; he pointed out that the extermination of historians could not be considered part of the struggle for the purity of Marxism-Leninism. Even Nosov's statement of self-criticism[40] did not spare him further censure in Ponomarev's concluding remarks: "Judging from Comrade Nosov's speech at the party history panel and from the note he has sent up, it is clear that he fails to understand the criticism. Moreover, between the lines of the note is the thought that the criticism was unjustified. . . ."[41]

The book was never put on sale. A few libraries obtained copies and apparently filed fewer than the usual number of entry cards. Coming upon it almost by chance raises the question in the finder's mind, What exactly is de-Stalinization? This gross event should not be underlined, for the fact remains that dissenting views, within limits that do not reduce them to trivia, do find their way into print.

The twin themes of Stalin and Pokrovskii received great publicity in 1962–1963. It is now part of the history of Soviet historiography that some of its representatives played a leading role in the de-Stalinization campaign. Some of their assertions were astoundingly candid. At an authoritative conference on history and sociology held in 1963,[42] A. L. Sidorov not only censured the view that the Leninist stage began in the 1930s, he argued that "after three decades, in many [respects] we have to return to the past in order to place the matter of concrete historical research on Marxist grounds."[43] The methodological problems now confronting Soviet social scientists were posed, according to Sidorov, by Pokrovskii in a speech in 1928 and by Lukin-Antonov.[44] a revolutionary historian closely associated with Pokrovskii and the man who replaced him as leader of the historical front. Nothing better, Sidorov continued, had been written about Marx as a historian since Lukin's report to the Communist Academy in commemoration of the fiftieth anniversary of Marx's death, i.e., in 1933.[45]

Nechkina did not attend the conference but forwarded a written statement that was included in the minutes. Except for her reluctance to name names, it is as sharp a condemnation of Stalin's practices as will be found. Like Khrushchev's speech, it confirmed the worst forebodings of Western contemporaries. The historian had to choose "between two 'evils,' risking [his] head or reproach for idleness; historians most frequently [chose] the latter; it was safer."[46] She asserted that despite great progress remnants of the cult of personality hang over historians.[47]

Circumstances thus were propitious for various writings on Pokrovskii and on the entire field of the history of Soviet historical scholarship. A brief classification of the literature is in order. First, the discursive essays on periodization, taken as a whole, constitute a distinctive body of literature. Second, a body of popular literature arose. *Izvestiia* devoted an article, that included a photograph, to the ninetieth birthday of V. I. Nevskii—a prerevolutionary Bolshevik who was an active historian and head of the Lenin library until the purges.[48] Numerous articles about Pokrovskii appeared, even one that reported dialogue between him and his wife and told the story of their meeting and courtship.[49] *Istoriia SSSR* has initiated a series of brief, popular articles on historians who participated in the October Revolution. A third body of literature, especially rich and timely, is the series of memoirs published in *Istoriia SSSR* since 1962. The editors of the journal proposed a set of questions about the educational and professional activities of Soviet historians and more than a half dozen major historians, such as N. M. Druzhinin, N. L. Rubinshtein, and A. L. Sidorov, plus some lesser known figures, have replied.[50] The result is, again, an enlargement of the body of known facts, some touching portraits of bygone figures, and disputes over past events and present trends. But the autobiographies embody a theme likely to interest any historian—the intellectual life of the authors, their attempt, under difficult circumstances, to master their craft and keep alive the memory of their nation. The authors also make valuable suggestions about research technique and the documentation of archival materials.[51] The fourth category is research; here we can specify subclasses of surveys, monographs, and encyclopedic research.

Though polemics about Pokrovskii and the 1920s continued after the Twenty-second Congress, they yielded the foreground to research: ascertaining facts from sources, including archives, and formulating conclusions of low generality. In evaluating the research we must take note, as was the case in our consideration of the earlier polemics, of divergent tendencies. There was, on the one hand, an upsurge of professional competence and, on the other, the persistence of some bad habits. Among the leading scholars in historiography is Professor Naidenov, who, in the essay mentioned above,[52] revealed a dialectical facility for showing how a given historical work fulfilled earlier efforts and predicted later ones. K. N. Tarnovskii, author of a monograph on the historiography of Russian imperialism,[53] has demonstrated the ability to synthesize the various sides of historians' writings and skill at presenting the ideas of others. A. A. Govorkov, a young historian at Tomsk University,[54] in an article devoted exclusively to one aspect of Pokrovskii's thought, showed how work on a narrow but strategically selected range of facts can have a wide range of implications. In general, works of this sort make authoritative assertions about the past resting on expertise in sources and critical mastery of the work of others. They manifest a striving for generality and operate at about the same level of abstraction as Western historical works.

Perhaps the work that manifests these virtues most strikingly is a brief monograph by L. V. Danilova,[55] in which she reconstructs the attempt in the late 1920s and early 1930s to apply the concept of feudalism to Russian history. Though she does not fully carry through the program of Sakharov, she clarifies by illustration the notion of *zakonomernost'* and indicates what is meant by the unity of theory and practice. She does so by untangling the threads of what was undoubtedly one of the most profound and extensive historical discussions in the twentieth century,[56] by taking note of the interaction between an author's sources, definitions, and conclusions. She even evokes something of the atmosphere of the past in indicating how political circumstances influenced the evolution of the discussion. Though these are bare suggestions on her part, they are more useful than references to economic categories and processes conventionally labeled by such value-laden terms as "the building of socialism." Her devotion to the past is complete; yet her narrative itself is an explication of the concept of feudalism and thereby serves present needs. Her work, moreover, has an oblique relationship to the current discussion of the "Asian means of production," a discussion which represents the first attempt to revise the Stalinist definition of historical materialism. The merits of Danilova's work are abundant and compelling even to one who feels keen dissatisfaction with the way she distinguishes between Marxist and non-Marxist scholarship and her explanations of an alleged collapse of bourgeois scholarship.

The reverse side of historiographical scholarship—the persistence of bad habits—is evident even in such prestigious works of the Institute of History as Volume IV of *Outline of the History of Historical Scholarship*,[57] and *History and Historians*,[58] an important collection of essays edited by Academician Nechkina. The factual store, once again, is enlarged, but assertions such as that Karl Mannheim was an apologist of Naziism are allowed to stand.[59] More serious flaws are the inability of some of the authors to digest their material and their unwillingness to answer questions that beg for treatment at every turn. Above all, they fail to convey anything of the inner life of the scholarly institutions and their relations to each other. This indisposition to reconstruct any of the decisions taken is doubtless a result of political constraint:

reluctance to awaken old issues that wracked the Communist party during its great upheavals or to raise names that are themselves issues. The only general evaluation stated is that the institutions contributed to socialist construction.[60]

It is Stalin's ghost that vitiates so much of the historians' efforts. They are quick to cite the harmful effects on personnel of the "cult of personality," but they are loath to concede that Stalin's intervention could have affected the body of ideas they are heir to.

In 1964, politics again impinged dramatically upon the debate about Pokrovskii and brought it to a new stage. The ouster of Khrushchev with the attendant call for objectivity has been taken to mean less discussion of the cult of personality. This is reflected in the continuing polemic between Naidenov and the Institute of History. In some respects the argument about the Leninist stage in historiography has become more refined. Once again we must pay respect to Naidenov's extensive knowledge and his ability to cast the problem in empirical terms.[61] He has designated some concepts as specifically Leninist, making it possible then in principle to confirm or disconfirm their presence in particular writings. His present opponent, V. G. Sarbei, a Ukrainian historian, seeks to affirm the existence of Leninism in the 1920s by reference to publication of Lenin's work and the general availability of his notions.[62] In this context the problem is one of knowing what was in peoples' heads without reference to their writings. Such an approach opens the door to endless debate without hope of agreement.

But the discussion is a sign of retrogression in its growing obscurity. Some passages have an almost allegorical character. Without knowledge of the debate in its earlier phases, the reader would be hard pressed to discern the differences of opinion. The historians allude to events and make suggestions about their significance, but they do not trouble to narrate them. Surely this expresses disrespect to the reader and is a disservice to the discipline. It means that the various activities of the historian are subordinated to the central task of propagating a particular world view.

The subject of this paper is too current to allow conclusions. Perhaps in ending we can usefully employ the Soviet technique of stating theses:

The discussion of Pokrovskii has brought him back to the revolutionary pantheon, but his most characteristic ideas continue to wander in disgrace.

The debate about the Leninist stage of historiography has momentarily taken a turn toward obscurity, but the sheer force of accumulated facts will probably force it into the open again.[63]

The historians' research is undistinguished except in its magnitude, but it has at least brought the matter within the ken of scholarship, and if the historians have failed to synthesize their material and clarify its interaction with political events, their efforts have significantly revised the norms of the profession.

If the concept of *partiinost'* has been diluted and is no longer taken as a call for falsification, no revision to liberalism has taken place.

Even though politicians continue to influence historians directly, they are not inclined to compel uniformity of opinion even on some questions that have political relevance.

The official version of Soviet history, which stresses the continuities of socialist construction, has suffered little revision, and still stands as an inroad to dogmatism.

NOTES

1. *Voprosy istorii*, no. 1 (1956), pp. 4, 11; no. 2, pp. 199–213.
2. *Ibid.*, no. 4 (1957), p. 5.
3. Moscow, 1959, col. 298.
4. *K voprosu o sushchnosti aziatskogo sposoba proizvodstva, feodalizma, krepostnichestva, i torgovogo kapitala*, Moscow, 1929; "Diskussiia o sotsial'no-ekonomicheskikh formatsiiakh," *Istorik-Marksist*, no. 16 (1930), pp. 15, 111–13, 126, 156.
5. Conversation with A. E. Lutskii, December 1966.
6. "Akademik M. N. Pokrovskii i ego rol' v razvitii sovetskoi istoricheskoi nauk," *Voprosy istorii*, no. 3 (1962), pp. 3–40; translated in *Soviet Studies in History*, I, no. 1 (1962), 23–50.
7. *Ocherki istorii istoricheskoi nauki v SSSR*, Moscow: Akademiia Nauk, 1963, III, 218–38.
8. N. L. Rubinshtein, "M. N. Pokrovskii—istorik rossii," *Pod Znamenem Marksizma*, nos. 10–11 (1924), pp. 189–209. Articles of value appeared that treated single aspects of Pokrovskii's work, but articles that

sought to characterize his life and work as a whole were either "nihilistic or apologetic." A possible exception is the chapter on Pokrovskii written by still another N. L. Rubinshtein in his *Russkaia istoriografiia*, Moscow, 1941. It is the most searching and profound work ever written on Pokrovskii.
9. *Voprosy istorii*, no. 3 (1962), p. 35.
10. *Ibid.*, p. 29.
11. *Ibid.*, pp. 29–30.
12. See L. Labedz, "Soviet Historiography between Thaw and Freeze," *Soviet Survey*, no. 15 (1957), pp. 1–13.
13. *Voprosy istorii*, no. 2 (1949), p. 6.
14. "O periodizatsii istorii sovetskoi istoricheskoi nauki," *Istoriia SSSR*, no. 1 (1960), pp. 77–91.
15. *Istoriia i sotsiologiia*, Moscow, 1964, p. 236.
16. M. N. Naidenov, "Problemy periodizatsii sovetskoi istoricheskoi nauki," *Istoriia SSSR*, no. 1 (1961), pp. 81–82.
17. "Velikaia Oktiabr'skaia Sotsialisticheskaia Revoliutsiia v osve-

shchenii (russkoi) istoriografii," in *Iz istorii velikoi Oktiabr'skoi Sotsialisticheskoi Revoliutsii,* Moscow, 1957.

18. "Velikaia Oktaibr'skaia Sotsialisticheskaia Revoliutsiia v sovetskoi isotoriografii," *Voprosy istorii,* no. 10 (1957), pp. 167–80.

19. *Ibid.,* p. 171.

20. *Ibid.*

21. *Ibid.,* p. 173.

22. *Ibid.,* p. 174.

23. *Ibid.*

24. "K itogam diskussiia o periodizatsii istorii sovetskoi istoricheskoi nauki," *Istoriia SSSR,* no. 2 (1962), pp. 57–78; translated in *Soviet Studies in History,* no. 3 (1962–63), pp. 40–57.

25. *Ibid.,* p. 67.

26. *Russkaia istoriia v osveshchenii ekonomicheskogo materializma,* Kazan, 1922.

27. Letter to the editor of *Istorik-Marksist,* no. 11 (1929), pp. 277–78.

28. *Istoriia SSSR,* no. 2 (1962), p. 69.

29. *Ibid.,* p. 62.

30. *Ibid.,* no. 1 (1961), pp. 82–84.

31. *Ibid.,* no. 2 (1962), p. 64.

32. "Nekotorye problemy metodologii istoriograficheskoi nauki" in *Metodologicheskie voprosy obshchestvennikh nauk,* Moscow, 1966, pp. 351–68.

33. *Pravda,* October 26, 1961.

34. *Ibid.,* February 4, 1962.

35. *Kommunist,* no. 3 (1962), pp. 15–46.

36. E. A. Lutskii, "Razvitie istoricheskoi kontseptsii M. N. Pokrovskogo," in M. V. Nechkina, ed., *Istoriia i istoriki,* Moscow; Nauka, 1965.

37. Moscow: Mysil, 1965–67. Edited by M. N. Tikhomirov, B. M. Khvostov, L. G. Beskrovnyi, and O. D. Sokolov, who wrote the sixty-six-page introduction and who seems to have been the most active editor. Even though the editors failed to realize their original intention of presenting some hitherto unpublished writings, the appearance of these volumes is an important event for the scholarly community and the public alike: at a stroke it broadened the range of tolerated opinion and value. The volumes are copiously and expertly edited.

38. *Netotorye voprosy bor'by KPSS za marksistskoe osveshchenie istorii bol'shevisma (1928–32),* Moscow: Vysha Shkola, 1962.

39. *Vsesoiuznoe soveshchanie istorikov,* Moscow: Nauka, 1964, pp. 22, 75, 210–11.

40. *Ibid.,* pp. 261–62.

41. *Ibid.,* p. 501; as translated in *Soviet Studies in History,* II, no. 1 (1963), 54.

42. *Istoriia i sotsiologiia, loc. cit.*

43. *Ibid.,* p. 74.

44. *Ibid.,* p. 177.

45. *Ibid.,* p. 175.

46. *Ibid.,* p. 235.

47. *Ibid.,* p. 236.

48. May 14, 1966.

49. *Literaturnaia Rossiia,* June 28, 1963.

50. Most, if not all, of these have been translated in *Soviet Studies in History.*

51. The most interesting in this connection are the memoirs of N. L. Rubinshtein, *Istoriia SSSR,* no. 6 (1962), pp. 88–114, and E. I. Zaozerskaia, *Ibid.,* no 3 (1964), pp. 139–49.

52. See above, note 17.

53. *Sovetskaia istoriografiia rossiiskogo imperializma,* Moscow, 1964.

54. A. A. Govorkov, "Problema sootnosheniia istorii i sovremennosti v proizvedenniiakh M. N. Pokrovskogo sovetskogo perioda," *Trudy Tomskogo Universiteta,* no. 178 (1965), pp. 66–85.

55. "Stanovlenie marksistskogo napravleniia v sovetskoi istoriografii epokhi feodalizma," *Istoricheskie Zapiski,* no. 76 (1965), pp. 62–119.

56. It is part of the discussion treated by Leo Yaresh in his essay "The Problem of Periodization," in Cyril Black, *Rewriting Russian History,* 2nd ed., New York: Vintage, 1962, pp. 34–76.

57. *Ocherki istorii istoricheskoi nauki v SSSR*, Moscow, 1966.

58. See above, note 38.

59. L. V. Cherepnin in *Ocherki istorii istorichoskoi nauki v SSSR*, IV, 159–60.

60. For a more detailed description of this state of affairs and an attempt to explain it with reference to the complexities of de-Stalinization and the lingering notion of *partiinost'*, see my review essay "Two Books on Soviet Historiography" in *World Politics*, XX, no. 2 (1968), esp. 335–49.

61. "O leninskom etape v istoricheskoi nauke," *Voprosy istorii*, no. 2 (1966), pp. 21–37; the editors appended a note to disassociate themselves from some of Naidenov's views.

62. "Eshche o leninskom etape v istoricheskoi nauki," *Voprosy Istorii*, no. 9 (1966), pp. 15–26.

63. This assertion proved unwarranted in its optimism. The celebration of the fiftieth anniversary gave evidence of further retrogression in the debate about Pokrovskii. It has almost reached the point where accurate description requires employment of such concepts as neo-Stalinism and de-rehabilitation. See the lead editorial in the anniversary issue of *Voprosy istorii*, no. 10, pp. 3–18, that glossed over the cult of personality and condemned the revival of nihilistic attitudes toward the past that allegedly occurred in the late 1950s and early 1960s, a clear warning to the leadership of the Institute of History. See also Naidenov's elaboration of his own interpretation of modern Russian history in the anniversary issue of the *Vestnik* of Moscow University, Historical Series no. 5, pp. 3–19. He combined his account with an enumeration of tasks for Soviet historians, a clear bid to become one of the party's leading spokesmen on historical matters.

PART II

ESSAYS ON SOVIET FOREIGN POLICY

PART II: ESSAYS ON SOVIET FOREIGN POLICY

Since World War II the Soviet Union has become one of the two most powerful states in the world and, as such, has played an increasingly important role in international politics. Not only has the Soviet Union continued to be the dominant power in Eastern Europe—although this dominance is somewhat less extensive than in the past—but it also has expanded its contacts and influence in Western Europe and in the developing countries. The articles in the second section of this book deal primarily with Soviet relations with the developing countries and the importance of the Sino-Soviet split on international affairs.

Roger Kanet presents a brief survey of the changes in Soviet attitudes concerning the developing countries during the past eighteen years. He shows how Soviet policy and ideology have been shifted from a position of almost total alienation from the newly independent states to one of very active involvement. He argues that the Soviets have changed their theoretical interpretations of conditions in the developing countries in order to make them fit more with reality.

Jaan Pennar presents an illuminating analysis of the historical background of Soviet involvement in the Middle East. He traces the development and oscillation of Soviet attitudes and policies and the rise of Marxist movements in the area since the Russian Revolution. In discussing Soviet attempts to present Central Asia as a model of development applicable to the Middle East, Dr. Pennar observes that "Soviet Turkestan is more like *Algérie française* and it is very doubtful indeed that the Arabs would want to exchange the *pieds noirs* for *pieds rouges.*" He concludes that the insistence of the Soviet leadership on following designs and politics laid down in Moscow has seriously impeded the development of Arab Communist parties over the past half-century.

Arthur Klinghoffer examines Soviet attitudes toward African views of the socialist path of development and points out the significant changes that have occurred during the past decade. From a denial of the possibility of an "African socialism," the Soviet leaders have moved to a tacit acceptance of non-Marxist varieties of socialism. Soviet writers have differentiated between "progressive" and "reactionary" socialism in Africa, with the primary criterion for judgment being the willingness or unwillingness of African leaders to adopt a friendly position toward Soviet policies. Professor Klinghoffer concludes with the argument that Soviet analysts "have shed many of their misconceptions about Africa" and have become more realistic in the perception and evaluation of the developments on the African continent.

In the final essay Chae-Jin Lee analyzes the differences in military strategy between the Soviet Union and Communist China and carefully examines the Chinese accusations against the Soviet Union. He points to the "striking dichotomy between China's theoretical de-emphasis of nuclear weapons and its strenuous efforts for their development." He also argues that the dispute between the Soviet Union and China has reached such a point that, as long as Mao Tse-tung and his supporters remain in power in China, "it is highly unlikely that they would accept a basic appeasement with the present Soviet leadership."

7

ROGER E. KANET
The University of Kansas

CHANGING SOVIET ATTITUDES TOWARD THE DEVELOPING COUNTRIES

In the past two decades or so, Soviet policy in the newly independent countries of Asia and Africa, as well as in Latin America, has shifted significantly from a position of almost total isolation from developments in the colonial and ex-colonial areas to rapidly expanding involvement. Soviet trade with the developing countries increased more than seven-fold from 1955 to 1968[1] and the Soviets now have diplomatic relations with most of the countries as Asia and Africa, as well as with a substantial number in Latin America.[2] At the same time that Soviet political, cultural, and economic activity in the developing world has increased so dramatically, Soviet views of these countries have also changed.

When Stalin died in 1953, the Soviet attitude toward the developing countries was still tied to his conception of a world split into two hostile camps, and Soviet views of "bourgeois nationalists" were extremely hostile. For example, in a speech to the Academy of Sciences in 1949, Evgenii Zhukov, a prominent Soviet specialist on Asia, stated that bourgeois nationalists in the colonies had gone over to the imperialist camp and that bourgeois nationalism was the most important

---

Parts of this article are reprinted with permission from "The Recent Soviet Reassessment of Developments in the Third World," *The Russian Review,* XXVII (1968), 27–41 and from "The Soviet Union and the Third World: A Case of Ideological Revision," *The Rocky Mountain Social Science Journal,* VI, 1 (1969), 109–16.

ideological weapon used by the imperialists in maintaining their colonial empires.[3] The big bourgeoisie who ruled the supposedly independent states—such as Nehru, Sukarno, and others—were condemned for their antidemocratic policies and were accused of acting merely as agents for their colonial masters.[4] According to the Stalinist position, only a revolutionary movement led by the Communist party could ever attain true independence. The logical extension of this attitude to the newly independent states was a policy of nonrecognition and subversion, and the wave of Communist-inspired insurrections which flooded South and Southeast Asia in the late forties was a result of this policy.

By 1953, it had become very clear that a policy of isolation and subversion had failed. Nowhere had a nationalist government been overthrown by Communists, and the Soviets—on the basis of the experience of the postwar period—began a total reassessment of their past policies. In an article published in 1963, long after Stalin's rigid policy had been replaced by one of cooperation with nationalist movements and regimes, a Soviet scholar admitted that many earlier Soviet writers on the colonial areas had not taken "full account of the meaning and historical significance of the events which were occurring" in Asia and Africa, because "the deadening influence of Stalinist dogmatism was too strong."[5]

At the Twentieth Party Congress in 1956, a new Soviet policy of *rapprochement* with non-Communist nationalist-revolutionary regimes and movements was outlined. Actually this revision of Soviet doctrine had begun soon after Stalin's death, but did not reach fruition until 1956. The new Soviet position included an invitation to countries outside the Communist bloc to join an expanding world-wide peace zone by instituting a policy of nonalignment with existing military blocs. It also included a positive evaluation of the role of nationalist leaders and nationalism in the world-revolutionary process. The three basic characteristics of Soviet writing on developing countries in this early period were: (1) an emphasis on the importance of the anticolonial movement for international affairs,[6] (2) a great optimism concerning developments in the Third World and the impending collapse of capitalism,[7] and (3) a lack of detailed information or ideological formulations concerning domestic developments in the Third World.[8]

The basic reasons for the oversimplified Soviet view of the developing countries—a view which has changed significantly in recent years—was a lack of knowledge and experience in these areas. Related to this was an attempt to develop broad general propositions which would apply to the historical process in all developing countries. Also, the Soviet preoccupation with the international implications of the anticolonial movement did not favor an emphasis on realistic analyses of socio-economic conditions in developing countries.[9]

Briefly, one could say that Soviet policy and ideology concerning developing countries in the 1950s were based on a small amount of factual information and a large amount of Marxist theory—theory which the rapidly increasing knowledge of Soviet diplomats and scholars has proven to be inaccurate or inapplicable in Asia, Africa, and Latin America. The increase in Soviet contacts and knowledge led eventually, not only to shifts in Soviet policies, but also to changes in Soviet theoretical statements about the developing world.

By the late 1950s, it had become evident that initial Soviet optimism about trends in the Third World were unfounded. With the exception of Cuba, no developing country had taken a socialist path of development—at least in Soviet terms—and none had aligned itself fully with the Soviet Union in international affairs. David Dallin has summarized the dilemma facing the Soviet leadership as follows:

> Although the process of decolonization continued and the number of independent nations was growing, and although "neutralism" was often preferred by the governments, all Soviet efforts to assume the role of guide and create a real alliance between the Soviet bloc and the "neutralists" and thus, in an evolutionary way, enlarge the number of "socialist" states were in vain.[10]

The failure of the fulfillment of original Soviet hopes led to a refinement of Soviet theory and policy on neutralism. Communist theoreticians began speaking more of the two sides of neutralism—a positive side that must be exploited and a harmful side which must be opposed.

One of the major attempts by the Soviets to fill the theoretical void concerning developing countries was the enunciation of the doctrine of the state of national democracy at the meeting of the Eighty-one Communist Parties in Moscow in November 1960 and its elaboration at the Twenty-second Party Congress a few months later. In presenting the idea of a state of "national democracy," the Soviets set forth the objectives that they hoped would be implemented in the developing countries. The major characteristics of this new type of state were to include: (1) the refusal to join military blocs or to permit foreign military bases on its territory; (2) a major effort to decrease Western economic influences in its economy; (3) the granting of democratic rights and freedoms to progressive political parties, labor unions, and other social organizations, including the Communists; and (4) the introduction of major social changes, especially agrarian reforms, in the interests of the people.[11]

Although the new doctrine was an innovation in Communist theory, it did not represent a basic change in Soviet policy, but rather a doctrinal implementation of the conclusions of the Twentieth Party Congress of 1956. The new theory represented a response to the real problems facing Soviet policy in the former colonies. According to the classical Communist theory of national liberation, the struggle for independence takes place in two stages. During the first of these, colonial peoples were to attain their independence from their foreign rulers and from the domestic feudal class in a revolution that would be both national and "bourgeois-democratic." During the revolutionary process the national bourgeoisie would have to turn to the workers and peasants for support against the colonial rulers, thereby creating the conditions for the development of powerful class organizations and, eventually, the conditions for the second, socialist, stage of the revolution which would be led by the workers under the guidance of the Communists.

The problem which faced the Soviets in the late fifties was the fact that in most of the newly independent states liberation from colonial rule had been accomplished without a revolution and that these countries were ruled by non-Communist dictators. The tasks of the first stage of the revolution, in the classical theory, had not been fulfilled. As a result of a number of discussions concerning the problems of the anticolonial movement, the Communists formulated the new strategy of national democracy, which would complete the tasks of the first stage of the revolution and lead to the attainment of the second, socialist, stage.[12]

The whole theory represented an attempt to pave the way for the gradual development of the necessary prerequisites for a socialist society in countries in which the proletariat is extremely weak. The role of the local Communists during the transition period represented by this type of state was to increase their power and gradually gain control of the alliance of workers, peasants, democratic intelligentsia, and a part of the national bourgeoisie. In his report on the Conference of the Eighty-one Communist Parties, Khrushchev clearly indicated that this was the role which local Communists had to play:

The correct application of Marxist-Leninist theory in the

liberated countries consists precisely in seeking the forms which will take cognizance of the peculiarities of the economic, political and cultural life of the peoples to unite all the sound forces of the nation, *to ensure the leading role of the working class in the national front,* in the struggle completely to eradicate the roots of imperialism and the remnants of feudalism, and to clear the way for the ultimate advance towards socialism.[13]

The Soviet hope obviously was that the transition from a state of "national democracy" to socialism would take place without violence. According to a Soviet writer, one function of the national-democratic state was that it "eases the carrying out of the future socialist changes in a peaceful, bloodless way and makes it possible to avoid an armed struggle and civil war, and in this the state of national democracy differs from the dictatorship of the proletariat."[14]

The new doctrine contained a number of innovations in Communist theory. First of all, the Communists were apparently willing to let the national bourgeoisie play out its progressive role, so long as it was unaligned with the West and strove for economic independence and social reform. Also, the role assigned to the trade unions represented a change in attitude, for never before in Marxist-Leninist theory was it argued that the trade unions could perform the tasks usually assigned to the Communist party. An additional innovation was the view that a peaceful road to power was possible for the Communists.

However, even those governments which the Soviets called progressive—such as those of Guinea, Mali, the UAR, Ghana (under Nkrumah) and Algeria—did not permit the creation or functioning of open Communist parties, and African and Asian leaders began claiming that they were developing their own brands of socialism. The Soviets, rather than antagonizing their new friends, did not push the idea of independent Communist parties and even acknowledged that these countries were building socialism. Rather than speaking of states of national democracy, the Soviets began to refer to "revolutionary democratic" states and to recognize that non-Communist governments were actually initiating policies which the Soviets themselves had earlier thought only a Communist regime was capable of introducing. Soviet writers began to argue that the Communists need not form independent parties, but should cooperate with the single-party nationalist regimes which had been established throughout Asia and Africa.

Beginning in 1963, the Soviets revised their attitudes toward non-

Communist, one-party regimes in the Third World, as well as toward the socialism advocated by the nationalist leaders of Africa and Asia. In an article published in 1962, Professor Ivan Potekhin, the dean of Soviet African scholars until his death two years later, had condemned the negative aspects of attempts on the part of African and Asian leaders to seek a "third way." According to him, "African Socialism," although it contained "sincere efforts of progressive individuals to find the transition to socialism which fits in with the special conditions of African reality," was also "used as a means to deceive the working masses in the interests of capitalist development."[15] Another Soviet specialist on developing countries was more blunt in his denunciation of ideas of a "third way": "There is not and cannot be any 'third path' and experience shows that the African peoples are not looking for one."[16] In this period, although the Soviets were willing to develop economic and political ties with one-party regimes, they were extremely critical of their political and ideological positions.[17] More recently, however, they have been much more lenient in their evaluation of these regimes. The reasons for this change in attitude seem to be easy to find. According to the "national democracy" doctrine, only the working class and its vanguard were considered capable of initiating the social revolution which was required for the development of truly independent states. However, some of the very regimes which banned the activities of local Communist parties also initiated radical measures of nationalization of "both domestic and foreign capital and were willing to rely on the support of the Soviet bloc in any ensuing conflict with the Western powers."[18] The question which the Soviet leadership must have asked itself was: "Why wait for the development of strong local Communist parties, if non-Communist nationalist governments were willing to carry out much of the program advocated by the Soviets?"

In an article published in *Kommunist*, the theoretical organ of the CPSU, R. Ulianovskii has outlined the new policy which is to be followed by local Communist parties. Rather than calling for the formation of strong Communist organizations, the Soviets now argue that "the most consistent and best trained Marxist-Leninist elements should play the role of friend and assistant" of the nationalist leaders:

> Upholding the principles of Marxist-Leninist doctrine, Marxists must be flexible and shrewd, in order not to antagonize the masses. They must constantly seek to find their allies among those social strata and groups which at

the moment do not fully accept the theory of scientific socialism, but who today make partial use of it and may fully arm themselves with it tomorrow.

Ulianovskii adds that the question concerns the initial approach to the building of socialism and not its detailed construction or completion:

> If the working people of an economically underdeveloped country, without a formed working class, had to wait for the possibility of forming a national proletarian distatorship in order to begin the transition to socialist development, this would mean that it was necessary to develop capitalism rapidly, in order that a working class might be created on the basis of capitalist industrialization and, subsequently, a Marxist-Leninist party might be formed on this base.[19]

Actually, before the shift in Soviet attitudes and policies toward the nationalist, one-party regimes in Africa and Asia had occurred, Soviet scholars were already questioning the foundations of the "national democracy" doctrine. First of all, the question of class structure in the developing countries was raised. Already in 1958 and again in the early sixties, Professor Potekhin admitted that classes, as defined in Marxism-Leninism, did not exist in Africa.[20] Two young Soviet economists, Gordon and Fridman, published studies of the class structure in the Middle East and North Africa in which they argued:

> An underestimation of the depths of the real sociopolitical differences between the modern proletariat, which is connected with large-scale capitalistic ownership on the one hand, and the majority of agricultural and artisan-handcraft workers on the other, will lead to an oversimplified understanding of the problems of the formation of the working class in Asia and Africa. An unconditional unification of all elements of the army of hired labor into an entity embracing almost one-half of the gainfully employed population would in reality be an admission that the proletariat has already become the most numerous class of society. Such an approach could produce an incorrect evaluation of the degree of capitalist development and arrangement of the class forces.[21]

Besides reevaluating the position of the workers, Soviet writers began to take a closer look at the role of the military and the intellectuals in the developing countries. Georgy Mirskii, a scholar at the Institute of World Economics and International Relations, called for more detailed study of the intelligentsia and the army, from whose ranks have come the "revolutionary and national democrats" in the developing area. Mirskii argued that the group of revolutionary leaders who were ruling in such countries as the UAR, Ghana, Guinea, and Mali could not be called members of the bourgeoisie, but was composed of progressive elements of the intelligentsia and the army, and the men who make up the class were truly striving to build the foundations for future socialism.[22]

In addition to reconsidering their views of the class structure and leadership of the nationalist regimes in the Third World, Soviet theoreticians began to analyze the economic policies of these leaders. According to the "national democracy" doctrine, only the active influence of the Communists would lead to the introduction of socialist programs in the developing countries. Domestic "progressive" forces were urged to bring pressure on their governments to initiate radical internal reforms. However, even without the existence of legal Communist parties, a number of African and Asian regimes did decide to select the noncapitalist path of development. For example, in discussions held in Moscow by the Institute of World Economics and International Affairs and published in its journal in 1964, Soviet scholars admitted that some developing countries had begun economic reforms which were aimed at both foreign and domestic capital. In these countries—especially Burma, the UAR and some African countries—the state sector was growing at the expense of the private sector of the economy. According to G. Akopian, "In a number of liberated countries of Asia and Africa not only have the principles of socialism been proclaimed, but the first practical steps to the realization of these principles have been made."[23] One Soviet writer went so far as to say: "If the conditions for proletarian leadership have not yet matured, the historic mission of breaking with capitalism can be carried out by elements close to the working class."[24]

Not only did the Soviets reassess the class structures of the developing countries and the role of the nationalist leaders in economic and political development, but they also shifted their attitudes toward the nationalist versions of socialism which have been expounded throughout Africa and Asia. As noted above, as late as 1962, Professor Ivan Potekhin had strongly condemned those who proposed a "third path" for the new states. However, more recent Soviet writing on the noncapitalist path of development has emphasized the progressive influence of such doctrines. After speaking of the great differences between scientific socialism and the various forms of national socialism, A. Avakov noted:

> However, all this cannot hide the fact that in the socialist doctrines of a nationalist type there are definite revolutionary and progressive beginnings. The existence of principles found at the heart of these doctrines can assist national progress, the development of revolutions of liberation, and their transition to the stage of national democracy.[25]

Another Soviet writer argued that the ideologies of the developing states are not the most important factor in evaluating their progressive nature. "Actually the real content of any revolution is determined . . . solely by the objective socio-economic content of the changes (chiefly in settling the question of ownership of the means of production) which the revolution brings about."[26] Revolutionary practice in such countries as the UAR, Burma, and Mali is said to be ahead of the development of ideological doctrine: "Social and economic reforms in these countries are often deeper and more radical than the theories 'elucidating' them. . . ."[27]

Since the Soviet reassessment of the nationalist regimes has led to the conclusion that these regimes are truly progressive, even though they have banned local Communist organizations, the Soviets have decided that their interests would be better served by not calling for independent Communist movements, but rather by having local Communists operate inside the single-party regimes. In late 1963 and early 1964, even before the new doctrines had been fully enunciated, the Algerian Communist party supported the establishment of a non-Communist, one-party state in Algeria. Ben Bella was declared a "hero of the Soviet Union" and the local Communists accepted positions within the nationalist government.[28] In April 1965, the Egyptian Communist party officially dissolved itself and declared that Nasser's single party was the only organization capable of carrying out the revolution in the UAR.[29] Obviously the leaders in Moscow had decided that the best means to maintain and increase Soviet influence in the Third World— at least in the "revolutionary" countries—was by infiltrating nationalist parties with individual Communists. This course has been followed in Algeria and the UAR, as well as in Mali, Guinea, and Ghana (until the 1966 overthrow of Nkrumah). European and African Communists have been sent to man training schools for party and labor leaders which have been constructed with Soviet aid. Soviet and East European economic and technical advisers have played important roles in economic planning in these countries.

However, even though the Soviets have been relatively successful in implementing this new program, they have found that the instability of the domestic political situation in many developing countries is a threat to the continued success of their policy. In recent years four of the leaders to whom the Soviets had given the most economic and political support were overthrown by military coups—Ben Bella, Keita, Nhrumah, and Sukarno. The Soviets now realize the weakness of a policy which is based largely on favorable relations with a single charismatic leader and are now encouraging the development of "vanguard" parties which would be able to institutionalize the revolutionary policies of individual leaders, even if the leader himself were to disappear. The Communist interpretation of Nkrumah's overthrow emphasizes the "absence of a well-organized vanguard party capable of rallying the masses to the defense of their gains."[30] Georgy Mirskii has written of the necessity for the Egyptian leaders "to train a new cadre of officials and extend the political education of the masses." He argues that a mass party like the Arab Socialist Union, although it has played a positive role in Egyptian life, "cannot act as a politically conscious vanguard. Socialist development is inconceivable without a party, without ideological work among the masses. That is precisely what the Egyptian revolution lacks, for from the very outset its leaders came from the middle strata, which had no social platform, and were inspired solely by the ideals of 'pure' nationalism."[31]

Since the proletariat is extremely weak in most African and Asian countries, "socialist consciousness' must be stimulated from the outside, with the cooperation of the international proletariat—i.e., of the Soviet Union and other Communist countries. Developing countries should look to the example of other backward regions which have made the transition from feudalism to socialism, such as Soviet Central Asia and Mongolia.[32] The major thrust of Soviet policy in the "progressive" states of the Third World is now support for revolutionary regimes. No longer do the Soviets call for freedom for Communist party activities as a sign of a progressive regime, as they did when the doctrine of "national democracy" was in vogue.[33] According to the more recent view, the only political prerequisites for progressive regimes are internal democracy for progressive elements, not necessarily Communists, and a strengthening of ties with the socialist countries.[34]

However, although most Soviet writers have emphasized the progressive nature of the "revolutionary democracies" during the past few years, the importance of these countries in the anti-imperialist movement, and the gains that the noncapitalist path of development was making in the creation of the prerequisites for socialism throughout Asia and Africa, a number of Soviet scholars have begun to question the assumptions underlying such optimistic statements. These questions have been based on increasing empirical data concerning conditions in the developing countries and the continuing failure of Soviet expectations to be fulfilled.

We have already seen that Gordon and Fridman have criticized the view which lumped the "modern proletariat" and "the majority of agricultural and artisan-handcraft workers" into one group, for "such an approach could produce an incorrect evaluation of the degree of capitalist development and arrangement of class forces."[35] Other writers have also argued that the class structure and other conditions in the developing countries are not nearly so favorable for a proletarian revolution as most earlier Soviet writers had assumed.[36]

In the area of requirements for economic development, Soviet writers have also made a number of significant changes. In the late fifties, most Soviet writers saw in industrialization a panacea for the ills of the developing countries. According to one economist, the development of heavy industry is essential for real independence, and those who warn against too much industrialization are those "who wish to perpetuate the economic backwardness of the underdeveloped countries and their dependence on imperialism. . . ."[37] Full industrialization was seen as the only means to improve the lot of the people. Later Soviet writers have become much more realistic in their appraisals of the possibilities for industrialization which exist in the developing countries. In a discussion in 1964, R. Ul'ianovskii admitted that many underdeveloped countries are unable to develop a complete industrial complex.[38] Others have noted the importance of agricultural development and the expansion of small handicraft industries as a means of getting production moving.[39] One writer has gone so far as to state that it would run counter to the urgent needs of developing countries to "renounce a purposeful use of the private sector in solving the serious technical and economic tasks of building up the productive forces. . . ."[40]

Other Soviet writers—especially since Khrushchev's removal from power—have seriously questioned general Soviet conceptions of the developing countries. First of all, some have questioned whether the national-liberation movement will automatically turn into a socialist movement, as most earlier writers had assumed. N. A. Simoniia has argued that the existence of the Communist camp can aid bourgeois leaders in the Third World as well as aid the revolutionary democrats. He has maintained that domestic social policy and the leadership of the workers is essential for the creation of socialism. In most of the developing countries, this is not the case and "one cannot speak of 'growing into socialism' as the dominant or general tendency in the development of national liberation revolutions."[41]

This is perhaps the frankest statement of the trend toward realism in Soviet writing on the developing countries since Khrushchev's fall. However, the trend began in the early sixties as the Soviets acquired more information about actual conditions in the Third World. As we have noted, the emphasis in most Soviet writing until 1964 was on the international importance of the national liberation movement as a part of the world revolutionary process. However, by 1964, even Khrushchev had begun to de-emphasize the priority granted to developing countries in Soviet policy and to speak of the construction of socialism and communism as the "primary international duty" of the socialist countries.[42]

Along with the new tendency to de-emphasize the role of the developing countries in Soviet priorities has come a realization among some writers that "scientific socialism" is not winning in Afro-Asia. They have pointed out that the noncapitalist path of development is not the same as the socialist path, but a lower stage of development, and that the most progressive of the developing countries are merely at the lower level.[43] In an analysis of the class struggle in the developing countries, D. Zarine noted the passivity of the semiproletarian groups in the countryside, the narrow-mindedness and chauvinism of the rural petty bourgeoisie, and the inadvisability of relying on "sudden action by the revolutionary forces or the carelessness of the reactionaries" to bring about rapid social revolution. According to Zarine, the "most important and difficult task of the revolution there is to prevent imperialist intervention."[44] This is far from the optimism expressed by most Soviet writers ten years ago.

Although a number of Soviet writers have criticized the optimism of the official Soviet line on developing countries during the past few years, the majority still emphasizes the progressive aspects of events in the "revolutionary democracies."[45] In spite of the numerous changes in emphasis in Soviet writings on the Third World, one thread has remained constant—the desire to expand Soviet contacts with and influence in the newly independent countries. This desire has been expressed, not only by increased diplomatic and economic relations, but also by the shifts in theoretical statements as outlined in the present study. The Soviets have been unwilling to antagonize leaders who are favorable to them by calling for the expansion of local Communist activity, but have rather called upon local Communists to work within the framework of existing political units. The Soviets have also shown that they are aware of the discrepancies between Marxist-Leninist dogma and the realities of the Third World and have modified dogma to fit more closely with reality. Their initial optimism has been tempered, and they now fear the revival of "reactionary influences" throughout much of the Third World. After more than fifteen years of concerted activity throughout Asia and Africa—and a shorter period in Latin-America—the Soviets can look upon significant success in the expansion of their influence, but they have not achieved—nor are they likely to achieve—their stated goal of the creation of a Communist commonwealth throughout the developing countries.

NOTES

1. From 271.8 million rubles to 2,037.1 million rubles. See USSR, Ministerstvo vneshnei torgovli, *Vneshniaia torgovlia SSSR,* Moscow: Vneshtorgizdat, for the appropriate years.

2. In September 1969 the Soviet Union had diplomatic representation in twenty-six of thirty-three non-Communist countries in Asia, including the Middle East; in thirty of thirty-nine independent African countries; and in eight Latin American countries, excluding Cuba. See U.S. Department of State, Bureau of Intelligence and Research, *Soviet Diplomatic Relations and Representation,* Research Memorandum, RSE-70, September 9, 1969.

3. E. M. Zhukov, "Voprosy natsional'-no-osvoboditel'noi bor'by posle Vtoroi Mirovoi Voiny," *Voprosy ekonomiki,* no. 9 (1949), pp. 57–58.

4. See, for example, V. A. Maslennikov, ed., *Uglublenie krizisa kolonial'noi sistemy imperializma posle Vtoroi Mirovoi Voiny,* Moscow: Gospolitizdat, 1953, pp. 43–44.

5. G. I. Mirskii, "Tvorcheskii marksizm i problemy natsional'no-osvoboditel'nykh stran," *Mirovaia ekonomika i mezhdunarodnye otnosheniia,* no. 2 (1963), p. 63.

6. In a speech before the Indonesian Parliament in 1960, N. S. Khrushchev stated that the major bond between the Soviet Union and the nonsocialist states of Asia and Africa was a "community of strivings and interests of our peoples concerning the fundamental problems of life . . . carrying on a decisive struggle for peace and peaceful coexistence." N. S. Khrushchev, *O vneshnei politike Sovetskogo Soiuza 1960 god,* Moscow: Gospolitizdat, 1961, I, 147.

7. See, for example, C. P. Zadorozhnii, *OON i mirnoe sosushchestvovanie gosudarstv,* Moscow: Gospolitizdat, 1958, p. 10.

8. The national bourgeoisie was now viewed as a positive force. See, for example, G. M. Gak, "Marksistsko-leninskaia teoriia revoliutsii i sovremennoe istoricheskoe razvitie,"

Voprosy filosofii, no. 5 (1958), p. 11.

9. See the excellent study of recent Soviet analyses by R. A. Yellon, "The Winds of Change," *Mizan*, IX (1967), 51–57, 155–73.

10. David J. Dallin, *Soviet Foreign Policy after Stalin*, Philadelphia: Lippincott, 1961, p. 523.

11. B. Ponomarev, "O gosudarstve natsional'noi demokratii," *Kommunist*, no. 8 (1961), pp. 43–45.

12. The discussions which were held in Leipzig in May 1959 were published as "The National Bourgeoisie and the Liberation Movement," *World Marxist Review*, II, no. 8 (1959), 61–81, and no. 9 (1959), 66–81.

13. N. S. Khrushchev, "For New Victories for the World Communist Movement," *World Marxist Review*, IV, no. 1 (1961), 21. Emphasis added.

14. G. Starushenko, "The National-Liberation Movement and the Struggle for Peace," *International Affairs*, no. 10 (1963), p. 5.

15. Ivan I. Potekhin, "Nekotorye problemy Afrikanistiki v svete reshenii XXII s"ezda KPSS," *Narody Azii i Afriki*, no. 1 (1962), p. 15.

16. G. Mirskii, "Whither the Newly Independent Countries," *International Affairs*, no. 12 (1962), p. 25.

17. See, for example, Khrushchev's statement at the Twenty-first CPSU Congress in 1959. In Leo Gruliow, ed., *Current Soviet Policies III: The Documentary Record of the Extraordinary 21st Communist Party Congress*, New York: Columbia University Press, 1960, p. 60. Three years later Khrushchev voiced a strong Soviet complaint about the treatment of Communists in developing countries: "Unfortunately, truths which are fully obvious to us Communists are not always acceptable to many leaders of the national-liberation movement. . . . Under contemporary conditions the national bourgeoisie has not yet exhausted its progressive role. However, as contradictions between the workers and other classes accumulate, it reveals more and more an inclination for agreement with reaction.

"Leaders who really hold dear the interests of the people and of the toiling masses will have to understand sooner or later that only by relying on the working class . . . can victory be achieved. . . . Either they will understand this, or other people will come after them who will understand better the demands of life." *Pravda*, May 19, 1962, pp. 2–3.

18. Richard Lowenthal, "Russia, the One-Party Systems, and the Third World," *Survey*, no. 58 (January 1966), pp. 46–47. In this article Lowenthal gives an excellent analysis of the shifts in Soviet doctrine.

19. R. Ulianovskii, "Nekotorye voprosy nekapitalisticheskogo razvitiia osvobodivshikhsia stran," *Kommunist*, no. 1 (1966), pp. 113–14.

20. See, for example, I. I. Potekhin, *Afrika smotrit v budushchee*, Moscow: Izd. vost. Lit., 1960, pp. 18–19.

21. L. Gordon and L. Fridman, "Osobennosti sostava i struktury rabochego klassa v ekonomicheski slaborazvitykh stran Azii i Afriki (na primere Indii i OAR)," *Narody Azii i Afriki*, no. 2 (1963), pp. 3–22. Translated in Thomas Thorton, ed., *The Third World in Soviet Perspective: Studies by Soviet Writers on Developing Areas*, Princeton: Princeton University Press, pp. 180–81. For a later study by the same authors see "Rabochii klass osvobodivshikhsia stran," *Mirovaia ekonomika i mezhdunarodnye otnosheniia*, no. 12 (1965), pp. 75–87, and no. 1 (1966), pp. 27–39.

22. G. I. Mirskii, "Tvorcheskii marksizm," p. 65. More recent Communist writings have reemphasized the potentially progressive nature of the military in developing countries. See, for example, A. Isken-

derov, "Problems and Judgments: The Army, Politics, and the People," *Izvestiia*, January 17, 1967, p. 2, translated in *Current Digest of the Soviet Press*, XIX, no. 3 (February 6, 1967), 9–10. Tigani Babiker, a Sudanese journalist on the staff of *Problems of Peace and Socialism*, has argued that the new generation of African military officers is drawn from the petty bourgeoisie and workers and peasants, has fought against colonialism, and is, therefore, "more likely to be imbued with hatred of imperialism, to find friends among the younger people, presently active in the revolutionary struggle, and to be more amenable to revolutionary ideas." "At the Cairo Seminar," *World Marxist Review*, X, no. 1 (1967), 54.

23. "Sotsializm, kapitalizm, slaborazvitye strany," *Mirovaia ekonomika i mezhdunarodnye otnoshenia*, no. 4 (1964), pp. 117, 119, and no. 6 (1966), p. 75. See, also, K. Ivanov, "National-Liberation Movement and Non-Capitalist Path of Development," *International Affairs*, no. 5 (1965), p. 61.

24. G. Mirskii, "The Proletariat and National Liberation," *New Times*, no. 18 (1964), pp. 8–9.

25. "Sotsializm, kapitalizm, slaborazvitye strany," no. 6, p. 66.

26. Ivanov, *op. cit.*, p. 65.

27. Tiagunenko, "Sotsialisticheskie doktriny obshchestvennogo razvitiia osvobodivshikhsia stran," *Mirovaia ekonomika i mezhdunarodnye otnosheniia*, no. 8 (1965), p. 85.

28. See Lowenthal, *op. cit.*, pp. 50–52 and V. Kaboshkin and Iu. Shchepovskii, "Alzhir: ot natsional'nogo osvobozhdeniia k sotsial'nomy," *Kommunist*, no. 16 (1963), pp. 115–19.

29. "Party Dissolved by Reds in Cairo," *New York Times*, April 26, 1965, p. 16.

30. Thierno Amath, "Some Problems of Tropical Africa," *World Marxist Review*, IX, no. 8 (1966), 33. One Soviet writer points to the examples of Mali and the UAR which are attempting to create vanguard parties inside the mass parties that have existed for a number of years. N. Gavrilov, "Africa: Classes, Parties and Politics," *International Affairs*, no. 7 (1966), pp. 43–44.

31. Georgy Mirskii, "United Arab Republic: New Stage," *New Times*, no. 48 (1965), p. 4.

32. G. F. Kim and P. Shastiko, "Proletarskii internatsionalizm i natsional'no-osvoboditel'yne revoliutsii," *Pravda*, September 14, 1966, p. 4.

33. See Khrushchev, "For New Victories," p. 21, and A. Sobolev, "National Democracy—The Way to Social Progress," *World Marxist Review*, VI, no. 2 (1963), 45.

34. I. Pronichev, "Nekapitalisticheskii put' razvitiia i ego mesto v istoricheskom protsesse," *Mirovaia ekonomika i mezhrunarodnye otnosheniia*, no. 12 (1966), pp. 7–8. A more recent and more explicit statement of this point is made by Y. Seleznyova: "Close alliance and cooperation with the Soviet Union and other Socialist countries . . . is an important condition for their [developing countries following a noncapitalist path] success." "Developing States and International Relations," *International Affairs*, no. 5 (1968), p. 72.

35. Gordon and Fridman, "Osobennosti sostava i struktury rabochego klassa," pp. 180–81.

36. See, for example, I. P. Iastrebova, ed., *Rabochii klass Afriki*, Moscow: Nauka, 1966, pp. 29–30.

37. G. Skorov, "Nekotorye ekonomicheskie voprosy raspada kolonial'noi sistemy," *Mirovaia ekonomika i mezhdunarodnye otnosheniia*, no. 4 (1958), p. 57.

38. "Sotsializm, kapitalizm, slaborazvitye strany," pp. 122–23.

39. O. Ul'rikh, "O gosudarstvennoi ekonomicheskoi politike v slaborazvitykh stranakh," *Mirovaia ekonomika i mezhdunarodnye otnosheniia*, no. 4 (1962), p. 98. For

a more recent argument in favor of an emphasis on agriculture and light industry, as well as heavy industry, see R. Andreisian and A. El'ianov, "Razvivaiushchiesia strany: diversifikatsiia i strategiia promyshlennogo razvitiia," *Mirovaia ekonomika i mezhdunarodnye otnosheniia*," no. 1 (1968), pp. 29–40.

40. V. Kondrat'ev, "Gana: vybor puti i preobrazovanie ekonomiki," *Mirovaia ekonomika i mezhdunarodnye otnosheniia*, no. 5 (1965), p. 54.

41. Simoniia points out that of the seventy-six states in Asia and Africa only four have elected communism and no more than seven are following a noncapitalist path of development. N. A. Simoniia, "O kharaktere natsional'no-osvoboditelnykh revoliutsii," *Narody Azii i Afriki*, no. 6 (1966), p. 14. For the earlier view, see G. F. Kim, who argued that "the national liberation movement" is a "constituent part of the world struggle of progressive forces for socialism and communism. . . ." "Oktiabr'skaia revoliutsiia i istoricheskie sub'by narodov Azii i Afriki," *Voprosy istorii*, no. 11 (1962), p. 21.

42. See *Pravda*, September 29, 1964, p.

1. Throughout 1965 and 1966 the Soviet press and Soviet ideologues continually referred to the international duty of building communism in the Soviet Union. See, for example, the editorial entitled "Zhiznenno neobkhodimoe delo," *Kommunist*, no. 5 (1965), p. 16, and a *Pravda* editorial of October 27, 1965, entitled "Vyshnii internatsional'nyi dolg stran sotializma."

43. See G. Mirskii, "On Noncapitalist Path of Development of Former Colonies," *Pravda, January* 31, 1965, p. 5, translated in *The Current Digest of the Soviet Press*, XVII, no. 5 (Feb. 24, 1965), 14. See also Pronichev, "Nekapitalisticheskii put' razvitiia," pp. 9–14.

44. D. Zarine, "Classes and Class Struggle in Developing Countries," *International Affairs*, no. 4 (1968), pp. 51–52.

45. See, for example, the article by Y. Seleznyova, *op. cit.*, p. 72, in which the author argues that the noncapitalist path "is regarded as a means for creating certain socio-material conditions which will pave the way for the transition to Socialism. This is the political, economic and ideological goal of progressive regimes."

8

JAAN PENNAR
Columbia University

THE ARABS, MARXISM AND MOSCOW: A HISTORICAL SURVEY

No modern Soviet author writing on the Arabs has unearthed anything significant that Marx might have said on the subject. Neither do the works of Lenin provide any relief. Whenever the latter is quoted it relates to national liberation in general and not the Arab countries in particular. The only original early Soviet thinker on Islam and revolution, Sultan-Galiyev, has still to be rehabilitated from an indictment delivered by Stalin and is therefore not quotable in Soviet writings. It is nevertheless useful to review some of the early Soviet thinking on Islam, even though its relationship to the Arabs was marginal.

The October Revolution ignited national feelings among the minorities in Russia. Rather than see the country dismembered into a number of independent states, small and large, the Bolsheviks decided to ride out the crest of the wave by sheer demagoguery. A Declaration of the Rights of the Peoples of Russia was issued, calling for self-determination, to be followed shortly by a manifesto to "all the toiling Muslims of Russia and the Orient." Drafted by Stalin, then commissar of nationalities, the manifesto called on "all those whose mosques and shrines were destroyed, whose beliefs and customs were trampled under foot by the tsars and oppressors of Russia! From now on your

This article is reprinted with permission from *The Middle East Journal*, XXI (1968), 433–47.

158

customs and beliefs, your national and cultural institutions, are declared free and inviolable! Build your national life freely and un-
hindered." Overnight, even the mullahs became socialist.

Stalin's right-hand man in the People's Commissariat for the
Nationalities was Mir Said Sultan-Galiyev, editor of the journal
Zhizn' Natsional'nostei (Life of the Nationalities). The journal he
edited contains several articles he authored on the subject of Islam,
communism, and what is known today as the Third World. He also
wrote on these subjects elsewhere. As Alexandre Bennigsen, French
expert on Turkic studies, points out, the main objective of the Muslim
revolutionaries, such as Galiyev, was the national liberation of their
countries from foreign tutelage, Western or Russian.[1] The only way
this was to be accomplished was through a socialist revolution, but
without a class war. "Since almost all classes in Muslim society have
been oppressed formerly by the colonialists," writes Sultan-Galiyev,
"all are entitled to be called proletarian." Religious leaders were to be
laicized but Islam was not to be destroyed and only religious fanaticism
was to be done away with. Eventually, a Colonial International was to
be established, merging the "oppressed" peoples of the Third World.
Sultan-Galiyev and his associates had no use for the Comintern. If a
revolution were to succeed in, say, Britain, its "proletariat will go on
oppressing the colonies and pursuing the policy of the existing bourgeois government." Galiyev's thoughts are known to have influenced
some of the Algerian FLN leadership. In the following quote Galiyev
interpreted the political implications of Western attitudes towards
Islam to his Soviet readers. It might have some pertinence to the
events of today:

> If West European imperialism, [which] began its
> initial penetration into Muslim countries with the "Cru-
> sades," did assume lately the character of pure economic
> struggle, then this struggle is also regarded as a political
> battle, i.e., a battle with Islam as a whole. It could not be
> otherwise, since conceptually the Muslims regard the whole
> Islamic world, without distinguishing nationalities and
> races, as one inseparable and single whole.[2]

The Colonial International was nipped in the bud in 1920 when
the Third International took over the arrangements of an Eastern
congress which was held in Baku. Karl Radek was particularly active
in these arrangements, which he believed would arouse the Muslim
world against the West. Referred to officially as the First Congress of

the Peoples of the East, the Baku Congress was apparently at its most tumultuous during Gregory Zinoviev's address calling for a holy war against British imperialism. There were only three Arabs among the slightly fewer than 1,900 delegates; to them, perhaps, such an appeal would have made sense. It has been pointed out that the leading Comintern organizers of the Baku Congress—Radek, Zinoviev and Bela Kun—were Jewish.[3] Their sympathies obviously did not lie with Zionism, however, since the subsequently published manifesto, based on the resolutions adopted at the Baku Congress, condemns "Anglo-Jewish capitalists" who drove the Palestinian Arabs from their lands in order to transfer these lands to Jewish settlers. The purpose was obviously to divide and rule. English colonialism in Egypt, "Mesopotamia" and "Arabia" was also condemned. No holy war occurred, of course, and the Comintern shifted its emphasis back onto the European proletariat in the hope of achieving revolution there. Sultan-Galiyev lasted in his post until June 1923, when he was expelled from the party as a "bourgeois nationalist."[4] In his indictment Stalin accused Galiyev not only of pan-Turkism and pan-Islamism but also of contact with the *Basmachis*—anti-Soviet guerrillas in Turkestan who proved to be a headache for the Communists for several years to come. After a stretch in prison, Sultan-Galiyev eventually vanished in the Stalinist purges of the 1930s.

Chronologically, the Baku Congress was preceded by the Second Comintern Congress by a few months. The Baku Congress was to find ways of putting into effect the theses on the national and colonial question adopted by the Second Comintern Congress. These theses are significant since they reflect Lenin's views, frequently quoted and misquoted since, on national liberation. The theses call for a close alliance of all national and colonial liberation movements with Soviet Russia and refer to a "revolutionary liberation movement" apart from the Communists in backward and undeveloped countries. This does not mean that the Communists should lose their identity:

> The Communist International has the duty of supporting the revolutionary movement in the colonies and backward countries only with the object of rallying the constituent elements of the future proletarian parties— which will be truly communist and not only in name—in all the backward countries and educating them to a consciousness of their special task, namely, that of fighting against the bourgeois-democratic trend in their own nation. The

Communist International should collaborate provisionally
with the revolutionary movement of the colonies and backward countries, and even form an alliance with it, but it
must not amalgamate with it; it must unconditionally maintain the independence of the proletarian movement, even if
it is only in an embryonic stage.[5]

Lenin's motives at the time may have been tactical. An alliance
with Kemalist Turkey would lighten the burden of capitalist encirclement. The only reference to Arab countries in the theses was the
appeal to expose the deception practiced by the British in Palestine
"under the pretense of creating a Jewish State" there.

M. N. Roy, an Indian delegate to the Second Comintern Congress,
added refinements to the Lenin thesis suggesting, among other things,
that landless peasantry could provide a mass basis for Communist
activity and should not be sacrificed to the middle-class nationalist
movement. Roy was to expand upon this at the Fourth Comintern
Congress in 1922. With special reference to Kemalist Turkey he noted:
". . . the bourgeoisie and the feudal military clique . . . may take in
hand the leadership of the national revolutionary movement [but] then
the moment arrives when these people inevitably betray the movement
and become a counter-revolutionary force."[6]

During the same session another speaker, Ravenstein, reviewed
the situation in the Arab world and concluded that the international
proletariat welcomed the strivings of the Islamic peoples for liberation
from Western imperialism, even though it may not be directed against
hired slavery or private property. It was useful as long as it under-
mined the rule of European capital.[7] At the Fifth Comintern Congress
in 1924 Zinoviev suggested, in his opening address, that if the fused
national-revolutionary and proletarian movements were to win the
colonies for socialism before a strong native bourgeoisie had emerged,
the capitalist stage of development could be skipped over. Lenin has
been cited to the same effect. The Comintern continued to advocate
collaboration with national liberation movements until the Kuomintang
broke relations with the Chinese Communist party in 1927. The following year, at the Sixth Comintern Congress, the Communists decided to
go it alone. The Communists, stated the Congress, "are the only sure
bulwark of the colonial peoples in their struggle for freedom from the
imperialist yoke."[8]

In the Arab world this meant, according to the instructions of the
Congress, that the "national-reformist" character of the Wafd party in

Egypt should be exposed, that the Communists there should prevent the trade unions from falling into the hands of bourgeois nationalists, and that the agrarian question should be correctly formulated in that country. Somewhat exceptionally, the instructions for North African Communists called for a fighting bloc of different revolutionary organizations although "the leading part must be secured for the revolutionary proletariat."[9]

Failure of Communist policies in Germany and the rise of Hitler forced the Comintern to change its tactics again. As decreed by the Seventh Comintern Congress in 1935, from now on it was the united front of the working class against fascism. In the Third World there was parallel establishment of "an anti-imperialist people's front." Arab delegates at the Congress spoke of the isolation the 1928 Comintern decision of going it alone had caused.[10] In their opposition to the Wafd party, the Egyptian Communists had called upon the workers to remove themselves from any national movement. This, of course, fell on deaf ears and for a while the Egyptian Communist party was doomed to total inactivity. In Syria the Communists insisted on their own program at a congress for national liberation with the result that their influence was restricted to a small number of delegates. Arab Communists had even failed to pay lip service to Arab unity. The delegates concluded that the Arab national bourgeoisie could not be considered servile to imperialism nor would it necessarily capitulate to imperialism in the future. Soviet commentators, in reviewing these Arab viewpoints twenty years later, regarded the 1935 decisions of the Comintern as important forward steps. What benefits redounded to Arab Communist parties is not clear, however. They were, and remained, weak.

Communism in the Middle East was introduced at the Comintern's initiative. Until the middle 1920s, however, it was only the predominantly Jewish Palestine Communist party that showed any activity. Its chairman, Haim Auerbach, noted at a secret meeting (the party was illegal) in Tel Aviv in 1927:

> We were the only Communist front in the Arab Orient and in the absence of anybody else we had to pay attention to every question. All the duties in relation to the revolution fell on our shoulders. We had to look into matters relating to Syria, Egypt, and Islamic congresses in Cairo, Mecca and elsewhere.[11]

The Comintern showed considerable concern for establishing Arab-based parties. It sent its agents to Syria, where it had limited success in creating Communist cells. The founding date for the Syrian Communist party is 1924. It folded the first year because it was composed, reads a Comintern survey, only of intellectuals. It was reconstituted a short time later on a wider base, and a joint Communist party of Syria and Lebanon was founded in 1930. The Armenians played a major role in the party until 1934, when an Arab leadership took over. It is from that date on that Khalid Bakdash (although Kurdish by birth) began his meteoric rise to become the foremost Communist leader in the Arab world. Separate Syrian and Lebanese parties were set up in 1943. It might be of interest to note that the united front tactics recommended by the Seventh Comintern Congress failed to engage Arab nationalist aspirations. Michel Aflaq, one of the founders of the Ba'th (Arab Resurrection) party in Syria, wrote that he stopped flirting with communism in 1936, because "the Syrian Communist Party became nothing more than an executive tool of its French parent Party and of the French Government in general."[12] Marxist study circles appeared in 1924 in Iraq and a Communist party was established in that country in 1927. Between the wars the Iraqi Communist party was small and largely student-based.

In Egypt, revolutionary socialist cells had already put in their appearance in 1918; a socialist party was founded a year or two later and renamed, in 1922, the Communist party of Egypt. The party was plagued, throughout most of the interwar years, by minority leadership (Greeks, Jews, Armenians, and Copts), government repression, and faulty tactics, which made it oppose the popular national liberation slogans of the Wafd party. It lost all effectiveness during the 1930s, and it was not until 1940 that the Communists again became active in Egyptian politics, this time as the left wing of the Wafd party, within whose ranks they remained until 1948.[13]

The situation was not much better in North Africa where Communist activities were more French than Arab. The French Communist party was, nevertheless, active in national liberation matters and backed the first North African Congress, which was held in Paris in 1924. At about the same time the French Communist groups in North Africa began recruiting from the indigenous population. In Algeria these ranks accounted for three hundred out of a total of twelve hundred in 1924–25.[14] This was in response to the directives of the Fourth Congress which read: "The creation of separate European Communist organizations in the colonies (Egypt, Algeria) is a concealed form of colonialism and only helps imperialist interests."[15] An Algerian Communist party came into being in 1936, although French tutelage continued.

The Stalinist era, the rise of Hitler, the Second World War and its consequences put a temporary damper on Communist attempts to convert the Middle East to communism. *Realpolitik* preceded ideology and Soviet arms penetrated the Arab World ahead of new Soviet theories on national liberation. As Walter Z. Laqueur put it: " . . . the Soviet reorientation in the Middle East in 1954–1955 did not come as the result of any startling new discovery made by Soviet Middle Eastern experts, nor did a new Marxist-Leninist analysis *precede* the change. The Middle East experts modified their approach after, not before, the politicians did. They continued to write in a critical vein on the Arab national movement for months after Shepilov had professed feelings of friendship for Colonel Nasser. If there had been a Leninist reappraisal of the Middle Eastern situation, it was carried out by the diplomats and the Presidium rather than by the experts—who followed a lead given from above."[16]

At the Twentieth Party Congress in Moscow in 1956, party stalwart Otto Kuusinen drew attention to the "sectarian errors" of Soviet ideologues in their evaluation of the role of Gandhi, who prior to the Congress had been regarded as a reactionary. Kuusinen also insisted that the theses of the Sixth Comintern Congress on the national liberation question be overhauled as also showing traces of sectarianism. The new directives rehabilitated many national political figures of the East.[17] This just about sums up the extent of the ideological concessions granted by Moscow to national liberation movements in the 1950s.

The 1960 Moscow Conference of Eighty-one Communist Workers' Parties is generally credited with putting forward the thesis of "non-capitalist development of the national democratic revolution." The Chinese Communists, incidentally, approved of this concept at the time but later began criticizing it. Basically, the "national democratic state," as explained in an article by B. Ponomarev in *Kommunist* a year later, was one where political action was based on the united front tactics wherein the Communists joined hands with other "progressive forces" in "defending its political and economic independence and struggling against imperialism," where a state sector of industry was being established and where "dictatorial and despotic methods of government" were being rejected. Somehow, no Arab country qualified, since Communists were being persecuted both in Egypt and Iraq at the time.

Concern for local Communists, however, became secondary as the

UAR and the newly independent Algeria began legislating socialist measures in the early 1960s. Encouraged by similar developments elsewhere in the world, e.g., Ghana, Soviet theoreticians in effect abandoned "national democracy" as a useful concept and switched to "revolutionary democracy," a concept which permitted Third World countries to progress along the noncapitalist path to eventual socialism and communism without Communist leadership, at least initially.[18] The keynote was struck by Karen Brutents, a leading Soviet theoretician on the subject, in an article which appeared in *Kommunist* toward the end of 1964:

> . . . in many former colonies and semicolonies, socialist development is both possible and necessary before class stratification has become sufficiently pronounced. Under such conditions, when . . . the proletariat has not yet developed into a leading force in social development, the intermediate strata, namely the peasantry, the lower urban classes and the democratic intelligentsia, acquire political independence and thus assume a particularly active role. The revolutionary democracy becomes their spokesman.[19]

Thus, to the FLN in Algeria and the ASU (Arab Socialist Union) in Egypt was ascribed a "national revolutionary" role as the world moved, in Soviet eyes, closer to socialism. As if in reciprocation for this vote of confidence, Egyptian Communists were released from prison and the Algerian Communists were invited to join the FLN. Communist parties as such were dissolved in both countries. Not all Arab Communists, however, took to this *coup de grace.*

At an Arab Communist meeting in Vienna in 1964, Nasser and the then Algerian leader Ben Bella were attacked as dictators. The final communique, however, favorably appraised Algerian developments and was hopeful about the Arab Socialist Union's ability to "permit the UAR to march towards socialism." But Khalid Bakdash, the doyen of Arab Communists and general secretary of the Syrian party, could not restrain himself from writing in the *World Marxist Review* the following year that "we do not consider it permissible to go so far as to deny the role of the Communist parties and to call for their dissolution."[20]

The mid-1960s saw the debate spreading to Soviet theoretical journals as well. One difficulty was that the officer class was the vanguard of the revolution in Egypt and, to a certain degree, in Syria. These revolutionary democrats were promptly dubbed "officer patriots" and a quotation was dug up in which Marx purportedly spoke of the patriotic role the native army played during the Sepoy Revolt in India. The background of the officer class was also brought into play. In Syria the upper classes refused to serve the French during the mandate. As a result, most graduates of the Homs Military Academy came from poor families and had chosen the military as the only way in which they could advance. This presumably assured their proletarian purity. After the Ghanaian army had ousted Nkrumah, further refinements were added to the army's revolutionary role. Writing in *Izvestia* in 1967, A. Iskenderov suggests that while a revolutionary movement can arise and develop without an advanced political party, such a party is needed to consolidate the victory of the revolution and the army cannot take its place. Furthermore, Karen Brutents asserts:

> . . . it was not the army of the Egyptian monarchy that carried out the revolution; on the contrary, it was the revolutionary forces that established their control over the army, virtually changing its nature and leading it in the attack against the reactionary and anti-national authority. *It was in the army that the revolution started and scored its first victory.* [Emphasis in the original.][21]

This sort of sophistry did not fit the facts. Reviewing some of the reasons for the Arab defeat in 1967, two Soviet journalists reporting from Cairo wrote that while the renewal of the officer corps went on during the years of revolution, it had not reached the top military leadership. Then, an officer-businessman type had emerged, creating a military bourgeoisie in the country. What is more, "far from all the important bureaucrats are 100 per cent socialists. How could they carry out a socialist policy? Thus far there is no answer to this."[22] The same writers note in a later article: "The middle classes of the UAR where many of the leaders of the Egyptian revolution had their origin are notorious for their inconsistency."[23]

Even before the June 1967 Arab-Israeli war, some pessimism crept into the Soviet theoretical formulation on Third World socialism. Broadly, Soviet theoreticians on the subject could be divided into two categories which, for the sake of convenience, could be described as the liberal and the conservative factions. The liberals have the upper hand in the more popular journals (*Mirovaia ekonomika i mezhdunarodnye otnosheniia* and *Aziia i Afrika segodnia*), while the conservative stronghold is a slightly more obtuse scholarly journal (*Narody Azii i Afriki*). The latter began challenging some of the positions taken by the former and the debate was on. Some of the points debated deal

with the "noncapitalist path," whether it will necessarily lead to socialism, and the role of the working class. As one conservative writer, R.
G. Landa, put it:

> Whether or not the noncapitalist development will lead to
> socialism depends in the first order on the operating posi-
> tions, the level of consciousness and organization of the
> working class. . . . The participation of broad masses of
> people in the realization of these goals will mean that an
> important step has been taken towards socialism.[24]

The liberals have since become more circumspect. One of them,
V. L. Tiagunenko, assures his readers: "The establishment of a vanguard party is an indispensable condition for the national-liberation
revolution developing into a socialist one."[25] In another article Tiagunenko describes such a vanguard party as conversant in Marxist-Leninist theory, but still maintains that the revolutionary development in
such countries as the UAR, Algeria, and Syria proves that it is possible
to move toward socialism in the absence of direct proletarian leadership as long as the revolutionary democrats rely upon the world system
of socialism.[26] And another writer, in *Pravda,* goes on to define the
"noncapitalist path":

> It is an alternative to capitalism. In the final analysis, it leads
> to the formation of a working class where there is none or
> where it is weak and to the strengthening of its important
> role in public life. All this takes place not on a bourgeois
> but on an anticapitalist basis, although the bourgeois ele-
> ments, with the striving for the accumulation of capital, as
> well as the pressure of petty-bourgeois sentiments, offer
> stubborn resistance.[27]

In any event, adds Tiagunenko, the "growing" of a national-
democratic revolution into a socialist one may take a few months in
some countries, as was the case with Cuba, and in others—several
years.[28] How many years is anybody's guess. A conservative commentator, N. A. Simoniia, surveys Asia and Africa and finds that, with the
possible exception of the UAR, Syria, Algeria, Burma, Mali, and
Guinea, in all other countries there has actually been—fairly rapid in
some countries, and slow in others—an evolution along the capitalist
road. For these reasons, he concludes, one cannot speak of "growing
into socialism" as the dominant or general tendency in the development
of national liberation revolutions.[29]

In the fall of 1966 the editorial boards of the *World Marxist Review*, published in Prague, and *Al-Taliah* (The Vanguard), published in Cairo, held a joint seminar in Cairo on "Africa—National and Social Revolution." Leftist and Communist delegations from twenty-two African countries were in attendance. The seminar had originally been scheduled to take place in Ghana. There was some trouble in Cairo, too. Four of the Egyptian organizers of the seminar were arrested three weeks before its start by the Egyptian Security Police. These included Lutfi al-Khuli, editor-in-chief of *Al-Taliah*. Upon the intervention of President Nasser, who also sent a greeting to the seminar from India, the four were set free. The seminar dealt largely with the difficulties, rather than the successes, of liberation movements in Africa. Aleksandr Sobolev, executive secretary of the *World Marxist Review*, set the tone. His speech was pragmatic and reflected the liberal line of Soviet theories on national liberation. Some of the remarks of Arab delegates are also pertinent.

Fuad Mursi of the UAR suggested that in his country the leading role is currently played by the small bourgeoisie and its spokesmen—the revolutionary intellectuals—and that the working class will not be able to occupy a leading position until "the peasant masses and revolutionary intellectuals recognize it as the leader."[30] Lutfi al-Khuli believed that "revolutionary parties in the countries which had recently gained independence should have the organization forms and tactics and the strategy suggested by the actual conditions in the particular country."[31] We are bringing about today in Africa, he continued, "a great political, libertarian and social revolution, at heart a radically different reality than the societies in Russia, China and Eastern and Western Europe. Our revolution is of an ambivalent character and the most recent."[32] He also added, however, that several of the revolutionary parties are more like clubs for revolutionary intellectuals who enjoy listening to their own voices and are not in tune with realities in their own countries. The UAR, Mali, Tanzania, the Congo Republic (Brazzaville), and Algeria were qualified at the seminar as bastions of progress in Africa. The meeting agreed with the view of Ali Yata, first secretary of the Moroccan Communist party, that these countries are in the forefront of the African revolution and that it is the "paramount" duty of every genuine revolutionary to support and defend them. There were no Chinese Communists or their supporters attending the seminar.

Ali Yata caused something of a sensation shortly before the seminar when the Soviet publication *Aziia i Afrika segodnia* (Asia and

Africa Today) reprinted an article of his on Islam. There were shades of Sultan-Galiyev in that piece of writing. The goals of socialism, wrote Ali Yata, are not contradicted by Islam. "I think," he continues, "that the Prophet Muhammad, like Moses and Jesus Christ, was a great social reformer."[33] At this time, he continued, Islam expressed, both subjectively and objectively, the feelings of community among Muslims, their solidarity and their aspirations for independence and progress. Soviet writers had previously pointed out that Arab Communists, particularly those from the Maghrib, felt that the goals of socialism could be attained under the sign of the crescent, but Yata's statement is the strongest on the subject to date. At any rate, the Soviets do not seem to be too worried: "As illiteracy is liquidated and the general cultural level is raised, the people will understand that the building of a socialist society is impossible under conditions where Islam and religious prejudices prevail."[34]

Arab Communist leaders met again in May 1967. The published statements indicate minor concern for the impending Arab-Israeli war.[35] Rather, the concern was with Mao Tse-tung and imperialism in general. The statements also approve of the "profound social and economic transformations" that have been carried out in the UAR, Syria, and Algeria, which are referred to as "liberated" Arab states, and pledge the support of Communists in defending, strengthening, and broadening these gains as these countries move along the path towards socialism. An appeal is made to Algeria, however, to have those "progressive forces" not now participating in the government join hands with those that are. Boumedienne (Bu-Midyan), it will be recalled, ousted the Communists from the FLN upon his assumption of power. Exiled, the Algerian Communists set up an Algerian Popular Resistance Party (ORP—*Organisation de Resistance Populaire*) which has been feuding with the FLN. In this feud, the Algerian Communists must have had some support from Moscow, since the radio facilities of the clandestine "Voice of the Iraqi People" have been made available to them to propagate their own views, which run counter, of course, to FLN. The May 1967 meeting also discussed the imprisonment of one thousand Communists in Iraq but failed to mention that there is a feud among the Communists in that country.

The Iraqi Communist party has had a checkered history. Factionalism was nothing new. During the 1940s it grew to be one of the largest parties in the Middle East. Repressed by the monarchy, the party sought to make good under the regime of General Kassem but failed to find a proper balance between the contending forces within and without. When Kassem was killed and his regime overthrown, the Communists suffered serious persecution. Sino-Soviet polemics serve best to illustrate the recent fate of the Iraqi party. In the 1964 Open Letter dispute the Chinese Communists had the following to say:

> The comrades of the Communist party of Iraq were once full of revolutionary ardor. But acceptance of Khrushchev's revisionist line was forced on them by outside pressure, and they lost their vigilance against counter-revolution. . . . In the armed counter-revolutionary *coup d'état*, leading comrades heroically sacrificed their lives, thousands of Iraqi Communists and revolutionaries were massacred in cold blood, the powerful Iraqi Communist party was dispersed, and the revolutionary cause of Iraq suffered a grave setback. This is a tragic lesson in the annals of proletarian revolution, a lesson written in blood.[36]

To which Suslov replied a few weeks later:

> How Peking understands proletarian solidarity can be judged by the CPC Central Committee's attitude toward the Baathist nationalists' repression of Salam Adil and other leaders of the Communist party of Iraq. In conversations with foreign delegations, the Chinese leaders rejoiced openly and maliciously at the brutal murder of the Iraqi comrades. Immediately after the Baath takeover they began to seek contacts with the assassins. As has now become clear, the Chinese representatives in Iraq wanted to take advantage of the fact that the Iraqi Communist party had become leaderless to create their own schismatic group there.[37]

But even as the decimated Iraqi party tried to rebuild itself, the clandestine "Voice of the Iraqi People" carried a statement by the party (dated September 30, 1967) which denounced an "opportunist renegade" group in the party for physically assaulting some of the party leaders, stealing party property, and attempting to kidnap a top leader. The group was allegedly led by a "renegade" number of the Central Committee.

The 1967 statements on the meeting of the Arab Communist leaders also contain a complaint about the "dismissal" of "progressive forces" in Sudan. The Sudanese Communist party was banned in December 1965 and its eleven deputies were ousted from the National

Assembly. The ban was adjudged as unconstitutional by the Sudanese High Court ruling a year later but the government has defied the ruling. The Sudanese Communist party was the only legal party in the Arab world in recent years. The Communist party of Syria, however, seems to enjoy all the benefits of legality without actually so being.

Party membership figures for the Arab countries are only available in Western estimates and therefore are not too reliable. For instance, party membership in Iraq is variously estimated at anywhere from two thousand to fifteen thousand. It is safe to assume, however, that there is no major Arab country without a hard core of at least one thousand party members. In any event, the Communists do not represent a mass movement among the Arabs. But Lenin proved that the party's strength lies in its organization and discipline and not in the number of its followers. Whether the Arab Communists can live up to Lenin's dicta is another matter.

The 1967 statements conclude with an appeal to respect the rights and democratic freedoms of the working class, to create conditions which would provide for its initiative and give it the opportunity to participate in industrial management and in bringing about reforms. A tall order from a small minority!

The 1967 statements on the meeting of the Arab Communist leaders were published in *Partiinaia zhizn'* on the eve of the Arab-Israeli war. What changes the war wrought in Soviet views on national liberation are none too clear but it would seem that for lack of an alternative the prewar views prevail. *Realpolitik*, of course, dictates the presence of friendly relations with Arab states formerly described as "reactionary." The war itself is cast in terms of national liberation theory. As stated by Brezhnev: "The essence of the Near East crisis consists in the antagonism between the forces of imperialism and the forces of national independence, democracy and social progress."[38] Fuad Nassar, the first secretary of the Jordanian Communist party, embroidered upon the theme in explaining that the conflict was not between Arab and Jew, the Arab states and Israel, but a repetition, in another form, of the 1956 tripartite aggression with the same aim of overthrowing the progressive regimes in the UAR and Syria, and sabotaging the progressive march of the Arab peoples.[39] The same line was echoed by the Moscow-approved wing of the Israeli Communist party, whose membership is largely Arab. But Meir Wilner, leader of the Israeli Communist party, also criticized "certain Arab countries" for having denied Israel's right to exist and for having permitted the sending of Palestinian commandos into Israel; this "has served the imperialists and the Israeli leaders as a pretext for their aggression." *Pravda* omitted this particular reply when it republished the original interview Wilner had granted to *Unitá*, organ of the Italian Communist party.[40] Be that as it may, the Soviets are obviously concerned with future developments in the area and what form they will take. One Soviet expert on the Middle East, Georgy Mirsky, sounded a cautiously optimistic note: "It is not excluded that the Left, socialist tendencies in the Arab world may gain ground as a result of the recent events."[41]

The way this should be brought about is outlined by Khalid Bakdash, the Syrian Communist leader. The Moscow *Za rubezhom* (Abroad) republished an August 1967 article of his which originally appeared in the presumably clandestine Syrian party organ *Nidal al-Sha'b*. The first task is, according to Bakdash, Arab rearmament, and the second the strengthening of friendly relations with the Soviet Union and other socialist countries. This should be followed by a reevaluation of political work, particularly sloganizing. In this area the Arabs should not give vent to emotions, "engage in dexterous conversations" and push for slogans and appeals which cannot be realized. But a progressive Arab nationalist cannot, Bakdash continues, look to socialist countries merely for military and economic assistance. Such an approach is too narrow. There should be a united front on all major problems, and mutual suspicions between all Arab revolutionary forces should disappear. The Communists and other progressive forces throughout the Arab world should thus join hands. As for the Syrian Communists, they should strengthen party discipline so that they would be equal to the task. Bakdash's prescription is orthodox Marxism and just falls short of recommending immediate Communist takeover.

Egyptian Marxists, who conceded to Bakdash that their experience, i.e., dissolution of the party,[42] need not necessarily be extended to other Arab countries, do not seem to be as militant. "We have committed major errors," admitted one Egyptian Communist to a correspondent of *Jeune Afrique;* "we have been 'drooling' so much during the years because Nasser had permitted us to participate in the national life and had given us posts in editorial offices and the university that we have let ourselves become anaesthetized. Yes, the majority of us have become *embourgeoisés*. We have lost all contact with the masses and these, abandoned to themselves, are completely disorganized. The truth is that we are tired and not at all prepared to return to prison."[43]

Six Arab delegates from the UAR, Morocco, Syria, and Israel

participated in what might be called the Second Baku Congress in September 1967. The affair lacked the luster of the first and was more in the nature of a sideshow to various events taking place in the USSR in connection with the fiftieth anniversary celebrations of the October Revolution. The Soviet leadership sent a message stressing the "profound bond between the national liberation movement and the struggle of the working class for the socialist reconstruction of society."[44] Lenin's alleged emphasis on the East was overemphasized in the keynote address by V. Iu. Akhundov, first secretary of the Communist party of Azerbaidzhan. To quote Sultan-Galiyev in 1919: ". . . almost all the attention of the leaders of the revolution was directed towards the West."[45] And one Egyptian delegate, Lutfi al-Khuli, deviated from orthodox Marxism even more by setting forth that "scientific socialism today is not the theory of the proletariat alone, but has become a great and powerful magnet for wider popular forces, especially in countries struggling for national liberation."[46]

It might well be asked what is meant by "scientific socialism." In Soviet parlance it is nothing less than the road to communism. But when Gamal Abdel Nasser spoke of "scientific socialism" he had in mind not Marxism, but scientific methods, as opposed to anarchy. Soviet authors persist, however, in an attempt to find a common ground between socialism as they know it and as it is practiced and preached in Egypt. O. E. Tuganova quotes Nasser to the effect that "I believe in an Arab expression of Socialism rather than Arab Socialism. I believe that there is only one kind of Socialism."[47] The quotation is correct and is taken from Nasser's reply to a question at an Arab student conference in August 1966. What the Soviet author failed to do, however, is to quote Nasser's complete answer. Herewith is the remainder of the reply, as reported by *Al-Ahram* (August 9, 1966):

> . . . and socialism has its principles. There may be differences between us and the Communists and I have already stated this at the conference of Popular Forces. We do not have the dictatorship of the proletariat, but we speak of democracy for the working people as a whole. Also we recognize religions. We do not believe in a bloody class struggle to eliminate a class by violence or force; and there may be other details. But I believe that there is one socialism and the ways of implementing it might differ from place to place.

Nasser was probably in greater agreement with the Soviets on the causes of the June 1967 Arab-Israeli war since he, too, maintained that "the real aim was to crush the socialist revolution in Egypt."[48] And a settlement of the consequences of this war, as the Soviets would put it, is also uppermost in the Arab mind. Once a *modus vivendi* has been established, however, the problems posed by socialism in the Arab world will again come to the fore.

The Soviet Union has its own Middle East in Central Asia and the Caucasus. Every so often the Soviets point to these areas, suggesting that the Arabs take them as an example. But Soviet Turkestan is more like *Algérie française* and it is very doubtful indeed that the Arabs would want to exchange the *pieds noirs* for *pieds rouges*. In independent Algeria both have been kicked out. Had the Soviets listened to Sultan-Galiyev, it is likely that communism would have been a powerful force in the Middle East. As this survey has shown, however, communism has always been foreign to the Arab body politic. But Sultan-Galiyev may have triumphed in spite of the Soviets. The concepts of socialism in the Arab world today are closer to his thinking than to the thinking of those who remained to guide the Soviet ship of state, long after he had been thrown overboard.

NOTES

1. Alexandre Bennigsen and Chantal LeMercier-Quelquejay, *Islam in the Soviet Union*, New York: Praeger, 1967. Quotations from Sultan-Galiyev in this paragraph are to be found in the referenced volume.
2. *Zhizn' natsional'nostei*, no. 29 (127), December 14, 1921.
3. Ivar Spector, *The Soviet Union and the Muslim World, 1917–1958*, Seattle: University of Washington Press, 1959, p. 52.
4. I. V. Stalin, *Sochineniia*, vol. V, 1921–1923, Moscow, 1952, pp. 301–12.
5. Jane Degras, ed., *The Communist International, 1919–1963, Documents*, vol. I, 1919–1922, London, Toronto, New York: Oxford University Press, 1956, pp. 143–44.
6. *IV Vsemirnyi Kongress Kommunisticheskogo Internatsionala, Izbrannye doklady, rechi i rezo-*

liutsii, Moscow: Gosudarstvennoe izdatelstvo, n.d., p. 267.
7. *Ibid.*, p. 261.
8. Degras, *op. cit.*, vol. II, 1923–1928, p. 533.
9. *Ibid.*, p. 546.
10. B. M. Leibson, K. K. Shirinia, *Povorot v politike Kominterna*, Moscow: Mysl, 1965, p. 227.
11. John Batatu, "Some Preliminary Observations on the Beginnings of Communism in the Arab East," *Islam and Communism*, ed., Jaan Pennar, Munich–New York: Institute for the Study of the USSR, 1960, p. 57.
12. Cited in Patrick Scale, *The Struggle for Syria*, London, New York, Toronto: Oxford University Press, 1965, p. 150.
13. Cf. Walter Z. Laqueur, *Communism and Nationalism in the Middle East*, New York: Praeger, 1957, p. 43.

14. Degras, *op. cit.*, vol. II, 1923–1928, p. 247.
15. *Ibid.*, vol. I, 1919–1922, p. 393.
16. Walter Z. Laqueur, *The Soviet Union and the Middle East*, New York: Praeger, 1959.
17. For an analysis, see Georg A. von Stackelberg, " 'Peaceful Coexistence' Between the Communists and the National Bourgeoisie," *Bulletin* of the Institute for the Study of the USSR, VII, no. 7 (July 1960), 3–10.
18. Cf. Georg A. von Stackelberg, "The Soviet Concept of the Revolutionary Democratic State and its Political Significance," in *Bulletin* of the Institute for the Study of the USSR, XIII, no. 4 (April 1966), 3–13.
19. *Kommunist,* no. 17 (1964), p. 30.
20. *World Marxist Review,* VIII, no. 12 (December 1965), 17.
21. *International Affairs* (Moscow), no. 1 (1967), p. 25.
22. *Za rubezhom,* no. 27 (June 30–July 6, 1967), pp. 7–8; English translation in *Current Digest of the Soviet Press,* XIX, no. 26 (July 19, 1967), 6–8.
23. *New Times,* no. 39 (September 27, 1967), p. 9.
24. *Narody Azii i Afriki,* no. 6 (1966), p. 38.
25. *International Affairs* (Moscow), no. 5 (1967), p. 58.
26. *Mirovaia ekonomika i mezhdunarodnye otnosheniia,* no. 1 (1967), p. 13.
27. R. Ulianovskii in *Pravda,* April 15, 1966, p. 4.
28. *Aziia i Afrika segodnia,* no. 2 (1967), p. 4.
29. *Narody Azii i Afriki,* no. 6 (1966), pp. 16–17.
30. *World Marxist Review,* X, no. 3 (1967), 61.
31. Cited in *Mizan,* IX, no. 2 (March–April 1967), 62.
32. Cited in *Jeune Afrique,* no. 305 (November 13, 1966), p. 21.
33. *Aziia i Afrika segodnia,* no. 8 (1966), p. 10.
34. K. I. Grishechkin, "Socio-economic Changes in the UAR and Scientific Socialism," *Ekonomika Afriki* (Moscow, 1965), p. 25.
35. *Partiinaia zhizn',* no. 11 (June 1967).
36. *Peking Review,* no. 14 (April 3, 1964), p. 18.
37. "The Soviet-Chinese Polemic: Suslov Speech—II," *Current Digest of the Soviet Press,* XVI, no. 14 (April 29, 1964).
38. *Pravda,* June 7, 1967.
39. *World Marxist Review,* X, no. 8 (1967), 68.
40. Radio Liberty Research Paper CRD 388/67, Munich, July 11, 1967.
41. *New Times,* no. 28 (July 12, 1967), p. 6.
42. *World Marxist Review,* IX, no. 10 (1966), 52.
43. *Jeune Afrique,* no. 351 (October 1, 1967), p. 23.
44. *Bakinskii rabochii,* September 20, 1967.
45. *Zhizn' natsional'nostei,* no. 39 (October 12, 1919).
46. *Bakinskii rabochii,* September 23, 1967.
47. *International Affairs* (Moscow), no. 5 (1967), p. 63.
48. Radio Cairo, July 23, 1967.

9

ARTHUR JAN KLINGHOFFER

Rutgers University

(Camden)

THE SOVIET VIEW
OF AFRICAN SOCIALISM

The Soviet view of socialism in the African states is directly related to the Soviet Union's foreign policy toward this part of the world, to the theoretical framework within which Soviet scholars assess events in underdeveloped areas, and to the tactics which Moscow advocates for the Communists on the African continent. The Soviet view contributes to the evaluation of African socialism, its future evolution, and its relationship to Marxist-Leninist socialism.

A reader of Uri Ra'anan's article on "The Third World in Soviet Perspective," which appeared in the January-February 1965 issue of *Problems of Communism,* or of the transcript of the 1964 Moscow conference on underdeveloped areas, which appeared as a special supplement to the November 1964 issue of the *Mizan Newsletter,* will realize that the attitudes of Soviet Africanists toward socialism in Africa are not monolithic. However, there is generally a Soviet line on each fundamental issue, which sets up certain guidelines for analysis, and the scholars and political ideologues all adhere to it, expressing their own concepts only through the filling in of minor details. It is to this basic line that this study is primarily addressed.[1]

DOES SOCIALISM EXIST IN AFRICA?

The late Ivan Potekhin, who became the leading Soviet authority

This article is reprinted with revisions by permission from *African Affairs,* LXVII, no. 268 (1968), 197–208.

on Africa during the Khrushchevian era, argued that there could be no such thing as "African socialism," although he maintained that there may be an "African road to socialism."[2] By this, he meant that there is only one variety of socialism, "scientific," "true," or "Marxist-Leninist" in Soviet parlance. It has the same characteristics no matter where it is established and Africa cannot create a unique brand of African socialism. The African socialism proclaimed by many African leaders is therefore not really socialism.

On the other hand, the paths taken to achieve socialism do differ in various places. Which path is taken depends on the relationships between social classes in the given area and on how these classes stand vis-à-vis the seat of state power. Multiple roads to socialism are possible and Potekhin recognized a specifically African road. Therefore, according to Potekhin, Africa may have unique means of achieving socialism but there is no room for any explicitly African brand of socialism. He claimed that although African socialists and scientific socialists agree on the end that the exploitation of man by man must be eliminated, they disagree as to what type of society can bring this about: a singularly African society which is ostensibly socialist or a Marxist-Leninist socialist society built under African conditions.

Soviet observers depict Africa as a major battleground in the struggle between bourgeois and socialist ideologies, but recognize the powerful attraction of nationalism as a complicating factor. Forever seeking explanations for the persistence of "incorrect" socialist views, they claim that African socialism is infused with bourgeois and petty-bourgeois notions. The colonial powers are charged not only with introducing bourgeois concepts but also with spreading the false socialist tenets of British and French socialism. As a result of this external barrage, which has been ceaselessly aided by the dissemination of imperialist propaganda, the African people have come to accept certain premises quite alien to the Marxist-Leninist doctrine of socialism.

Soviet writers contend that most African leaders improperly understand socialism because they do not live in advanced industrial countries and are greatly isolated from the outside world. This latter point is not altogether persuasive and indeed runs counter to the claim that exposure to the external world is responsible for the adoption of certain bourgeois ideas. Another frequent Soviet argument is that the thinking of many African intellectuals is eclectic and pervaded by petty-bourgeois views.

According to Soviet analysts, many African leaders proclaim their belief in some variety of socialism but actually use socialist slogans only to deceive the masses. These men understand the socialist aspirations of their people but are intent upon personal enrichment or "improving capitalism." The analysts feel that private property must be completely abolished, as capitalism often masquerades under many guises.

Soviet African specialists recognize many forms of African socialism, some of which they deem progressive and others of which they consider reactionary. One of the main criteria used in determining the nature of Africa's socialist regimes seems to be the foreign policy postures of countries in question, especially their attitudes toward the Soviet Union. Guinea, Mali, and Ghana (prior to the overthrows of Keita and Nkrumah) usually were perceived as the African nations most closely approaching Marxist-Leninist positions, while the sub-Saharan countries of former French Africa—with the exception of Guinea, Mali, and the Congo (Brazzaville)—generally were viewed as more prone to collaboration with the imperialist powers. Senegal and the Ivory Coast in particular were often the targets of vitriolic Soviet attacks.

It was claimed in Soviet writings that the working people of Guinea and Mali, prior to the removal of Keita, supported their governments and that the "broad people's masses" played an active political role. Although local capital was weakly developed, there was a sharp class struggle in these countries. Soviet authors praised the voluntary work programs and the somewhat communal system of land tenure and declared that Guinea and Mali had the preconditions for taking the "non-capitalist path." During the last several years, the Congo (Brazzaville) has joined the list of those singled out for praise while post-Nkrumah Ghana and post-Keita Mali have been demoted from the ranks of progressivism. In 1961, the Communist party of the Soviet Union took the unprecedented step of inviting delegates from the non-Communist ruling parties of Guinea, Ghana, and Mali to its Twenty-second Congress, and the leaders of these countries were all honored with Lenin Peace Prizes: Touré in 1961, Nkrumah in 1962, and Keita in 1963.

Aspects of African socialism favorably regarded by Soviet writers are a national monetary system, which is viewed as a necessary attribute of state sovereignty and a bastion of economic independence; mutual assistance programs; common land ownership; a strong state sector of the economy; a state bank; and state control over exports and transportation. Most African socialist governments have established one-party systems but Soviet analysts rarely discuss this facet of African socialism. The most probable reason is that these one-party systems are not Communist and many of them actually suppress the

Communist parties and movements within their countries. Soviet authors usually look favorably upon the mass parties in power but are wary of approving them as a general principle since they hope for the establishment of Communist regimes in Africa. In addition, some one-party states (such as the Ivory Coast) have been labeled "reactionary." V. Kudriavtsev, a leading Soviet political analyst, has summed up Soviet thinking on this touchy issue of one-party regimes:

> The question of a one-party or multi-party system is extremely complicated. Its solution depends on the concrete conditions existing in each African country, on the alignment of class forces within it, on the way the country develops, and on many other things. No set pattern or dogmatic, tidy propositions are possible.[3]

Soviet relations with Senegal have recently become more cordial and Soviet attacks on the views of Léopold Senghor have therefore abated. However, it should be pointed out that Senghor was for a long time viewed as the prime example of a reactionary African socialist. He was consistently accused of speaking for the big bourgeoisie, of having close ties to French capitalists, and of representing "the bureaucratic top crust." His brand of humanistic socialism was seen as a camouflage for capitalism and was purportedly supported by the neo-colonialists. Félix Houphouët-Boigny was vilified in similar terms.

IS AFRICA UNIQUE?

Many African socialists claim that there are no classes in Africa and that the traditional African societies which existed prior to the arrival of the colonialists were socialist. Both of these contentions are disputed by Soviet political experts, who aver that the African countries are now experiencing bitter class struggles and that class differentiation was beginning in Africa even before the colonial powers disrupted the course of African social evolution. These experts reject the African socialist assertion that the African nations can return to the precolonial socialist way of life, since they take the position that such a way of life did not exist just prior to the advent of colonial rule.

Soviet writers outline a definite sequence of historical development which they claim is pertinent to the African continent, as well as to other parts of the world.[4] Under the primitive-communal system, clans and tribes are the primary social groupings. These clans and tribes have common languages and cultures, have no classes, and are based on ties of kinship. When several tribes amalgamate, a nationality *(narodnost')* is created. A nationality has a common language, territory, and culture but not a common economy. It may have a system of slavery but is usually primarily feudal. Communal landholding is replaced by a system of feudal exploitation, and class differentiation proceeds rapidly.

As feudalism develops into capitalism, the nationality changes into a nation *(natsional'nost')*. Private landholding becomes prominent and a landless capitalist class forms in the towns. Nations are composed of antagonistic classes and a nation may contain people of many races. There is no relationship between race and nationhood. According to Ivan Potekhin, there were no nations in Africa until the end of the nineteenth century.

The Soviet analysis of African historical development is marked by a recognition of three basic stages: tribalism, nationality, and nation. The corresponding forms of economic relationships are communal, feudal, and capitalist. Therefore, as far as Soviet critics are concerned, Africa is certainly not classless and most of it has not been since long before the arrival of the colonialists.

In regard to the contemporary period, Soviet Africanists minimize the extent of class hostility between the working class and bourgeoisie and instead call for a united front, including these two classes, to oppose the imperialists. They declare that the foreign firms, not the native African bourgeoisie, are the chief exploiters of the African working class and they also recognize that political independence can be achieved under national bourgeois leadership. Another of their views, derived from the writings of Lenin, is that nationalism in exploited nations has a democratic content.

Soviet political analysts write about a world revolutionary process and also discern an international class struggle. The former includes the world socialist system (Communist countries), the international workers' movement, and the national-liberation movement and is an alignment of the main progressive forces against international imperialism. The latter refers to the Soviet claim that the class struggle in underdeveloped countries cannot be viewed just in terms of the classes present in those countries. Although peasants usually constitute the majority of the population and the working class is relatively weak and disorganized, the manner of evolution may be the same as that experienced where the working class is the leading force. This is possible since the socialist (Communist) countries, in which the working class purportedly is in power, can act as the leader of an international alliance of workers and peasants. Therefore, the underdeveloped countries can conceivably construct socialism despite the fact that their own working classes are far removed from the seat of state power.

Soviet theorists maintain that Africa has its own individuality, which can affect its transition to socialism, but Africa cannot have its own ideology and form of socialism. They cite many unique aspects of African life and state that Africa must strive to gain self-respect following the humiliating period of colonialism. They also charge colonial authorities with denigrating African history and culture and instilling a belief that Africans are inferior and uncreative. However, these analysts are careful to stress that it is because of its colonial experience and not from any racial factor that Africa is unique. Marxism-Leninism recognizes a class struggle, not racial solidarity. Another important reason for minimizing racial differences, which has been implicit in the Soviet exchanges with the Chinese, is the Soviet fear that the Chinese are attempting to align the nations of Asia, Africa, and Latin America on a racial basis. The Soviet Union is primarily a white power and Ivan Potekhin hastened to note that imperialism and the white race are not synonymous. He pointed out that Africans have many friends of the white race.

Accordingly, Soviet Africanists oppose the idea of *négritude,* which is most prominently put forth by Léopold Senghor. They are averse to this racial concept, partly because it includes only Negroes, and *négritude* is considered to be "antiracial racism." Soviet writers aver that Negroes are not "intuitive" and therefore different from "analytical and logical" whites. Pan-Africanism presents different problems and is viewed equivocally by Soviet analysts. Although wary of its racial element, the Soviets are encouraged by its extension to the Arab nations of Northern Africa. Praising the unification of the African peoples in the struggle against imperialism and colonialism, they are hesitant to support any pan-national movements (such as pan-Africanism or pan-Islam) because they are based on ethnic or religious differences and supposedly gloss over the class struggle in each country. The economic facet of pan-Africanism, on the other hand, is cordially accepted by Soviet observers, since African economic cooperation reduces reliance upon the formal colonial powers.

Marxism-Leninism generally recognizes an incompatibility between socialism and religion, as the Marxist view is still maintained that religion is the "opiate of the masses." In their writings on Africa, however, Soviet theorists increasingly contend that socialism and religion are compatible. This is a concession to the African socialists, since many of these leaders emphasize the religious values of their cultures, and is offered to make the Soviet model more palatable to religious African nations (and also to improve relations with certain African socialist leaders like Nyerere and Touré). Soviet writers usually couple attacks upon religion with statements to the effect that despite many negative aspects, religion may exist in a socialist society. One leading Soviet Africanist has stated:

> The Communist outlook and philosophy is indeed atheistic. But the doors of the majestic edifice of socialism are not closed to believers. . . . Communists are convinced that religion will die out in time, but not by way of violence or decrees of any sort, rather as a result of the dissemination of scientific knowledge, the growth of literacy and culture of human beings. Consequently, Islam cannot serve as an obstacle to taking the road to socialism.[5]

BLUEPRINTS FOR AFRICA'S FUTURE

According to Soviet scholars, the nations of Africa must proceed to either capitalism or socialism. There is no third path. However, it is often affirmed that the African nations have a choice between these two paths and this, to some extent, denies historical inevitability. Skipping the capitalist stage of development is considered possible and the "noncapitalist path" is advanced as a realistic alternative for the "progressive" countries in Africa. Soviet writers believe that Africans are greatly attracted to socialism, of one variety or another, and they claim that scientific or Marxist-Leninist socialism is receiving ever wider dissemination. The desire of most Africans to avoid the evils of capitalism is also a persistent theme.

What are the prerequisites for taking the noncapitalist path? Soviet authors cite many. The bourgeoisie which promotes capitalism must be weak or absent and the middle bourgeoisie also must not be numerous; the capitalist enterprises must belong to foreign firms rather than to native capitalists; the petty-bourgeoisie must be similar to the working class and must not support capitalism; communal land tenure under which land cannot be bought or sold is desirable; the working class should have a high degree of consciousness and organizational ability; and, of course, the powerful world socialist system (Communist countries), which enabled colonial areas to become independent, must play a significant role.

Examples of successful leap-frogging over capitalism include Mongolia, the Kazakh Republic, and peoples of the Northern USSR, and their models of development are frequently advocated by Soviet writers. Another method of transition to socialism is the "national democratic state," under which nationalist leaders can lead their revolutions into the socialist stage. The concept of a national democratic state was first put forth in December 1960, a few months prior to Cuba's affirmation that its revolution was of a "socialist" nature, and evidence points to Cuban events as an important influence upon the formulation of this concept. Countries now considered to be progressing toward a national democratic state are Guinea, Congo (Brazzaville), Algeria, the Egyptian Arab Republic, and Burma.

State capitalism and agricultural communes are considered to be steps forward toward socialism. Although certain negative aspects are cited, the former are deemed both economically and politically progressive. The large state sector benefits the people, opposes imperialism, and is greatly different from state monopoly capitalism in the advanced Western countries. State capitalism in underdeveloped countries opposes monopolies while state-monopoly capitalism permits the monopolies to control the state machinery. State capitalism can aid the transition to socialism as the public sector gradually eliminates the private sector. Soviet spokesmen also maintain that the communal and cooperative agricultural systems practiced in Africa, which feature the absence of private landholding, are capable of advancing the African nations toward socialism.

Another view espoused by Soviet analysts is that many Africans of nonproletarian origin favor the development of scientific socialism in their countries. This appears to contradict the orthodox Marxist tenet that class determines consciousness, but Soviet writers do just that. Y. Tomilin stated: "The social origin of an African intellectual is not the main factor determining his political views. ... Of all strata in African society the intelligentsia is best prepared to take in Socialist ideas."[6] Other writers frequently assert that the ideology of people can change and that nonproletarians are able to undergo an ideological evolution and eventually become Marxist-Leninists. This line of reasoning became prominent early in 1962 (it should be remembered that Fidel Castro declared himself a Marxist-Leninist in December 1961), and there is much evidence to the effect that Cuban developments prompted the Soviet theorists to emphasize this new position. Of course, Communists such as Mao Tse-tung have used similar arguments many times in the past.

In accord with this reasoning, Soviet spokesmen foresee the radicalization of the African nationalist parties, and pro-Soviet members of these parties are encouraged to steer them further toward the position of scientific socialism. The most progressive African nationalists are called "revolutionary democrats," and, in the words of one Soviet observer, "the Communists believe that life itself, the logic of the struggle, a study of the experience of socialist countries will lead these people to scientific socialism."[7] Even African military leaders may be included among the ranks of revolutionary democrats, and Soviet analysts come to terms with the recent spate of officers' coups in Africa by recognizing the political importance and possible progressivism of African military men.

Soviet writers stress the purported ideological evolution of the African leaders toward scientific socialism and hope that the African nationalist parties will eventually become parties of the Marxist-Leninist type. However, the formation of Communist parties in the African countries is not ignored, since they provide an alternative to the radicalization of the nationalist parties. In the traditional Communist style, African Communists attempt to increase their influence within the nationalist parties but, at the same time, preserve their own organizational base and develop it as a rival source of strength. Many African regimes, especially the Arab states of Northern Africa, persecute the Communists in their nations, since they see them as agents working against the existing order. However, Soviet leaders usually do not let such actions obstruct their cordial diplomatic relations with these nations. In this respect, African Communists are subordinated to the exigencies of the Soviet Union's foreign policy, one aspect of which is good will towards most Afro-Asian leaders and states.

THE DYNAMICS OF SOVIET INTERPRETATION

Beginning with Nikita Khrushchev's rise to power in 1955, Soviet writers have come to recognize many positive aspects of African socialism and to believe that African socialism can evolve into scientific socialism. Cordial state relations with most African nations have been accompanied by a coming to terms with African socialism on an ideological plane and *Realpolitik* has therefore found its reflection in the analyses of the journalists and academic writers. The Soviet approach toward Africa has been marked by a fairly realistic assessment of the chances for Communist influence in that continent, and the rigid doctrinal tenets of the Stalinist period have given way to the realization that there are tremendous differences between the political and economic relationships in various African countries. While they are optimistic about the rise of socialism in Africa and about the anti-imperialist posture of the new African political regimes, Soviet theorists are nevertheless cautious and careful to point out the supposedly dualistic nature of the bourgeoisie, state capitalism, the peasantry, nationalism, and other forces at work in African states.

Ideological erosion has been a by-product of the Khrushchevian and post-Khrushchevian outlook on Africa, as the cherished theoretical concepts have become tempered by their adjustment to the realities of life on the African continent. The basic precipitate of this doctrinal dilution has been the realization that the underdeveloped nations play a key role in the world revolutionary process and that the proletariat of most Asian and African states is not yet ready to establish its hegemony in the national-liberation movement and in the process of nation-building. Prospects for the advent of scientific socialism appear brighter in the former colonial areas than in the advanced industrial countries of the West and the tenets of Marxism-Leninism have been revised to meet this changing situation. New concepts accepted by Soviet theorists include the views that there may be different roads to socialism and that socialism may be achieved through a peaceful transition. Closely related is the new idea that independence may be won despite the fact that the proletariat does not lead the independence struggle.

One way to view the interaction between Soviet theory and practice is to distinguish between long-term and short-term foreign policy objectives. Ideology generally plays a more significant role in regard to basic aims than it does in regard to everyday tactical maneuvers. Another distinction of great relevance has been made by Zbigniew Brzezinski. He differentiates between doctrines and action programs and considers both to be facets of ideology. Doctrines are basic beliefs which shape one's concept of history and the dynamic forces in the world, while action programs are specifically related to the short-term policies through which change is initiated in any given situation. Doctrines rarely change while action programs must change to keep abreast of reality. "Without the doctrine, ideology would be just a static dogma. Doctrine linked with action program gives modern ideology its religious fervor, its sense of constant direction, as well as its freedom of maneuver in the use of political power to achieve that which must be."[8]

In their long-term view of history, Soviet foreign policy analysts adhere to certain fundamental doctrines: there is a definite progression of historical stages and the advent of both socialism and communism is inevitable; economic forces are at the base of society and they determine the prevalent political structure; the evolution of history is directly related to the conflicts between various socio-economic classes; imperialism and capitalism will always be fundamental enemies of the Soviet regime. However, doctrine is often relegated to a minor role in the formulation of short-term action programs. Especially in regard to recent Soviet policy toward the African states, doctrine has taken a back seat as the Soviet Union has developed cordial relations even with military dictatorships not prone to collaboration witth the socialist (Communist) countries. Time purportedly favors the Communist cause, and it is believed that Africa will move into the Communist orbit when the time and conditions are appropriate. Therefore, the short-range objective is to turn the African nations against the West; the long-term objective is to win these nations over to the Soviet camp. The former objective has been partially realized, although Soviet overtures have had little to do with molding the views of African leaders, while the Soviet Union has met with little success in regard to its latter objective. However, as action programs have come to predominate over doctrines, ideology has been increasingly whittled away by the intricacies of power politics.

Soviet political analysts realistically understand that the African nations are not prepared for the Soviet brand of socialism and they therefore seek to outline paths of development for these nations which can bring them to scientific socialism in the near future. They also attempt to foster imitation of the Soviet model, since such elements as collectivization, state ownership of the means of production, and centralized one-party regimes may tend to increase the chances for Soviet influence in these countries and, at the same time, advance them on the road to socialism. It is quite evident that most African leaders favor some variety of socialism, but the Soviet model presents certain points for hesitation; among other things, the Soviet Union's program of agricultural collectivization has not produced the expected results, and there is fear that imitation of the Soviet system and increased economic ties with the Soviet Union might lead to Soviet political domination of the African states.

TOWARD TOMORROW

Since 1955, Soviet writers have shed many of their previous misconceptions about Africa. The preoccupation with rigid class differentiations has given way to the recognition of new, flexible, more realistic, and almost trans-class categories such as "revolutionary democrats" and "progressive intelligentsia," and the idea that only the proletariat can secure complete independence and build socialism has been replaced by a new analysis which recognizes the significant role of the national bourgeoisie. National peculiarities in socialist construction have also come to be tolerated, and even advocated, by Soviet theorists. However, many misconceptions about the African situation remain.

Soviet observers base their analyses on the assumption that the African nations must follow either the capitalist or scientific socialist path and fail to realize that these nations may adopt a path unique to the African continent. They also describe almost all African political events in terms of class struggle and therefore largely ignore the roles of racialism, tribalism, regionalism, and personal charisma. Their reluctance to attribute an important role to racialism is apparently related to the facts that the Soviet Union is generally considered to be a white power and that the Chinese are trying to use the racial theme to their own advantage. Tribalism and regionalism are rarely discussed, as Soviet scholars do not recognize that differences between politicians and political parties are often based more on tribal and regional animosities than on ideological differences brought about by contrasting class backgrounds. The role of tribalism in countries such as Uganda and Kenya is hardly mentioned, nor is the role of regionalism in the Congo (Kinshasa) or Dahomey. With such a gap in their theoretical framework, it is not surprising that Soviet writers often proffer analyses divorced from reality. Another great impediment to their comprehension of African politics is the failure to take into account the role of personal charisma or the personalization of power. The ascendancy of African leaders and the popularity of these men among the masses are seen as the products of class forces, and the magnetism of men like Nkrumah, Kenyatta, Banda, and Touré has not been recognized.

Soviet theorists constantly discuss the role of the African proletariat, despite the fact that this class is minuscule in almost all African countries. While acknowledging that the proletariat is not now capable of dominating African politics, Soviet articles nevertheless discuss the size of the proletariat in various countries, its class consciousness, its influence upon the political process, and its task during the existence of a national democratic state. This preoccupation with the proletariat is highly unrealistic because of the weakness of this class and because a class evaluation of African society sheds little light upon its true mechanics.

Socialism of some sort appears to be a fundamental part of the programs of nation-building throughout Africa, since it is directly pertinent to the problems of underdevelopment and the initiation of radical economic and political reforms. However, most African leaders will probably continue to adapt the teachings of Marx, Lenin, and others to the specific needs of the African peoples and will avoid political alliance and ideological conformity with the Soviet Union. The Africans value their independence too dearly to turn from one master to another, and they also try to assert their identity, long suppressed by the colonial powers, through their ideological pronouncements. African socialism itself incorporates many diverse viewpoints and is intended to serve both as a philosophical and practical guide for African development. Basic socialist precepts are applied to the African environment and, despite certain similarities between African socialism and scientific socialism, the African leaders will not become Soviet satraps. In the spirit of Léopold Senghor, they will assimilate but not be assimilated.

NOTES

1. The most significant Soviet journals which include discussions about political and theoretical developments in Africa are *Aziia i Afrika segodnia* (Asia and Africa Today), *International Affairs, Kommunist, Mirovaia ekonomika i mezhdunarodnye otnosheniia* (World Economics and International Relations), *Narody Azii i Afriki* (Peoples of Asia and Africa), *New Times,* and *Sovetskaia etnografiia* (Soviet Ethnography). Valuable non-Soviet English language sources include *Current Digest of the Soviet Press,* translations of the *Joint Publications Research Service, Mizan,* and *Soviet Periodical Abstracts.* The author's book, *Soviet Perspectives on African Socialism,* was published by Fairleigh Dickinson University Press in 1969.

2. Until his death in September 1964, Ivan Potekhin was the doyen of Soviet Africanists and served as director of the African Institute of the Academy of Sciences. His research encompassed numerous fields but his major studies were concerned with contemporary political developments and ethnography. Among his best known books are *Africa: Ways of Development; Afrika, 1956–1961; Afrika smotrit v budushchee* (Africa Looks into the Future); and *Formirovanie natsional'noi obshchnosti iuzhnoafrikanskikh bantu* (Development of the National Consciousness of the South African Bantu).

3. V. Kudriavtsev, "Africa's Hopes and Anxieties," *International Affairs,* no. 11 (November 1963), p. 45.

4. For an interesting discussion of this topic, see Ivan Potekhin, "De quelques questions méthodologiques pour l'étude de la formation des nations en Afrique au Sud du Sahara," *Présence Africaine,* no. 17 (December 1957–January 1958), pp. 61–65.

5. Iu. Bochkarev, "Communists Are Doughtiest Fighters for National Independence," *Kommunist,* no. 5 (March 1963). See Joint Publications Research Service, no. 18768, pp. 24–25.

6. Y. Tomilin, "The Intelligentsia of Tropical Africa," *International Affairs,* no. 6 (June 1967), pp. 39–40.

7. Bochkarev, *op. cit.,* p. 26.

8. Zbigniew Brzezinski, *The Soviet Bloc,* New York: Praeger, 1961, p. 387.

10

CHAE-JIN LEE
The University of Kansas

STRATEGIC ASPECTS OF THE SINO-SOVIET DISPUTE: A STUDY OF RECENT CHINESE ARGUMENTS AND POSITIONS

It is a truism that the problems of war and peace have significantly contributed to the gradual deterioration of Sino-Soviet relations for more than a decade. Even when the conflict between Moscow and Peking was not widely known, a number of serious disagreements existed in the crucial area of strategic calculations and preparations. In brief, the Chinese Communists never accepted the role of a junior partner in military and doctrinal arrangements with the Soviets, but persistently pursued the status of a big and independent global power. The most dramatic dispute in this respect emerged in the summer of 1963 when the top-level conference of Soviet and Chinese leaders proved futile and the Soviet government signed a partial nuclear test ban treaty with the United States and Great Britain. In the exchange of subsequent letters and pronouncements both Moscow and Peking presented a long list of their divergent strategic arguments which clearly showed total absence of mutual confidence. Consequently, the practical utility of the 1950 Sino-Soviet alliance substantially diminished, and neither party could thereafter rely upon their erstwhile allies and comrades.

Both in theory and in practice, the Chinese directly challenged Moscow's foreign policy, which placed high priority on a world-wide détente with the United States. The Soviet leaders indicated that war was no longer a desirable and meaningful instrument of politics in the nuclear age. They also feared a possibility that local wars involving the nuclear powers might escalate into another world war. As a pragmatic alternative to the threat of nuclear holocaust, they advocated the use of less risky methods of peaceful competition against the forces of imperialism and reaction. This moderate policy, however, ran counter to the requirements of militant revolutionary strategy and tactics which Mao Tse-tung espoused and undertook. He obviously supported the priority of armed insurgency, particularly in developing areas.

Indeed, the glorification of war is an integral element of Mao's political and military thought. In "Problems of Strategy in China's Revolutionary War" (December 1936), he stated: "War is the highest form of struggle for resolving contradictions . . . between classes, nations, or political groups."[1] And, in the course of the recent Cultural Revolution, the Chinese attached a very special importance to Mao's military doctrines, ranging from "people's war" to "paper tiger." In claiming the universal validity of his teachings, they went as far as to insist that his doctrines were "the most comprehensive, the most scientific and the greatest military theory representing the peak of Marxist-Leninist theory in this sphere."[2] Explicit in this kind of excessive idolization of Mao is their conscious campaign to show the absolute superiority of China's revolutionary and military model over that of the Soviet Union.

In order to discredit Moscow's "capitulationism" and "opportunism" in international affairs, the Chinese offered a variety of arguments aimed at exposing what they regarded as the strategic weakness of the United States. The principal cliché used for such a purpose was Mao's celebrated thesis that all imperialists, reactionaries, and revisionists are "paper tigers." This slogan was profusely assailed by the Soviet leaders as being "illogical" and "erroneous." On the fiftieth anniversary of the Soviet Armed Forces, for example, Defense Minister Grechko made it unmistakably clear that "present-day imperialism is far from a paper tiger" and that "the most dangerous thing is to underestimate the opponent."[3] Despite its appearance of naiveté, the paper-tiger notion was originally adopted as an ideological and strategic cover for China's actual military inferiority to the United States. It preached strategic contempt of imperialist power as a "paper tiger" in the view of historical determinism; nevertheless, it required tactical respect and prudent appraisal of imperialist superiority as a "real tiger" in any specific short-range context. Thus, the notion was mainly used to dispel fear of U.S. military strength, to boost revolutionary morale, and to counterbalance the arrogance of any superior power.

Another major reason for the alleged strategic weakness of the U.S., according to Peking's contention, was the global overextension of its resources, human and material, which were thinly spread and thus vulnerable to the wave of anti-imperialist revolutions. Therefore, the Chinese observed that the United States was in a "position of passivity, ready for a beating." The crucial argument here is that once United States power is pinned down in several critical areas, its mobility and effectiveness elsewhere is limited. For this reason the Chinese promoted simultaneous revolutionary storms against the United States and encouraged armed struggles in such countries as Laos and Thailand, in addition to Vietnam. Whatever merit the Chinese strategy may have, the Soviets are not willing to instigate more local crises which might lead them to the threshold of nuclear war.

In an attempt to repudiate Moscow's "nuclear fetishism," defined as a blind belief that nuclear weapons decide everything, the Chinese deliberately belittled the strategic importance of nuclear weapons and nuclear blackmail. In his famous article, "Long Live the Victory of People's War" (September 1965), Defense Minister Lin Piao asserted that nuclear weapons were incapable of saving U.S. "imperialism" from its historically predetermined doom and of suppressing the indomitable revolutionaries. He added:

> However highly developed modern weapons and technical equipment may be and however complicated the methods of modern warfare, in the final analysis the outcome of a war will be decided by the sustained fighting of the ground forces, by the fighting at close quarters on battlefields, by the political consciousness of the men, by their courage and spirit of sacrifice. . . . The spiritual atom bomb which the revolutionary people possess is a far more powerful and useful weapon than the physical atom bomb.[4]

This theoretical de-emphasis of nuclear weapons was first enunciated by Mao Tse-tung. At the Moscow meeting of Communist and Workers' Parties in November 1957, he said that it was the imperialist system, and not mankind, that would perish as a result of nuclear war. It was further suggested in "Long Live Leninism!" (April 1960) that after the nuclear war the victorious people would very swiftly create on the ruins of imperialism a civilization thousands of times higher than the capitalist system and a truly beautiful future for themselves.[5]

In a later rebuttal, the Soviets argued that the use of class-blind nuclear weapons would be suicidal both to capitalism and to socialism. They also denounced China's "adventurist," "inhuman," and "bestial" conception of nuclear war, which might sacrifice half the population of the world just to build a higher civilization on corpses and ruins.[6] It was Moscow's intention to project an international image of China as a belligerent and irresponsible power bent on provoking a world war. But one should not take China's reiteration of militant assertions at face value, nor should one misconstrue them as showing China's reckless desire to initiate a nuclear war. For in the course of polemical exchanges both Moscow and Peking tended to distort and exaggerate the views of the other. Conceivably, the Chinese used those arguments to reassure their revolutionary self-confidence and to deter any aggressive temptations on the part of the super-powers.

Even before their acquisition of nuclear capabilities, the Chinese were fully aware of the destructiveness of nuclear weapons. Obviously, they were simply unable to wage a total "tit-for-tat" struggle against the nuclear-equipped U.S. power. The verbal bellicosity was perhaps the only available, though dangerous, method whereby a proud nation like China could expect to obtain some propaganda objectives and compensate for its relative military weakness. To dispel the unfavorable implications of the Soviet propaganda, the Chinese affirmed a fairly consistent public stand that "(1) China wants peace, and not war; (2) it is the imperialists, and not we, who want to fight; (3) a world war can be prevented; and (4) even in the eventuality that imperialism should impose a war on the people of the world and inflict tragic losses on them . . . the future of mankind would still be bright."[7]

There is a striking dichotomy between China's theoretical deemphasis of nuclear weapons and its strenuous efforts for their development. It is because the Chinese definitely recognized certain prerequisites for their great power status, anti-U.S. struggle, and strategic independence from Moscow's nuclear protection. For these objectives they adopted measures for ideological regimentation, political mobilization, and military modernization. But the highest priority in their military programs has long been accorded to the development of independent nuclear capabilities. Although the Soviets in the mid-1950s helped China to build its first three nuclear reactors and testing sites, they gradually took a series of steps, both persuasive and coercive, against China's further nuclear programs. In 1959 the Soviet Union unilaterally nullified the agreement on new technology for national defense concluded between Peking and Moscow in October 1957, and refused to give China an atom bomb and the technical data concerning its manufacture that had earlier been promised. This was soon followed by the withdrawal of Soviet scientific and technological personnel from China and the drastic reduction in Soviet export of strategic materials to China. The Soviet Union also accepted in 1962 Secretary of State Dean Rusk's proposal for nondissemination of nuclear information to nonnuclear countries, and subsequently concluded the tripartite test ban treaty.

The logic of China's nuclear argument against the Soviet Union was analogous to the French case against the United States. First, if Moscow were earnest about observing the Sino-Soviet alliance of 1950, it would hardly oppose China's possession of nuclear power. Again, as Moscow's promise of nuclear protection for China was unreliable and chauvinistic, it was necessary for China to rely first on its own nuclear arsenal against the U.S. threat. The Chinese felt—not without reason —that the Soviet Union had failed to fulfill its responsibilities as their ally on a number of critical issues, especially in their confrontations with U.S. "imperialists" over Taiwan in 1958 and with Indian "reactionaries" over the border disputes in 1962. Thus, the crisis of credibility between Peking and Moscow was truly profound. Like Charles de Gaulle, Mao Tse-tung realized the basic inefficiency of the conventional alliance system in a nuclear age, for no nation, confronted with the risk of its own destruction, would jeopardize its survival for its ally.

As the Chinese were determined to obtain nuclear weapons, the Soviets grew increasingly apprehensive that China might initiate or force a direct nuclear clash between Moscow and Washington. They were also wary of further nuclear proliferation following Chinese explosions and of an increase in China's influence on revolutionary movements in developing countries. To discourage China's nuclear policy, the Soviets argued that, first, Soviet nuclear power was still sufficient to guarantee China's external security; secondly, an enormous economic expense was needed for nuclear projects; and, finally, China's possession of nuclear capabilities would increase the number of U.S. atom bombs pointed at China and thus the danger of nuclear war. In reply, the Chinese upheld the principle of "self-reliance" in national defense. They admitted their poverty, but added that they would "neither crawl to the baton of the Soviet leaders nor kneel before the nuclear blackmail of the U.S. imperialists." And they maintained that as the U.S. already had many atom bombs poised against China, it would not make much difference if the U.S. added a few more.[8] In reality, these presumptuous politico-military polemics only strengthened China's resolution to be independent of the Soviet Union's protective shield and to accelerate its nuclear programs.

In October 1964, China successfully conducted its first nuclear explosion. After this, it took only two years and eight months to test its first hydrogen bomb in June 1967. It is worth noting that the U.S. spent seven years and four months in the interval between two such tests and the Soviet Union, three years and ten months. In fact, the remarkable progress and the size of China's successive tests far exceeded the predictions made by U.S. scientists and spokesmen. As a result, China demonstrated its strategic potentialities and entered the most exclusive of international power clubs. The Chinese may utilize this instrument to discredit the U.S. policy of peripheral military containment and to obstruct the nuclear policies of Moscow and Washington. The limited tests, however, can hardly provide them with an assurance of national security. They simply do not possess a sufficient stockpile and sophisticated means of delivering nuclear weapons to establish effective deterrence against the United States or the Soviet Union. Even with their independent nuclear capabilities the Chinese remain insecure.

Perhaps apprehensive of a potential preemptive attack by the United States or by the Soviet Union against their nuclear installations, the Chinese took great pains to stress that their nuclear weapons would be used only for defensive purposes, declaring that "at no time in no circumstances will China be the first to use nuclear weapons."[9] To cover up their nuclear development, they proposed a world-wide summit conference to discuss the question of total nuclear disarmament, and a denuclearized zone of the Asian and Pacific region, including America, Russia, Japan, and China. If either utopian proposal is ever implemented, China will be its chief beneficiary because the elimination of nuclear arsenals will definitely increase China's relative power position vis-á-vis Moscow and Washington. In the meantime, however, the fact that such proposals of China's are not taken seriously by other major powers can be used to justify its further nuclear projects.

In a more serious attempt to limit the options of U.S. nuclear policy, the Chinese ambassador quietly proposed at Warsaw that China and the United States conclude a joint agreement not to be the first to use nuclear weapons against the other. But this proposal quickly disappeared in 1966 when he rejected America's counterproposal that such a mutual undertaking should be reciprocated by China's acceptance of the nuclear test ban treaty.[10] For the Chinese considered the treaty one of the "frauds" which Moscow and Washington perpetrated to oppose China's nuclear programs. Moreover, unlike the Soviets, the Chinese in effect held a fundamentalist position that any piecemeal arms control measures, short of total disarmament, were unwise and impracticable during the existence of imperialism. At the Twenty-sixth United Nations General Assembly, the Chinese refused to support the Soviet proposal for a world disarmament conference on the ground that the proposal neither set out a clear aim or put forward practical steps for its attainment. Instead, they reiterated that the Soviet Union, together with the United States, should undertake the obligation not to be the first to use nuclear weapons in any circumstances and to dismantle all nuclear bases and installations set up in foreign countries.

In view of the rapid progress of Chinese nuclear programs and the mounting pressure from Congress, Defense Secretary Robert McNamara announced in September 1967 that the United States had decided to start building a thin antiballistic missile system against China by the end of 1967. Although this decision might as well have been directed against the threat of a missile attack by the Soviet Union, the Chinese immediately regarded it as the result of a "tacit understanding" reached by President Johnson and Premier Kosygin at their Glassboro talks. "All this," declared *People's Daily* (October 10, 1967), "reveals the insidious scheme of the U.S. imperialists and the Soviet revisionists to step up their military collaboration against China."

When the United Nations finally adopted the treaty on nonproliferation of nuclear weapons in June 1968, an editorial of *Izvestia* (June 21, 1968) triumphantly called it "an important milestone" toward the goal of achieving general and complete disarmament. In appraising its significance, the editorial reiterated the consequences of nuclear proliferation and said that "the globe, if saturated with nuclear weapons, would be like a gigantic powder keg, ready to explode at the slightest spark." As clearly expected, the Chinese claimed that the treaty was produced solely to meet the common needs of the two nuclear overlords, who were colluding ever more closely to strengthen the "anti-China, anti-Communist, anti-people and counter-revolutionary alliance." And they argued that the treaty itself was another unfair and unequal "fraud" because (1) it allowed the Soviet Union and the United States to produce nuclear weapons and increase the number of their nuclear bases; (2) it deprived the nonnuclear states of their right to develop nuclear weapons for self-defense; (3) it restricted the use of atomic energy for peaceful purposes; and (4) it greatly increased, rather than reduced, the possibility of nuclear blackmail.[11]

The last point is of particular importance. In theory, the Chinese denounced the Russian and American assumption that the further spread of nuclear weapons would necessarily increase the chances of a nuclear war. An increase in the number of "peace-loving" nuclear powers, they rather contended, would restrain the temptation of nuclear blackmail and consequently would create the conditions for total nuclear disarmament. Furthermore, it was their position that every state should retain the sovereign right to decide the question of its own nuclear development, and this right should not be usurped by the present nuclear powers. In September 1965 Foreign Minister Chen Yi specifically said: "China hopes that Afro-Asian countries will be able to make atom bombs themselves, and it would be better for a greater number of countries to come into possession of atom bombs."[12]

This argument against the nonproliferation pact was primarily intended to dispute the validity of Soviet and American nuclear policies. It may be a propagandistic statement of "principles" designed to promote China's self-assumed role of representing the interests of nonnuclear countries. More important, it may also reflect China's probable long-range strategic calculations that further proliferation will produce a highly complicated set of nuclear checks and balances which can in turn confuse or shatter the present state of comparatively simple nuclear imbalance. For only such a complex situation may ever camouflage China's continuing strategic inferiority and upset the nuclear coordination between the United States and the Soviet Union. Even if this analysis is correct, it does not suggest that the Chinese would seriously encourage or assist independent nuclear development programs of their neighboring rivals like India and Japan. Indian or Japanese possession of nuclear weapons—under the present political leaderships—will surely amount to strengthening the anti-China nuclear cordon and to undermining China's prestige as the only nuclear power in Asia.[13]

Even in the milieu of a violent political convulsion, the Chinese allocated the greatest portion of their military expenditures to nuclear and missile fields and made special efforts to protect the normal functions of those scientists and technicians involved in these fields. In the sixteen-point decision on the Cultural Revolution adopted in August

1966, they issued a conspicuous instruction: "Special care should be taken of those scientists and scientific and technical personnel who have made contributions."[14] In the initial stage of the revolutionary upsurge, therefore, the rampaging Red Guards left a small group of nuclear scientists and missile specialists intact and strictly avoided nuclear institutes and test sites. But, as the rebellious movement permeated every sector of China's social and bureaucratic fabric, it finally reached the Scientific and Technological Commission for National Defense, which had planned and supervised a series of successful nuclear tests. In particular, Chairman Nieh Jung-chen of the commission, known as the father of China's atom bombs, was the object of a severe accusation and evidently wrote a statement of self-criticism. Only after Premier Chou En-lai personally intervened in the confused commission and its institutes, was Nieh Jung-chen saved from public disgrace and were the scientists allowed to continue their work.

The Cultural Revolution revealed the actual or imagined conflict of two military lines taken by Peking's ruling circles over the questions of whether China should develop the most advanced science and technology and whether China should take the road of self-reliance or depend on the Soviet Union in the development of nuclear weapons. Those who followed the "proletarian military line" of Mao Tse-tung and Lin Piao criticized the "bourgeois reactionary military line" pursued by such "revisionists" as Liu Shao-chi and Lo Jui-ching (ex-chief of the General Staff of the People's Liberation Army). According to a multitude of public denunciations, Liu and Lo were jointly held responsible for a crime of submission to the pressures of U.S. "imperialists" and Soviet "revisionists." "In a vain attempt to turn China into an appendage of Soviet revisionism," charged the Maoists in the Scientific and Technological Commission, "China's Khrushchev [Liu] advocated the dependence of China's national defenses on Soviet atomic bombs and tried in a variety of ways to hamper our development of up-to-date science and technology."[15] In the process of building and training the army, it was alleged, Liu and Lo ignored the goals of political education and ideological revolutionization and followed the Soviet revisionist road in publicizing the omnipotence of modern weapons and professional experts. It is likely that Liu and Lo, as a powerful pro-Soviet lobby in Peking, approved of a reconciliation with Moscow to provide for China's military improvement and industrial progress and of a common action with Moscow against the United States in Vietnam and elsewhere in Asia.[16]

The proper relationship between "men and weapons" and between "red and expert" occupied a central place in Mao's military thought, and involved the question of priorities in military training and preparedness. In his "On Protracted War" (May 1938), Mao said: "Weapons are an important factor in war, but not the decisive factor; it is people, not things, that are decisive. The contest of strength is not only a contest of military and economic power, but also a contest of human power and morale."[17] Mao's "close comrade-in-arms," Lin Piao, added that the greatest combat effectiveness lies in men armed with Mao's thought. Although the Soviets called it "naïve" and "criminal" to ignore modern military techniques, the essence of Mao's and Lin's arguments was not to ignore them in practical defense preparations, but to de-emphasize them in theoretical and ideological perspectives; they simply reasserted the principles of "politics in command" in military affairs and the necessity of political consciousness and ideological indoctrination among soldiers and officers.

Added to the disharmony among Chinese leaders over military policies was a pervasive lack of central authority in Peking during the Cultural Revolution. The disturbances and difficulties in economic life, transportation facilities, educational institutions, and local administrations—all these undoubtedly contributed to a considerable lag in the development of China's intercontinental ballistic missile, which was predicted to be tested before the end of 1967. However, judging by China's nuclear experiences, sophisticated scientific staff, and political commitments, it is highly likely that China will produce operational ICBMs by the mid-1970s and would be able to wage a nuclear war against the United States or the Soviet Union before the beginning of 1980. This distinct prospect of China's offensive nuclear capabilities complicates its strategic and political relations with both Moscow and Washington.

Conceivable options for the Soviet Union were so far three-fold: first, to preempt China's growing nuclear strength in a surgical manner; second, to conclude a *modus vivendi* with China; or, finally, to establish an effective shield against China's potential nuclear attack. Whereas the first alternative was too risky to be implemented because China is obviously more populous, capacious, and powerful than Hungary or Czechoslovakia, the Chinese were reluctant to accept the second one except on their own terms, a price too high to be paid by Moscow. Given this dilemma, it is plausible that the Soviet Union deployed the anti-missile defense system around its industrial centers and nuclear installations not only against the United States but also against China.

When the Soviet Union agreed in July 1968 to discuss with the United States the question of restricting and reducing strategic nuclear weapons systems, a *People's Daily* (July 8, 1968) commentator promptly declared that both countries went a step further to form an "anti-China nuclear military alliance" under the cloak of nuclear disarmament. The direct charge of a U.S.–Soviet "alliance" completed a long sequence of Chinese complaints, and also symbolized a complete reversal of the 1950 Sino-Soviet alliance.

Notwithstanding their position of military and economic inferiority, the Chinese boldly proceeded to challenge the two super-powers simultaneously in an attempt to gain their ambitious political objectives. To carry out this formidable task, they intentionally predicted the worst possibility that the United States and the Soviet Union would consolidate an alliance with all reactionary forces and would eventually initiate a large-scale war against mainland China. This propaganda theme was evidently calculated to prepare the Chinese population for all contingencies and to project China's image abroad as a source of true revolutionary inspiration. It was also aimed at generating international moral pressures against Moscow's "active collusion" with the U.S. policy of diplomatic isolation and military containment of China. "In Asia," *Peking Review* (December 25, 1967) pronounced, "the Soviet revisionist clique has worked closely with U.S. imperialism in organizing a counter-revolutionary 'holy alliance' and a ring of encirclement against China." In Peking's view, therefore, the Soviet Union was slandering China and working up anti-China opinion to the best of its ability; it was applauding and assisting every anti-Chinese act organized by Japan, India, Indonesia, Burma, and "all other puppets and satellites" of the United States in Asia. To deter any serious contemplation of military attack, though, the Chinese frequently repeated a warning that any foreign invasion would be frustrated by the huge armed forces and militia at their disposal and by the invincible magic of a people's war. Yet, Gen. Huang Yung-sheng, chief of the General Staff, was quick to add in 1968: "We must raise our vigilance, intensify preparedness against war, and must be ready at all times to smash all provocations and invasions by imperialism, revisionism and reaction."[18]

As another recent example of global military cooperation between Moscow and Washington, the Chinese cited the fact that the Soviet Union and Eastern European countries had proposed the abolition of military blocs in Europe and the establishment of a European collective security system. The objective of this Soviet policy, they argued, was to help the United States to bring about a stabilized Europe and shift the emphasis of its military deployment eastward so that the United States could pull out of Western Europe several hundred thousand combat troops, transfer them to Asia, throw them into the Vietnam war, and threaten China. Indeed, the Chinese were increasingly apprehensive and clamorous about a new American policy which they thought shifted its "counter-revolutionary global strategy" from Europe to Asia with concomitant concentration of its overseas forces and bases around mainland China. When the State Department announced in May 1967 its intention to withdraw from West Germany thirty-five thousand troops and four fighter-bomber squadrons (which constituted 15 percent of U.S. troops in West Germany and 50 percent of its combat aircraft there), the Chinese found a more compelling reason to criticize Moscow's détente policy in Europe. In particular, they noted that the U.S. decision came right on the heels of the Karlovy Vary conference of European Communist and Workers' Parties, where Brezhnev reiterated the notion of "European peace and security."[19]

In response, the Soviets contended that the concentration of U.S. forces in Asia was rather China's own fault because its adventurist and expansionist policy, especially its nuclear programs, provoked U.S. escalation around China. The goal of Mao's foreign policy was, according to "Ernest Henry" in *Literaturnaya gazeta,* to build a "new celestial empire" through military conquest of his neighboring countries—even with the risk of global nuclear confrontation. It was further suggested in *Kommunist* that, as a result of the Cultural Revolution, which represented "psychological indoctrination of the nation in a spirit of chauvinism, militarism and preparation for war," Mao's policy fomented war hysteria, threats, and border incidents with neighbors.[20] On the fiftieth anniversary of the Bolshevik Revolution, Brezhnev argued, *inter alia,* that the very chaos caused by Mao's fanatic policies weakened China's strategic posture against imperialism and thus impaired the interests of the socialist commonwealth.[21] Although Foreign Minister Gromyko, in his report to the Supreme Soviet in June 1968, optimistically noted that Mao's adventurist position and hostile subversive activity against the Soviet Union were only a "historically transient stage," the Soviet government took some precautionary measures against China's militant challenge. It issued a series of strong protests against the angry Red Guards' anti-Soviet provocations ranging from attacks on the Soviet Embassy in Peking to their intrusions into Soviet merchant vessels at Chinese ports.

The most sensitive question in Sino-Soviet military relations is the continuing border controversy and its accompanying armed clashes.

Ever since Mao Tse-tung publicly deplored the Soviet troop concentrations along the border in July 1964, there have been an increasing number of episodes concerned with hostile activities along the long frontier.[22] For example, it was reported in 1966 that the Soviet Union had transferred six divisions from Eastern Europe to the Amur River area or deployed seventeen divisions against the five hundred thousand Chinese forces. According to China's own account, Soviet military aircraft intruded into China's air space 119 times during 1967; moreover, from October 1964 to March 1969, the Soviet Union provoked 4,189 border incidents, two and a half times the number of those provoked from 1960 to 1964.[23] Perhaps in an effort to remind Peking of Moscow's superior muscle, the official journal of the Soviet Defense Ministry, *Krasnaya zvezda* (*Red Star*, September 9, 1966), prominently displayed a picture of the medium-range missile located near Lake Baikal, which could easily reach Peking or Manchuria. And, in January and March 1967, a large number of Soviet Politburo and Secretariat members, including Brezhnev, Kosygin, and Podgorny, crisscrossed the Soviet Union attacking the "tragic" error of the Maoist leadership.

The territorial conflict reached the most explosive level during 1969, when a series of bloody armed clashes took place along the Ussuri River and the Sinkiang border. After Moscow's repeated hints of a possible nuclear attack against China, Chou En-lai invited Kosygin to Peking in September 1969. Both leaders discussed the border question, trade, and other issues, and evidently agreed to hold a high-level border discussion. Although the subsequent negotiations between Deputy Foreign Ministers Vasily V. Kuznetsov and Chiao Kuan-hua helped ease the dangerous border tensions, there appeared no visible hope for concluding a comprehensive territorial settlement.

As the border dispute inevitably entails the acute problem of national pride and territorial integrity, it continues to be a dangerous source of tensions between Peking and Moscow. However, the possibility of massive military confrontation seems remote; for the costs of such a grotesque venture would be mutually intolerable, particularly to their respective positions in the international revolutionary movement. Moreover, the strategic and tactical disadvantages that China would be forced to bear in the face of the Soviet attack are abundantly clear. In a discussion of this question, General Samuel B. Griffith concluded:

> Here, China's geographic situation lays vital areas in both
> Sinkiang and Manchuria open to converging attacks which

the Russians could mount in security and push home vigorously. Avenues of approach to critical targets are good, terrain generally suitable for tanks, and Soviet air bases relatively close to targets. In short, the Soviets hold both areas as hostages of sufficient value to deter the Chinese from provocative actions along the Sino-Soviet frontiers.[24]

If, indeed, the Chinese considered any direct military challenge against Moscow or Washington both unwise and risky, they had all the more reason to maximize the use of political means against the two super-powers. Since the united front had proved successful in their domestic revolutionary experiences, they projected this model into their foreign affairs to form and mobilize what they termed "the broadest possible international front" against imperialism and revisionism. This front, they predicted, would ultimately include more than 90 per cent of the total world population; hence, the "rural areas of the world" —Asia, Africa, and Latin America—would encircle and overcome the "cities of the world"—North America and Western Europe. Exclusion of the Soviet Union and Eastern Europe from the front was justified on the ground that the anti-imperialist struggle was inseparable from the antirevisionist struggle.

The Soviet Union, however, proposed that both Peking and Moscow, for the benefit of the international Communist movement and for the common interest in the anti-imperialist struggle, should diminish their conflict and strengthen their united action against the United States in Vietnam. No doubt this argument appeared reasonable and attractive for those who were deeply concerned with Hanoi's predicament. But the Maoists intrinsically suspected Moscow's intentions to fight imperialism, as they found a distinct revisionist and bourgeois tendency in the Soviet Union. After reiterating his "hope" to restore friendship and unity with China, Premier Kosygin observed at the Supreme Soviet in August 1966 that the position of the socialist commonwealth would be even stronger if comprehensive cooperation with China were assured.[25]

This theme was a shrewd one calculated to blame China for the continuing Sino-Soviet rift and even for the insufficiency of international assistance for Hanoi. Ten days after Kosygin's speech, the Chinese Communist Party Central Committee not only rejected his proposal, but also reaffirmed an absolutely uncompromising position. Its statement declared:

... to oppose imperialism, it is imperative to oppose modern revisionism. There is no middle road whatsoever in the struggle between Marxism-Leninism and modern revisionism. A clear line of demarcation must be drawn in dealing with the modern revisionist groups with the leadership of CPSU as the center, and it is imperative resolutely to expose their true features as scabs. It is impossible to have "united action" with them.[26]

But China's search for "Marxist-Leninist" orthodoxy vis-á-vis Russian "revisionism" is largely antithetical to the idea of organizing the broadest possible united front against the United States. The simultaneous and ambitious endeavors which the Chinese carry on against the two more resourceful powers tend to be a costly and counterproductive tactical mistake. Such endeavors also reduce the China-sponsored international front to a rather exclusive, assertive, and dogmatic minority in world affairs. One serious outcome of China's tactical blindness and political intolerance is the alienation or antagonism of an increasing number of Communist parties and neutral countries. Only a handful of extreme Communist groups—mostly splinter parties—remain faithful to Peking's self-righteous leadership.

The Cultural Revolution and its militant foreign policy, notably the Red Guards' extremely xenophobic activities, damaged China's international respectability and sowed the seeds of its diplomatic setbacks in Africa and Southeast Asia. Moreover, Moscow's persuasive campaign for united action, coupled with its military commitments in Vietnam, effectively isolated China in the world community and in the international Communist movement. In addition, *Izvestia* suggested that the Chinese reached a "tacit understanding" with the United States at Warsaw that they would not take any direct military action in Vietnam if the United States did not attack them or invade North Vietnam. It also reported—with obvious implications—that China had sold several thousand tons of steel to the United States to be used in Vietnam.[27] In fact, the absence of a unified socialist front weakened Hanoi's position in the battlefield as well as at the negotiation table. In Vietnam, Mao's line remained basically passive and noncommittal; he did not significantly increase China's troop deployment along the Vietnam frontier, nor did he issue credible warnings against the United States.

On the other hand, to undermine Moscow's growing role in Vietnam, the Chinese employed a series of arguments: first, Moscow adopted the dual tactics of sham unity but real split in relation to Vietnam; secondly, Moscow's aid to Vietnam was deplorably small, and most of its military supplies were obsolete and inefficient; and, finally, Moscow eagerly helped the United States to peddle its "peace swindles" and to bring the Vietnam issue into the U.S.–Soviet orbit. When President Johnson proposed peace talks with North Vietnam by partially stopping the bombing in the northern part of Vietnam in 1968, the Chinese immediately warned Hanoi against the illusion of negotiations with the U.S. and advised it to continue a protracted people's war until complete victory. In trotting out this "new peace fraud," purportedly made in collaboration with the Soviet Union, a commentator of *People's Daily* (April 15, 1968) claimed Johnson's real aim was to gain a breathing spell on the Vietnam battlefield so as to further expand the war. The Chinese evidently reasoned that the prolongation of the Vietnam conflict would pin down and weaken U.S. strength and also militate against the Soviet thesis of peaceful coexistence. But the Chinese propaganda which implicated Moscow in Washington's "peace conspiracy" invited a pointed reaction from Moscow. For example, B. Zanegin asserted in *Izvestia* (May 23, 1968) that, in addition to rejecting Moscow's proposals for a "joint rebuff" of the United States, the Chinese hampered the transit of Soviet aid supplies to Vietnam and attempted to impose on the Vietnamese people a protracted war on the Chinese model. All these efforts, he said, were designed to create a buffer between China and U.S. forces in Southeast Asia and to gain the time necessary for developing China's own nuclear-missile potential. In effect, Zanegin meant that since Peking's policy toward Vietnam was thoroughly selfish and destructive, Hanoi should not heed Peking's opposition to a negotiated settlement of the Vietnam war.

As the preliminary peace talks between Hanoi and Washington started in Paris with Moscow's blessings, the Chinese suddenly refrained from making any direct public reference to the talks. For the time being, they seemed to take a relatively detached "wait-and-see" approach. Whereas Peking disliked Hanoi's acceptance of the talks, it was conceivable that Hanoi felt that its negotiating position in Paris would have been enhanced if Peking's support was obtained. It was the Soviet Union that reported a sharp conflict of opinions developing between Peking and Hanoi in regard to the peace negotiations. For example, *Literaturnaya gazeta* said that at the beginning of June the Red Guards staged hostile demonstrations in front of the consulates of North Vietnam in Nanking, Kunming, and Canton; in Nanking, the

Red Guards even demanded that the Vietnamese consul denounce the Paris talks.[28]

After the Soviet Union occupied Czechoslovakia in August 1968, the Chinese violently assailed Moscow's "social imperialism" and simultaneously launched unmistakable criticism against the Paris talks. At the diplomatic reception held in Peking on September 2, 1968, Premier Chou En-lai told the North Vietnamese ambassador that "the peace talks scheme on Vietnam is jointly devised by U.S. imperialism and Soviet revisionism," and observed that because of the Soviet invasion of Czechoslovakia the United States would definitely demand a "higher price" on the Vietnam question. After asking all those who cherished the slightest illusion about Moscow and Washington to wake up, Chou ominously concluded: so long as the Vietnamese people persevere in a protracted war and oppose "capitulation and compromise," they will surely win final victory.[29] Thus, the peace talks further aggravated the already tense conflict between Moscow and Peking, and became a test of the relative merits of Soviet and Chinese strategic arguments.

But the causes and variations of strategic conflict between Moscow and Peking are too complex and profound to show any clear future direction. Neither country is presently prepared to risk a total war, nor flexible enough to take major steps toward a political accommodation. Notwithstanding an occasional appearance of tactical maneuvers, these two equally proud powers continue to follow basically stagnant and unimaginative policies. Indeed the limiting preconceptions and obsolete stereotypes, derived from competing doctrines, rival national interests, cultural differences, and historical distortions, persist to the detriment of creative and progressive policies. The fact that the Soviet Union and Communist China have transformed their relationship from "allies" to "enemies" only vividly reaffirms the characteristic polycentric trend in the international Communist movement and the irretrievable disintegration of the postwar bipolar international system. It also proves how deceptive the myth of "proletarian internationalism" can be in the face of conflicting strategic interests and how prevalent "ethnocentric parochialism" can be in power politics.

And yet, despite the exchange of hostile strategic arguments and dangerously provocative vituperation, both Moscow and Peking so far have maintained a considerable degree of self-restraint to avoid a decisive military showdown or a diplomatic rupture. The Chinese often sounded reckless and adventurist, but in practice they deviated from the implications of their pronouncements. This gap between words and deeds became the subject of a Sino-Soviet controversy, too;

Moscow denounced the "ulterior motive" of China's intentional "bellicose tone" and "phony militancy." In the process of realistic strategic assessment the Chinese upheld the supremacy of vital security interest, recognized their limited resources and capabilities, and averted a major armed confrontation with the Soviet Union along the unstable frontiers. They also carefully emphasized the defensive purpose of their nuclear power. If an ultimate military bluff is considered necessary by them in a certain crisis, they might threaten to use atom bombs as a means of deterrence or bargaining leverage, but not to the extent of inviting a total nuclear war. It will take years before the Chinese nuclear capabilities constitute a genuine balance of terror against the Soviet Union or the United States. Until they come to terms with the reality of the nuclear situation and with the futility of an endless arms race against the two super-powers, the Chinese will continue to assume the exorbitant economic and military burden of a perennial security dilemma.

As long as Mao Tse-tung and his immediate associates remain in a position of leadership in China, it is highly unlikely that they would accept a reconciliation with the present Soviet leadership. In the event of a direct military confrontation with the United States, they may not count on Moscow's assistance; rather, they may anticipate cooperation between Washington and Moscow. The reverse may also be true; in the event of a U.S.–Soviet war, the Chinese are likely to act in a manner consistent with the conditions of their own security and prestige. Although the conflict between Moscow and Peking substantially reduced a possibility of coordinated offensive action, it did not rule out that of common defensive efforts. It is not entirely improbable that, as political realists, the Soviet and Chinese leaders, if faced with a vital common threat from the United States, might forge at least a temporary alliance. The eventual direction of all these possibilities depends upon a combination of various unpredictable factors—including the outcome of the Vietnam war, the consequences of China's Cultural Revolution, the development of nuclear capabilities, and the disintegration of Eastern Europe. In essence, therefore, the strategic dispute between Moscow and Peking is still in the state of flux.

NOTES

1. *Selected Works of Mao Tse-tung*, Peking: Foreign Languages Press (hereafter cited as FLP), 1964, I, 180.

2. See, for example, *Peking Review,* X (August 11, 1967), 11.

3. *Pravda,* February 28, 1968, in *Current Digest of the Soviet Press,* XX (March 13, 1968), 11–16.

4. *Long Live the Victory of People's War!* Peking: FLP, 1965, p. 57.

5. For Mao's Moscow speech, see the Chinese Government statement of September 1, 1963, in *People of the World, Unite For the Complete, Thorough, Total and Resolute Prohibition and Destruction of Nuclear Weapons!* Peking: FLP, 1963, pp. 41–42; and see *Long Live Leninism!* Peking: FLP, 1960, p. 22.

6. See the Soviet government statement of August 21, 1963, in *People of the World . . .* , pp. 181–208.

7. See the Chinese government statement of September 1, 1963, in *ibid.,* p. 43.

8. *Ibid.,* pp. 19–28.

9. For Khrushchev's plan to eliminate Chinese nuclear installations, see Harold C. Hinton, *Communist China in World Politics,* Boston: Houghton Mifflin Co., 1966, pp. 476–83; and, for China's postdetonation press communiques, see *Peking Review,* VII (October 16, 1964, May 21, 1965, May 13, 1966, October 28, 1966, January 1, 1967, and June 23, 1967).

10. For the exchange of proposals at Warsaw, see Kenneth T. Young, "American Dealings with Peking," *Foreign Affairs,* 45 (October 1966), 84–85; for the Chinese account, see *People's Daily,* June 20, 1966.

11. *People's Daily,* June 13, 1968.

12. See *Vice-Premier Chen Yi Answers Questions Put By Correspondents,* Peking: FLP, 1966, p. 5.

13. However, Morton Halperin suggests that China would gain more advantages than disadvantages from Indian or Japanese nuclear armament, in *China and Nuclear Proliferation,* Chicago: Chicago University Press, 1966, pp. 36–42.

14. *Peking Review,* IX (August 12, 1966), 10.

15. *Ibid.,* November 3, 1967, p. 15.

16. For a succinct discussion of factional disputes, see Donald S. Zagoria, *Vietnam Triangle: Moscow, Peking, Hanoi,* New York: Pegasus, 1967, pp. 63–98.

17. *Selected Works of Mao Tse-tung,* Peking: FLP, 1965, II, 143.

18. *Peking Review,* XI (August 9, 1968), 14.

19. For some of these points, see *ibid.* (May 12, 1967), pp. 30–31, and (December 25, 1967), pp. 40–43.

20. *Literaturnaya gazeta,* nos. 39 and 40 (September 27 and October 4, 1967), in *Current Digest of the Soviet Press,* XX (January 24, 1968), 3–7; and *Kommunist,* no. 7 (May 1968), in *ibid.,* XX (June 26, 1968), 9–13.

21. *Pravda,* November 4, 1967, in *ibid.* (November 22, 1967), p. 12; nevertheless, *People's Daily,* June 4, 1967, claimed that the cultural revolution was "more deep-going and larger in scale than the Paris Commune, the October Revolution and all past revolutions in China" and that it made China all the more powerful and consolidated.

22. See Dennis J. Doolin, *Territorial Claims in the Sino-Soviet Conflict: Documents and Analysis,* Stanford: Hoover Institution, 1965.

23. See *London Times,* November 5, 1966, *Der Spiegel,* November 7, 1966, and *Peking Review,* XI (September 20, 1968), 41 and XII (May 30, 1969), 6.

24. *The Chinese People's Liberation Army,* New York: McGraw-Hill, 1967, p. 283. For a different assessment, see Harrison E. Salisbury, *War Between Russia and China,* New York: Norton, 1969.

25. *Pravda,* August 4, 1966, in *Current Digest of the Soviet Press,* XVIII (August 24, 1966), 11–19.

26. "Communique of the Eleventh Plenary Session of the Eighth Central Committee of the Communist Party of China," *Peking Review,* IX (August 19, 1966), 7.

27. See *Izvestia,* December 20, 1966, and August 24, 1967; *Peking Re-*

view, X (April 28, 1967), countered with a report that the American Dow Chemical Company had imported from the Soviet Union four shipments of magnesium—the rare strategic material for napalm and aircraft manufacture—to "commit further brutal atrocities" in Vietnam.

28. No. 26 (June 26, 1968), in *Current Digest of the Soviet Press,* XX (July 17, 1968), 21.

29. *Peking Review,* XI (September 6, 1968), 6–7.

NOTES ON CONTRIBUTORS

WILL ADAMS, Professor and Chairman, Department of Political Science, William Jewell College. Ph.D., Columbia University (1968). Professor Adams has written articles that have appeared in *American Journal of Comparative Law* (1970), Robert Linder *et al.*, eds., *Politics and Protest: Christianity and Contemporary Affairs* (1968) and Joseph Dunner, *Dictionary of Political Science* (1964). At present he is revising his doctoral dissertation on Soviet criminal law for publication.

NICHOLAS DeWITT, Associate Professor of Economics and Government, Director of the International Survey of Educational Development and Planning, Indiana University. Ph.D., Harvard University (1962). Professor DeWitt's publications include *Soviet Professional Manpower—Its Education, Training and Supply* (1955), *Education and Professional Employment in the U.S.S.R.* (1961), "Educational and Manpower Planning in the Soviet Union," in Mark Blaug, ed., *The World Year Book of Education 1967: Educational Planning,* and numerous other articles in books and academic journals.

GEORGE M. ENTEEN, Associate Professor of History, The Pennsylvania State University. Ph.D., George Washington University (1965). Professor Enteen's publications include articles on the teaching and writing of history in the USSR in *World Politics* (1968) and in *The Russian Review* (1969) and a forthcoming book entitled *M. N. Pokrovskii and the Society of Marxist Historians.*

ERIK P. HOFFMANN, Assistant Professor of Political Science, State University of New York at Albany. Ph.D., Indiana University (1967). His publications include "Communication Theory and the Study of Soviet Politics," *Canadian Slavic Studies* (1968) and "Methodological Problems of Kremlinology," in Frederic J. Fleron, ed., *Communist Studies and the Social Sciences* (Rand McNally, 1969). He is presently working on two studies of contemporary domestic politics in the Soviet Union.

ROGER E. KANET, Associate Professor of Political Science, University of Kansas. Ph.D., Princeton University (1966). Professor Kanet's publications include articles in *The Russian Review, Canadian Slavic Studies* and *Soviet Studies* and an edited book entitled *The Behavioral Revolution and Communist Studies* (1971).

ARTHUR J. KLINGHOFFER, Associate Professor of Political Science, Rutgers University (Camden). Ph.D., Columbia University (1966). His publications include articles in *Africa Report, African Affairs,* and other journals. He is author of *Soviet Perspectives on African Socialism* (1969) and co-author with Roger Kanet of the forthcoming *The Soviet Union and Africa.*

CHAE-JIN LEE, Associate Professor of Political Science, University of Kansas. Ph.D., University of California at Los Angeles (1966). Professor Lee's publications include articles in *Pacific Affairs, Asian Survey, Military Review, Vietnam Perspectives,* a monograph on *Communist China's Policy toward Laos* (1970), and an article in Wesley R. Fishel, ed., *Vietnam: Anatomy of a Conflict* (1968).

JAAN PENNAR, Visiting Scholar, Research Institute on Communist Affairs, Columbia University. Ph.D., Princeton University (1953). Dr. Pennar's publications include *The Politics of Soviet Education,* co-author (1960), *Islam and Communism,* ed. (1960), and articles in *Problems of Communism, Mizan* and other academic journals. Until 1970, he was Counselor on Institute Relations at the Institute for the Study of the U.S.S.R.

PAUL L. ROLEY, Associate Professor of History, Western Washington State College. Ph.D., University of Illinois (1966). Professor Roley's publications include reviews in *Slavic Review, The Russian Review* and *The Historian* and a forthcoming work on Soviet policy toward Eastern Europe during World War II, to be published by Blaisdell.

ROBERT SHARLET, Assistant Professor of Political Science, Union College. Ph.D., Indiana University (1968). Professor Sharlet's publications include articles in *Slavic Review, Canadian Slavic Studies* and *Journal of Developing Areas* and a book entitled *Soviet Modernization: An Interpretation of Communist Political Development* to be published by Pegasus in 1971.